THE BATTLE FOR
IWO JIMA 1945

DERRICK WRIGHT

SUTTON PUBLISHING

This book was first published in 1999 by
Sutton Publishing Limited

This paperback edition first published in 2003
Reprinted in 2007 by Sutton Publishing,
an imprint of NPI Media Group Limited
Cirencester Road · Chaford · Stroud · Gloucestershire · GL6 8PE

British Library Cataloguing in Publication Data
A catalogue record for this book is available from the British Library.

ISBN 978 0 7509 4544 8

Typeset in 11/14 4pt Sabon.
Typesetting and origination by
Sutton Publishing Limited.
Printed and bound in England.

For Bert Clayton

Contents

Acknowledgements

In writing a book about a battle of over half a century ago, the author had to rely heavily on the good will of the veterans of that battle to supply information and personal accounts. This was something I approached with considerable trepidation, expecting some rebuffs from Americans who would query why a British author was examining their military history. Thankfully, my doubts were soon dispelled: everywhere, my requests for information were greeted with courtesy and enthusiasm, truly '*Semper fi*'.

I am particularly grateful to Col. Charles Waterhouse, USMC Ret., for permission to reproduce some of the superb paintings from his great book, *Marines and Others*. Many thanks go to Mr Taro Kuribayashi for unique information and photographs of his father, to Mr Joe Rosenthal for a definitive account of the famous flag-raising on Mt Suribachi, to Gen. Paul W. Tibbets for information on the bombing campaign against Japan, and to Dale Worley for allowing me to quote from his moving 'unofficial' Iwo Jima diary.

For permission to quote from their books on the battle, I am indebted to Maj. John Keith Wells, 'Chuck' Tatum, John Lane and Mary Hartman. For valuable information on the role of Navy Corpsmen, and for reviewing Chapter 7, many thanks to Stanley E. Dabrowski. For personal accounts of their experiences on Iwo Jima, and for interesting information about the battle, my thanks go to the following:

William A. Almond, Col. Joseph H. Alexander, Bill Alexander, Travis L. Budlong, Capt. Clifton J. Cormier, Roland Chiasson,

Clayton N. Chipman, Herman J. Dupont, Ross Doll, Robert R. DeGeus, Eric L. Doody, Col. E.J. Driscoll Jr, Chuck Davis, Isidore Finkelstein, Richard A. Fiske, George J. Green, Frank V. Gardner, Marshall Harris, Dr Sam J. Holman, Capt. Teruaki Kawano, Joe Kobylski, Al Kirtley, Dr Michael F. Keleher, Bill Konop, Col. Jim Leffers, Russell J. Lacher, Arthur E. Light, William L. MacAllister, Edward Maffei, Elbert Phillips, Vaughn B. Russell, Robert M. Rennie, Walt Sandberg, Col. Shelton Scales, Peter Santoro, John Spencer, Robert F. Tindall Jr, Roland S. Tolles, Alan Wood, Peter M. Walker and Cy Young. Special thanks to my two most consistent and accommodating American contacts, Bert Clayton, Editor of the 5th Division's *Spearhead News*, and John Lane, author of the fine book, *This Here is 'G' Company*.

The wartime photographs of Iwo Jima are reproduced courtesy of The National Archives, Washington DC, the United States Marine Corps, the US Navy, or as credited in the text. Maps and other drawings are by the author.

Preface

'How do you remember that far back?' several people have asked.

'That is not the problem,' I tell them – 'the problem, is how do I forget?' (John Keith Wells)

As the final hours of 1944 ebbed away, a mood of mounting optimism was sweeping the free world. After five years of bitter conflict and oppression in Europe, no one realistically doubted that Hitler's evil empire was on the point of collapse.

The cream of the German Army lay dead in the vast expanses of Russia, and the victorious Red Army was sweeping across Poland in the north and encircling Budapest in the south. In Italy, the Allied armies had advanced to the Gothic Line, and despite appalling weather, were pushing towards the River Po and Milan. In the west, Hitler's last mad gamble, the breakout in the Belgian Ardennes, had fizzled out in December with severe losses. The American 3rd Army of Gen. Patton was driving towards the Rhine at Mannheim, while the British and Canadian forces in the north had just liberated Antwerp on the Belgian coast. In the air, the USAAF and the RAF enjoyed total command of the skies, as the pathetic remains of the Luftwaffe and its demoralized crews were grounded through lack of fuel.

From Britain, the US 8th Air Force pounded the Nazi oil industry by day as the RAF hammered German cities by night, culminating in a devastating attack on Dresden in February 1945 which created a firestorm in which 136,000 people perished. As the noose grew tighter, the demented Führer continued to issue bizarre battle strategies to non-existent armies until he finally retired to his Berlin bunker with his mistress, Eva Braun, where they committed suicide on 30 April 1945.

In the Pacific, the Japanese had been rolled steadily back to the limits of their defensive perimeter around the homeland. The heady days of conquest at Pearl Harbor, the Philippines, Singapore, Burma and the East Indies were now a fading memory as the Japanese Army faced defeat on all fronts.

At sea, the picture was even bleaker, as the Americans, now in possession of the largest Navy the world had ever seen, hounded the remains of the Imperial Navy to the very shores of Japan. Gen. MacArthur fulfilled his promise to return to the Philippines, and by the end of 1944 his troops were advancing through the island of Leyte. In Burma, British and Commonwealth forces of the 14th Army had pushed the Japanese back from the borders of India and were advancing on Mandalay, while in the east, Adm. Chester Nimitz's Marines had blasted a trail from Tarawa in the Gilbert Islands to Eniwetok, Peleliu and Saipan, Guam and Tinian in the Mariana Islands, where huge airfields were being carved out of the jungle for the assault on the Japanese mainland by B29 Superfortress bombers.

While no one doubted that Japan would be defeated, what was in doubt was the cost in human lives. The Shinto religion practised by the Japanese decreed that death was merely a transitory event, not to be feared, in which the spirit moved from one plane to another, where it would be reunited with those of its ancestors. Courage, honour, loyalty and self-sacrifice were lauded, together with a contempt for death. The divinity of the Emperor was a paramount belief, and in battle, the ultimate disgrace was to surrender or be taken prisoner – far better to die or commit suicide.

The Americans were fully aware of the resilience and commitment to ultimate self-sacrifice of the Japanese soldier. At Tarawa, of a garrison of some 4,700, only 17 Japanese allowed themselves to be captured, and at Peleliu, only 406 survived from a total of 11,000 – and many of these prisoners were Korean labourers who did not share the Japanese death wish. The Joint Chiefs of Staff viewed the impending invasion of the Japanese mainland with horror. The prospect of a drawn-out campaign of attrition against the Japanese – both military and civilian – in which every town, village and field would be defended to the death was appalling. Marine planners had already calculated a 60–70 per cent casualty figure for the first waves of assault troops, and a well-known general had privately suggested that these men should all write farewell letters to their families, to be left with the postal service for later despatch.

Air Force General Curtis LeMay had made a trip to Washington to plead his case for increased area bombing of Japanese cities – he was firmly convinced that a few more months of his incendiary raids would see the government bowing to civilian demands for an end to the war. Nevertheless, plans for the invasion continued to be implemented, while at the highest levels of government, the Manhattan Project – the manufacture and testing of an atomic weapon – was pushed forward at a frantic pace.

As the American bombing campaign grew in intensity, a tiny island roughly halfway between the Marianas and the Japanese mainland had now assumed tremendous importance. Iwo Jima – Sulphur Island – was the only island on the B29 bombers' route to Japan that was capable of housing airfields. For the Americans, it was a thorn in the side of the 20th Air Force: Japanese fighters could attack the Superfortress bombers on their flights to and from Japan, and the radar station on the island gave the homeland two hours' warning of an impeding raid. In US hands, these threats would be eliminated, and the Air Force would have the added bonus of an emergency landing site for damaged planes returning from their very long missions, and a base for the long-range P51 Mustang fighters to escort the bombers to the heart of Japan.

For the Japanese, Iwo Jima, part of the prefecture of Tokyo and therefore officially Japanese territory, was the last line of defence before the mainland. The military knew that the Americans would attempt to occupy the island, and were equally determined that they would extract a huge price in Marine casualties that would possibly make the US Government have second thoughts about an invasion of Japan. Therefore, on Monday 19 February 1945, Iwo Jima, some 660 miles south of Tokyo, became the scene of one of the bloodiest battles of the Second World War. Three Marine divisions landed in what the planners had expected to be a ten-day operation, but for thirty-five days they were locked in a deadly war of attrition with a Japanese force for whom surrender was not an option.

Commanded by a brilliant general and entrenched in an amazing labyrinth of underground tunnels, chambers, gun emplacements and command posts, the Japanese, forewarned of the American invasion and resigned to dying at their posts, were determined to take as many Marines with them as possible. 'Do not plan for my return,' wrote the commander of the island, Lt.-Gen. Kuribayashi, in one of his last letters to his wife. His words would also prove a prophetic epitaph for many thousands of US Marines. Five weeks later, 6,766 US personnel lay dead, and nearly 20,000 were wounded. Of the Japanese garrison of 21,060, only 1,083 remained alive at the end of the battle.

Maps

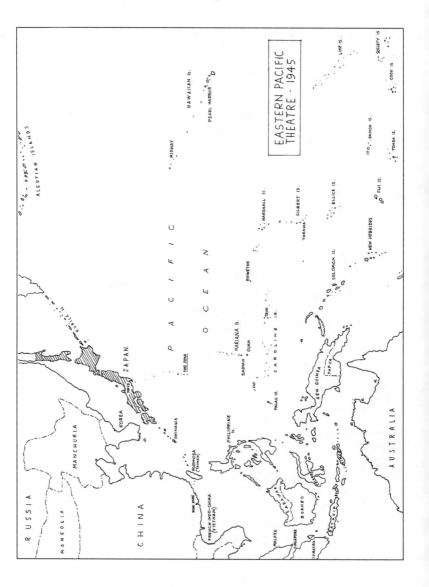

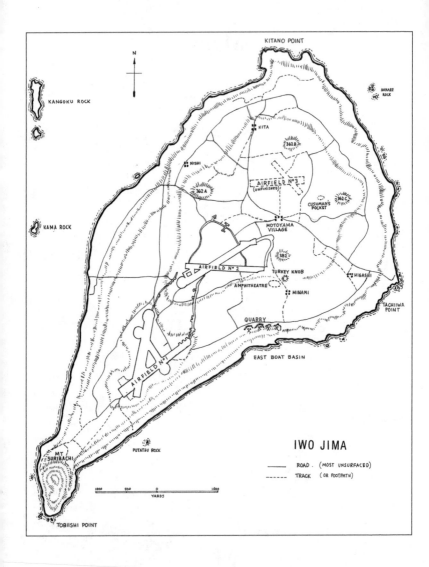

KITANO POINT

KANGOKU ROCK

N

MANABE ROCK

KITA

362 B

NISHI

AIRFIELD Nº3
(UNFINISHED)

362 A

CUSHMAN'S POCKET

362 C

KAMA ROCK

MOTOYAMA VILLAGE

382

AIRFIELD Nº 2

TURKEY KNOB

HIGASHI

AMPHITHEATRE

MINAMI

TACHIIWA POINT

QUARRY

EAST BOAT BASIN

IWO JIMA

PUTATSU ROCK

MT SURIBACHI

ROAD . (MOST UNSURFACED)

------ TRACK (OR FOOTPATH)

1000   500   0   1000
YARDS

TOBIISHI POINT

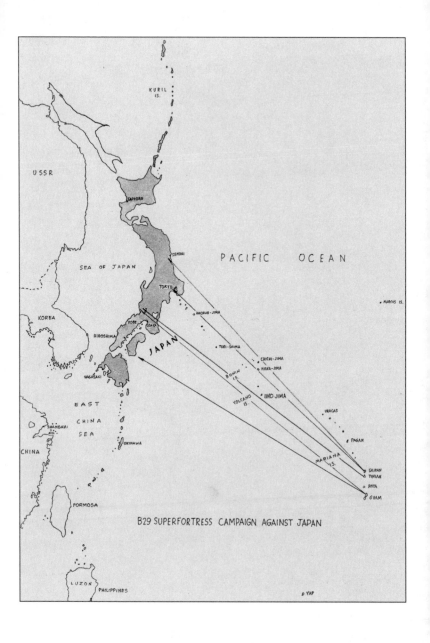

B29 SUPERFORTRESS CAMPAIGN AGAINST JAPAN

One

No Sparrows and No Swallows

In the beginning, Iwo Jima was just an unknown island in the north Pacific Ocean. In the end, it was to become the island of death. The Nanpo Shoto is a chain of bleak islands stretching for 750 miles into the Pacific from the edge of Tokyo Bay. With the exception of a few barren outcrops, the three principal groups are the Izu Shoto, the Bonin Islands, and at the end of the chain, the Volcano Islands. The islands aroused little interest over the centuries, although it is recorded that in 1543 a Spanish captain called Bernard de Torres visited the Volcano Islands, and the Bonins were briefly explored by Sadayori Ogasawara, a Japanese mariner, in 1593. Much later, in 1673, an Englishman called Gore set foot on Iwo Jima and named it Sulphur Island after the foul-smelling clouds of gas he saw rising from the earth. He professed an intense dislike of the place, and rapidly departed – an action that would have met with the US Marines' approval nearly three hundred years later.

Over the years, there were brief attempts at colonization, the most successful being in the 1830s, when a strange group consisting of British, Portuguese, Italians, Hawaiians and a sole American called Nathaniel Savory of Massachusetts sailed to Chi-Chi Jima and claimed the island on behalf of the British Crown. By 1891, the Japanese had asserted sole authority over the whole of the Nanpo Shoto, and began a discreet colonization of the inhabitable islands, finally bringing them under the jurisdiction of the Tokyo prefecture.

When in 1941 the Japanese Empire launched its attack on Pearl Harbor and America and Japan went to war, the population of Iwo Jima numbered 1,091. The islanders occupied a number of small villages, the capital, Motoyama, Nishi, Kita and Minami being the largest. The principal industry was the refining of sulphur, the only natural commodity, although this was supplemented by a small sugar cane plantation and some fishing. A great deal of the food for the island was brought in by ship, and water was a constant problem – there was no natural supply, and a system of concrete cisterns had to be constructed to collect rainwater, but even so, water was still imported.

Iwo Jima is 660 nautical miles south of Tokyo, and 625 miles north of Saipan in the Mariana Islands – almost halfway, a location that was to give the island immense importance later in the war. From the air, Iwo Jima has been described as resembling a pork chop, others see an ice cream cone: For the Marines who fought there in 1945, it simply looked like Hell: 'I don't have to worry about going to Hell,' said one veteran, 'I've been there already.'

The island is some 4½ miles long, with its longest axis running from south-west to north-east; it tapers from 2½ miles wide at the northerly section to a mere ½ mile in the south, giving a total land area of around 7½ square miles. At the base of the island lies Mt Suribachi, a 550 ft high dormant volcano – a strategically important feature with commanding views over most of the island. The beaches that stretch north and north-east from Mt Suribachi are terraced at various heights and widths by storms and constant wave action. There is no harbour or anchorage on the island, and the surf conditions, even in good weather, are not particularly conducive to landing operations.

In the centre of this lower part of Iwo Jima lay Airfield No. 1 (the Japanese used the prefix Motoyama for the three Airfields on the island, but for simplicity, they will be referred to in this book as 'Nos 1, 2 and 3'). Airfield No. 1 was constructed on a plateau, and had three runways, together with taxiways and revetments. Further north, at the wider part of the island, a second plateau, roughly a mile in diameter, housed Airfield No. 2, and a little further north lay the as yet unfinished third airfield.

The ground that slopes away from this northern plateau is a mass of gorges, valleys, ridges and hillocks – perfect ground for defensive fighting. At various points all over the island, foul-smelling clouds of sulphurous vapour are vented from fissures in the earth. The north-easterly shore of Iwo Jima, between Kitano Point and Tachiiwa Point – a distance of some two miles, is a mass of steep cliffs leading to barren, rocky shores. The climate is variable – cool from December to April (63–70°F), and warmer from May to November (73–80°F), and the annual rainfall is around 60 in. The poor soil allows only coarse grass and stunted trees to grow – Army Major Yokasuka Horie wrote to his wife: 'It has been written in the geographical books that this is an island of sulphur, – no water, no sparrows and no swallows.'

As early as March 1944, reinforcements were on the way to Iwo Jima. The Japanese High Command watched with increasing alarm the inexorable progress of Adm. Nimitz's Marines across the Pacific from Tarawa to the Marshall Islands and on to Peleliu, Saipan, Tinian and Guam. They knew that with airfields in the Marianas, the Americans would be looking to Iwo Jima, the only island in the whole of the Nanpo Shoto range capable of housing major airfields, as a halfway haven for their Superfortress bombers. After centuries of obscurity, the island had assumed a position of major strategic importance.

In May 1944, Lt.-Gen. Tadamichi Kuribayashi was summoned to the office of Gen. Tojo, the Japanese Prime Minister, and informed that he would be the next commander of the garrison on Iwo Jima. Whether by accident or design, the appointment was a stroke of genius. Kuribayashi, descendant of a long and distinguished military line, was also a Samurai, the warrior caste of Japan that has its origins in the middle ages. At 53, he could look back on a career spanning thirty years, including a spell as an attaché in America.

Like another great Japanese commander, Adm. Yamamoto, he had witnessed at first hand the vast industrial potential of America, and was of the opinion that war with it was futile. Kuribayashi had followed the progress of the war with growing dismay. The heady days of victory in 1941 and 1942 were over, and the forces of the Empire were being rolled back on land and sea – he knew that an Allied victory was now inevitable. Certain in the knowledge that the Americans would eventually secure Iwo Jima, he viewed the appointment as both a challenge and a death sentence: 'Do not plan for my return,' he wrote in one of his frequent letters to Yoshii, his wife.

Kuribayashi had carefully studied the tactics of the Japanese commanders on the various islands that had fallen to the US Marines in the Pacific – Tarawa, Kwajalein, Peleliu and the Marianas – and realized that previous methods of defence had failed. Nowhere had the attempts to thwart an invasion on the beaches worked, even at Tarawa, where shallow water on the reefs surrounding the island of Betio had forced large numbers of the invaders to wade hundreds of yards to the beach under murderous fire, and he regarded the traditional *banzai* charge as little more than frenzied suicide.

He was intrigued by the battle for Peleliu in the Palau Islands, where the Japanese commander had conducted a fighting retreat into the Umurbrogol Mountains and waged a suicidal battle of attrition among the caves valleys, gorges and rocks. This was a different concept – as the commander had put it: 'It is most urgent to lead the enemy to confusion and destruction by concentrating firepower from our strongpoints remaining in his midst, even though partially trampled under foot by landings, and to carry out strong counter-attacks from previously planned and prepared positions.' Kuribayashi approved of this strategy – the enemy would not be defeated, but they would pay heavily for every inch of Iwo Jima.

Once he had arrived on the island, Kuribayashi lost no time in implementing his strategy despite opposition from Gen. Osuga and Col. Hori, two of the Army staff who had been with the original reinforcements sent out in March. His first order was for the return of all civilians to the homeland – their presence would serve no useful purpose, and they would be a drain on the limited supplies of food and water. With the arrival of more troops and Korean labourers, a massive programme of tunnelling got under way. Cave experts were flown in from Japan to advise the Army on important aspects of the programme, such as reinforcement of strongpoints, ventilation and direction.

The tunnellers had an important advantage, since most of the sub-surface of the island was made up of soft pumice-like volcanic rock which could be cut relatively quickly with hand tools. In the nine months available to the defenders before the invasion, an astonishing complex of tunnels, caves, gun emplacements, pillboxes and command posts was constructed. It was found that the volcanic ash mixed well with cement, and provided a cheap and convenient building material – when reinforced with steel wire, the Japanese were able to provide their bunkers with up to four feet of defensive protection. Many of the tunnels and all of the command posts, some of them up to seventy-five feet underground, were wired for electricity, and in the northern part of the island in particular, the tunnels linked positions that were up to half a mile apart. Tunnels were built above other tunnels, and 'spidertraps' (covered pits in the ground) were arranged so that during the battle, Marines often found themselves destroying one position only to find the same enemy sniper popping up minutes later from another position fifty or sixty yards away. Many Marines, resting during the night, reported hearing voices and movement coming from the ground beneath them, and after the capture of Mt Suribachi at the southern end of the island, many of the defenders joined the troops fighting in the north by by-passing the Marine lines through one or other of the labyrinth of tunnels.

The tiny 'Grasshopper' spotter planes used to locate enemy positions often returned with the news that they hadn't seen the enemy at all, only groups of Marines. Private First Class (Pfc) Jesse Cass, a BAR man with the 4th Division, writes:

> I landed on Iwo on the fourth day. I was assigned to cover three flamethrowers and we spent two days burning out Jap positions near the quarry. On the third day we were closing in on a cave when a mortar shell landed among us. One of the flamethrower guys was killed and I got a piece of metal in my face – they carried me away and I was on a hospital ship before night. During the whole of my time on Iwo Jima I never saw a Jap.

A new command was based in Iwo Jima – the 109th Infantry Division, which was supplemented by troops originally destined for the defence of Saipan. By the time of the American victory in the Marianas in July, the defences of Iwo Jima were formidable. Supplying the island was a problem: with no harbour of its own, the transport ships were compelled to dock at Chichi Jima in the Bonin Islands, where supplies, weapons, troops and ammunition were transferred onto small vessels for the 150-mile trip to Iwo Jima.

This route soon attracted the attention of the Americans, and became a target for bombers and submarines operating from the Marianas. An early casualty was the 26th Tank Regiment, deployed from Yokahama on 14 July, which fell victim to the submarine USS *Cobia* when it sank the transport *Nisshu Maru* with the loss of twenty-eight tanks. Aware of the Japanese build-up on Iwo Jima, the US Navy sent a Task Force under Rear-Adm. Joseph J. Clark to attack the island on 15 June. Aircraft from seven carriers pounded the airfields and engaged the Japanese fighter force in fierce dogfights in which ten of the Japanese planes were shot down. The following day, the Japanese failed to intercept the Americans, and the Navy planes bombed and strafed the island at will, destroying a number of aircraft on the ground, and taking many photographs of the installations and terrain which were of great value when compared with later shots to evaluate the progress of the build-up of the Japanese defences. Clark made a third visit on 24 June, and this time the enemy responded by sending up their entire fighter force of eighty planes, but the pilots were young and inexperienced, and only fourteen of them escaped the Hellcats and Corsairs of the Navy.

In June, Maj. Yoshitaka Horie was sent to Iwo Jima to become a member of Gen. Kuribayashi's staff. As an officer who knew and had served under the General and survived the war, his observations are of great value. Horie was aware of the tunnels that were being constructed throughout the island: 'In order to connect with each defensive position we planned to make 28,000 metres of underground tunnels, and began this work in December 1944, but by the time the American forces landed on Iwo Jima, we had only made 5,000 metres.' However, in view of the masses of subterranean workings that were discovered after the battle, this is a major underestimation.

Gen. Kuribayashi issued a document to his troops called the 'Courageous Battle Vows', in which he explained what was expected of them:

We shall dedicate ourselves and our entire strength to the defence of this island. We shall grasp bombs, charge enemy tanks, and destroy them. We shall infiltrate into the midst of the enemy and annihilate them. With every salvo we shall, without fail, kill the enemy. Each man will make it his duty to kill ten of the enemy before dying. Until we are destroyed, to the last man we will harass the enemy with guerrilla tactics.

With his defences prepared and his men ready to fight to the finish, Kuribayashi waited serenely for the approaching American invasion force: 'I sing some songs and go to bed by six,' he wrote to his wife.

Two

Superfortress

The stories of the battle for Iwo Jima and the bombing campaign waged by the 20th Air Force against the Japanese mainland are irrevocably linked. Prior to the invasion of Saipan, Tinian and Guam (the three largest islands in the Marianas group) by the Marines of the 2nd, 3rd and 4th Divisions, the B29 Superfortress bombers had been limited to carrying out raids on the southern islands of Japan from bases in central China. Beleaguered by problems – including the need to fly all their aviation fuel over thousands of miles of inhospitable country, poor navigation by inexperienced crews, and the limitation of small bomb loads – the offensive had proved to be ineffective. Now, with the establishment of five huge airfields 1,500 miles south-east of Tokyo, the way was open for a massive offensive against the whole of the Japanese mainland.

The main obstacle to these missions was Iwo Jima. Situated halfway between Japan and the Marianas, it had two active airfields, with a third under construction. The B29s heading north were constantly under attack from fighters on the island, and the radar station on Mt Suribachi, primitive as it was, was capable of giving the homeland two hours' warning of an impending attack.

As the airfields on the Marianas took shape, Japanese bombers flying from Iwo Jima made frequent raids, destroying aircraft and installations. It was obvious that Iwo Jima had to come under American control, not only to neutralize the enemy attacks, but to provide a forward refuge for damaged bombers, as a base for air–sea rescue operations, and for P51

Mustang fighters to escort the Superfortresses on the second leg of their long trip to Japan.

A number of years before the outbreak of the Second World War, far-sighted planners within the Air Force had explored the concept of a 'super-bomber'. Working on the assumption that Germany would overrun Europe in a future war, the Air Force chiefs envisaged an aircraft with a range of 5,000 miles or more, a top speed of 400 m.p.h., and a large bomb load. The outbreak of the war in 1939 gave the programme an added impetus, and specifications were given to the four largest aircraft manufacturers – Boeing, Consolidated-Vultee, Lockheed and Douglas. By early 1940, the choice had narrowed to two, Boeing and Consolidated, and both were given contracts worth over $85,000 to proceed with wind tunnel tests. Concurrently, the Wright Aeronautical Corporation was commissioned to produce a larger and more powerful version of its Cyclone radial engine which had proved to be so successful in the B17 Flying Fortress. In September 1942, the Boeing option, the B29, made its maiden flight in Seattle, and the world's most advanced bomber was born.

The revolutionary design produced a number of 'firsts': the first bomber to have pressurized areas for the crew, allowing the plane to fly at very high altitudes, and the first to have a remotely-controlled gunnery system. The only manned gun was in the tail, the remaining four low-profile turrets were controlled by gunners operating computers that calculated target speed, distance, altitude and direction.

To give the aircraft the speed the specification demanded, the B29 was designed with long, narrow wings, a feature known as high wing loading, common on modern airliners, but novel in the 1940s. High wing loading results in high landing speeds – which was to provide difficulties for the first crews – and, of course, high landing speeds means long runways, an added task for the Seabee construction crews hacking the wartime airfields out of virgin jungle.

Unfortunately, the Superfortress programme did not proceed as smoothly as the Air Force or Boeing had anticipated. The new Wright Cyclone R-3350 engines were prone to overheating problems – indeed, the second B29 prototype crashed into a meat-processing factory on the edge of Boeing's airfield near Seattle with one of its engines blazing, resulting in the death of the chief test pilot, Edmund T. Allen, and ten members of the project development team, and the whole programme was delayed for many months. In their attempt to make the huge engines as light as possible, the manufacturers had compacted the front and rear rows of cylinders and made wide use of magnesium in place of the usual aluminium in the construction of a number of the components. With an inadequate air flow, the engines overheated, and the combustible magnesium burned through the engines and into the main wing spars. To alleviate the problems, the oil flow to the exhaust valves was increased, cowl flaps were redesigned to increase the flow of air, and baffles were installed to redirect the air flow through the nacelles. Despite the improvements, fire remained a serious problem for a long time, even when the bombers became operational in the Marianas.

The production of the Superfortress was spread over four massive plants – the Boeing works at Renton in Washington, Glen Martin's works at Omaha in Nebraska, and two new facilities specially constructed for the B29 project, at Wichita in Kansas and Marietta in Georgia. Additional sub-contract work for items such as gun turrets and undercarriages was given to companies previously unconnected to aircraft production, the Chrysler Car Company, the Fisher Body

Division of General Motors, the Goodyear Tire and Rubber Company, and a host of smaller manufacturers.

Even before the Marines had completely liberated the islands of the Marianas, the bulldozers of the Army Air Force engineers and the Seabees were busy carving great swathes out of the jungle and scrubland to provide the airfields for the Superfortresses. Five huge sites were constructed, two on Guam, two on Tinian and one on Saipan. Each airfield was virtually a small town, apart from the usual workshops, administration facilities and communication centres, shops, banks, post offices and cinemas sprang up to service the large numbers of air and ground staff. On Guam, at the height of operations in 1945, there were 65,000 Air Force and 78,000 Navy personnel alone.

The five Wings of the B29 force, the 21st Bomber Command, came under the direct supervision of the Commanding General of the Air Force, Gen. Henry 'Hap' Arnold, in Washington, and the first local commander was Brig.-Gen. Haywood S. Hansell Jr – 'Possum' to his friends. Upon his arrival on 12 October 1944, Hansell, very much aware of the very limited experience of his new B29 crews, initiated an intense training programme which culminated in a raid on the Japanese base at Truk on 28 October. The bombing results were not encouraging, and three of the eighteen planes taking part failed to locate the target. Further training raids were carried out on the two airfields on Iwo Jima in preparation for the first major raid on the Japanese mainland.

Hansell was an advocate of daylight precision bombing. Having served with the 8th Air Force in Britain and witnessed the excellent results the B17 Flying Fortresses had achieved in virtually wiping out the German oil industry, he was confident that similar methods would devastate the Japanese war industry. Following a photo-reconnaissance flight over the capital on 1 November, plans were laid for the first attack on Tokyo since the famous 'Doolittle' raid of 1942.

As dawn broke on 24 November, 110 Superfortresses thundered down the runways of Isley Field on Saipan and headed north. Led by Gen. O'Donnell in 'Dauntless Dotty', the crews settled down for their 7½-hour flight to the Japanese mainland. In the back of their minds, they were aware that their chances of recovery were slim should they have to ditch their aircraft in the vast areas of ocean between the Marianas and Japan – what would befall them should they have to bail out over the Japanese mainland was something they tried not to think about.

The target for this first raid was the Nakajima aircraft engine works in the Tokyo suburb of Musashino. Warned by the radar station on Iwo Jima, the enemy put up a heavy anti-aircraft barrage, and forty fighters made some rather cautious interceptions. Once the bombers had formed up on their bombing run at altitudes of 27,000–33,000 ft, the crewmen were astonished to find themselves approaching the target at speeds of over 450 m.p.h. Bombardiers struggled with their bombsight calculations as the target area raced towards them – a task that was not helped by heavy cloud conditions.

What the B29 crews had discovered was the jet stream, the sub-stratospheric wind that blows between the troposphere and the stratosphere, which was virtually unknown at that time. As a result, the raid was a failure, eight bombers were damaged and one shot down, and the bombing was scattered, few bombs hitting the target.

Three days later, a force of eighty-one Superfortresses returned to Musashino, but this time the jet stream raced the bombers over the target at over 550 m.p.h., and it remained unscathed. All the evidence showed that daylight precision bombing under these conditions was impossible. In subsequent raids, the jet stream and stiffening Japanese opposition played havoc with Hansell's strategy. Other targets were selected, and some improvements were forthcoming, but 'Possum' was becoming disillusioned, and in a bitter attack on his crews he announced: 'In my opinion you people havn't earned your pay over here. Unless you do better, this operation is doomed to failure.' Under mounting pressure from the 20th Air Force HQ in Washington for better results from the attacks on the principal Japanese cities, controversy arose between Hansell and the policy makers in Washington, led by the 20th Air Force Chief of Staff, Lauris Norstad, over the issue of area bombing versus precision bombing.

The start of 1945 saw morale in 21st Bomber Command at a low ebb. Of the 188 crew members who had died so far, 116 of them had been lost at sea when damaged aircraft had been forced to ditch in the Pacific with no refuge on the 1,500-mile return trip. A complex rescue network had been assembled – submarines between Japan and Iwo Jima, and destroyers and flying boats elsewhere – but with such vast areas of water to cover, the success rate was depressingly low.

By mid-January 1945, the chiefs in Washington had decided that Hansell must go. His replacement was Curtis Le May, a brilliant tactician who had formerly been in command of the 3rd Division of the 8th Air Force in England, where his tough stance had earned him the nickname 'Iron Arse'. The cigar-chewing General surveyed the problem in his cool, logical way – daylight high-altitude precision bombing did not work, so why not try a completely different approach.

On 9 March, the crews assembled for their briefing and were left speechless by what they heard. They were to attack Tokyo at night, at altitudes of 6,000–10,000 ft, and as if that were not enough, all bomb bay fuel tanks were to be removed (they would not need the extra gas if they did not have to climb to the usual 30,000 ft), all guns and their operators were to go, apart from the tail-gunner who was retained for observation purposes only, and the bomb load was to be all-incendiary.

There was talk among the crews of a 'suicide mission', and some pilots who had not served under Le May before openly doubted his sanity. Le May's answer was forthright: 'If this raid works the way I think it will, we can shorten the war.' But privately, he knew his career was on the line, and he admitted to a colleague: 'I was very nervous about the mission.'

Le May's great gamble paid off. Guided by Pathfinder planes, 334 Superfortresses saturated a three-mile by five-mile area of Tokyo with napalm-filled incendiaries, and a firestorm soon developed. At its centre, the temperature reached a staggering 1,800°F. Gen. Thomas S. Power, who led the raid, climbed to 20,000 ft to survey the scene: 'It was a hell of a good mission,' he later told Le May.

Only fourteen aircraft were lost, and of these, five crews were recovered by the air–sea rescue services. Reconnaissance pictures showed that nearly 16 square miles of the city had been totally destroyed, and the official death count was 83,793 killed and 40,918 injured. Eager to capitalize on his success, Le May launched a series of similar raids on major cities like Nagoya, Osaka and Kobe, with equally devastating results.

By now, the Japanese airfields on Iwo Jima had been captured by the Marines after bitter fighting, and bombers damaged during the raids on the mainland had a halfway refuge on their return. By April, squadrons of P51 Mustang fighters were operational, and could escort the bombers on the last leg of their missions. Forming up behind the B29s, the Mustangs were guided to Japan, and provided excellent cover. The statistics showed a dramatic reduction in bomber losses.

There was little respite for the Japanese as city after city was engulfed in flames. So frequent were the attacks that at one time Le May's planes ran out of incendiary bombs, and only a mammoth effort by the Navy replenished their stocks. The *kamikaze* attacks on the amphibious forces off the shores of Okinawa caused Adm. Nimitz to request the bombing of all nearby Japanese airfields, but once this task had been completed, Le May swiftly returned to the task of devastating Japan.

In conjunction with the firestorm raids on Japan's major cities, 21st Bomber Command, at the request of Adm. Nimitz, began OPERATION STARVATION, the mining of most of the routes used by Japan's merchant shipping. Beginning on the night of 27 March, the 313th Wing, operating from North Field, Tinian, began the systematic mining of the harbours of Tokyo, Kure, Hiroshima, Sasebo, Tokuyama and Nagoya, together with strategic areas of the East China Sea, the Sea of Japan and the Inland Sea. The results were dramatic: from an initial 18 ships sunk in April, the count rose to 83 in May, and 85 in June. Despite frantic minesweeping operations, major ports were paralysed for up to ten days at a time: 'You were eventually starving the country,' said the commander of the minesweeping force after the war. The 313th Wing dropped a total of 12,053 mines, the largest operation of its kind ever undertaken, and earned the warm praise of Adm. Nimitz.

Meanwhile, Le May's relentless bombing campaign continued unabated, and city after city virtually disappeared in flames. As the enemy fighter opposition was gradually driven from the sky by the Iwo Jima-based Mustangs, the B29s took to dropping leaflets to warn the civilian population of the next target for destruction.

Civilian morale was near breaking point as thousands fled the cities for the open countryside. In one three-month period alone, the Superfortresses had wiped out 105 square miles of the centres of Japan's six major cities, and the Minister of Home Affairs considered defence measures 'a futile effort'. Le May never wavered in his belief that his bombing campaign would end the war, even to the point of going to Washington to tell the Joint Chiefs of Staff of his conviction that Japan could be burned into surrender.

In June, a mysterious unit called the 509th Composite Group arrived at North Field on Tinian, and was assigned a compound that was isolated from the other Bomb Groups. The crews were given training missions to fly, and did not partake in the regular bombing missions assigned to the other units. None of the crews talked about their work. In fact, few of them, apart from their commander, Col. Paul W. Tibbets Jr, knew exactly what they were expected to do. This all changed on the morning of 6 August, when Col. Tibbets, piloting 'Enola Gay', dropped a single bomb into the centre of Hiroshima – eight days later, the war was over.

Bombing Japan was a hazardous business. Not only were the distances involved wearing on the crews, but the ever-present dangers of ditching in a cold and remote area of the North Pacific in an 80-ton bomber meant that the chances of survival were poor. Even worse was the prospect of bailing out over Japan: many crews were known to have been beheaded, and the lucky ones were imprisoned in grim POW camps. After the war, horrific cases of airmen being displayed in cages and even buried alive were verified.

As soon as the fighting had ceased, many Superfortresses were sent on missions to Japan to drop food and other supplies for camps known to hold allied POWs. The 444th Bomb Group was employed on a number of these missions, and Chuck Davis, a navigator with the Group recalls one in particular:

On 23 August 1945, we flew to nearby Saipan to have supplies loaded with parachutes and packed into our bomb bays. Then, back to Tinian – we had a briefing as to where we were to go and what to look for, because the Japanese had been instructed to paint the roofs of each camp with big letters 'PW'. We and another B29 from our Group were given the longest mission of all.

Our target was a camp deep in the mountains of northern Hokkaido, along a canyon on the Ishikari River. We were told that the prisoners worked in coal mines in this area. Our route to Hokkaido began at 4.00 a.m. and took us over Iwo Jima and to the coast of northern Honshu at Sendai. I must mention that not all Japanese were aware that the war was over, and some planes had been shot at, and one was even brought down, so we were apprehensive as we crossed the coast and flew north over Japan from there.

When we reached the gulf north of Honshu and neared Hokkaido, we had to fly close to the water because a typhoon had just entered the area, and we had to navigate by sight if we were to see our designated landmarks. In fact, we were so low that as we crossed the beach, a small boy threw a rock at us! So when we came to the major Hokkaido city of Sapporo at a few hundred feet off the ground we must have spooked the inhabitants no end, because people were running in all directions, and trucks, cars, and locomotives were heading out of town.

We picked up our river north of the town, and snaked along with the hills along each side getting steeper as we went. The clouds were getting lower and rain was beginning to fall as we saw the tell-tale 'PW' on a roof beside the river. We were elated, not from our skill in getting there, but that there was a camp there after all and some of our guys may be in it. We had to fly up and around into another canyon so that our drop path into the camp area came from the same direction as our first pass.

This time, we could see people running and waving as we opened our doors and jettisoned the cargo. Unfortunately, the wind blew some 'chutes over the river, but that didn't seem to bother those on the ground, because we could see them crossing the river in pursuit. By this time, the typhoon had caught up to us in buckets of rain and visibility near zero. We were left with two choices: fly through the mountains or get above the storm. We chose the former, and after what seemed like an eternity, we reached the coast. What a beautiful sight the ocean was, even with the typhoon still going strong.

The other B29 Superfortress caught up with us about twenty miles out of Iwo Jima, when they lost an engine and requested priority landing status. By now Iwo were streetwise and knew that B29s have no trouble landing with one engine out, so they denied the request.

Seconds after, it called Iwo again to say that a second engine had stopped and they wanted a straight approach. Still Iwo was adamant, and told them to make a standard approach. By this time, we were about to call for landing instructions, but decided to let our sister ship have first choice. It was then that we heard them call Iwo that they had lost the third engine – this got Iwo's attention!

By then they were a couple of miles out, and Iwo cleared them for a direct approach, but alas it was not to be. Their next transmission was a Mayday call saying that they had lost their fourth engine because they were completely out of fuel. We were circling overhead and could watch the entire drama unfold. Their plane made a wheels-up ditching, and came to a stop. As it bobbed in the ocean, we could see a rescue boat heading for them. Then crewmen began scrambling onto the fuselage and wings. By the time the boat arrived, we could see that all had exited the plane and were making their way to the boat. Don't ask why, but they then attached a line to the plane and began towing it to shore.

By then, it was about a mile offshore, but as expected, it began to sink, and the tow was abandoned. However, all the crew were saved and returned safely to their home base. Our stay on Iwo Jima that time was much more leisurely, and we were able to see some of the island.

The crews of the 20th Air Force were eternally grateful to the Marines for taking Iwo Jima. It has been estimated that the lives of 24,761 Superfortress crew were saved during the bombing campaign because of its availability.

Chuck Davis is one of those crewmen who sings the praises of the liberators of Iwo Jima, and recalls his introduction to the island:

It was a bright, clear day, one of those days one could stay in bed or head for the beach. However, we were up long before the sun, being briefed for our next mission, a medium-level daylight run up the Inland Sea to Osaka. Our and another Group's target was the Sumitomo aircraft parts plant. Our Wing, along with Wings from Guam and Saipan, was part of an all-out effort of 600 planes hitting the Osaka–Nagoya area that day.

Everything was uneventful until we joined formation of perhaps 70–100 planes to make the first run. At that point, the lead plane developed engine trouble and fell out of formation. As the deputy leader took over, he radioed (over clear air) that we were to change altitude, and gave the new altitude over the air! The plane off our left wing was immediately hit by anti-aircraft fire and broke in two. Several in the formation were seriously damaged and crews injured after our altitude was gratuitously given.

We received our share of holes, but fortunately no one was hurt, but one of our engine's fuel lines was knocked out and leaking, which meant that we were heading for our first visit to Iwo Jima, along with more than one hundred other B29s carrying over 1,100 crewmen.

Along with our apprehension over the engine problem, we discovered to our great delight that one of the 500 lb demolition bombs had stuck up in our bomb bay. We could just imagine the delight the Iwo tower would also feel when we told them what we had to land with!

The Second Pilot was delegated the chore of walking along the catwalk in the bomb bay with the doors open and manually releasing the 500 lb baby, hopefully on some unsuspecting Japanese war activist who felt that he was far from the combat zone. With the bomb gone, we headed away from Honshu until we picked up the Iwo Jima radar beacon on the scope.

Our feeling on seeing that beacon was as if we had just run out of gas in our new '39 Ford on the crest of a hill and there was a gas station at the bottom! But Iwo was not ready. We came along with over a hundred other B29s with the same thought in mind: fuel, repairs, medical help and rest. Planes were stacked wingtip to wingtip the entire length of both sides of the runway and any other place that was strong enough to take the weight. Some even got stuck in the black volcanic ash that seemed to be everywhere after the Seebees finished the runways.

Iwo's facilities were overwhelmed, and there was only time for Band-aid repairs, so as soon as one plane was patched up and fuelled, it left for its home field – rest was out of the question. I think that we were on the ground not much more than an hour, if that. With hose clamps and enough fuel to get us to Tinian, we were in the air again, saying a prayer for those Marines who gave us a second chance. Yes, the 20th Air Force loved Iwo Jima! God bless all that made it so.

Three

Operation Detachment

I knew we would win – we always did.
(Lt.-Gen. Holland M. Smith)

Mounting a large-scale amphibious assault against a heavily defended island is a daunting task, as the Marines had learned to their cost at Tarawa and a host of other Pacific islands. Gen. Patton once said 'In landing operations, retreat is impossible', but by 1945 the US Marine Corps had fine-honed the technique at Eniwetok, Peleliu and the Marianas until it developed a mastery it still enjoys to this day.

At Iwo Jima, the Joint Expeditionary Force Commander was Adm. Richmond Kelly Turner. Since the pioneering days of seaborne landings at Guadalcanal, Turner had led every major amphibious operation in the Pacific, and was the obvious choice. In overall command of OPERATION DETACHMENT was Adm. Raymond A. Spruance, Chester Nimitz's right-hand man since June 1942, when Adm. 'Bull' Halsey had plucked him from relative obscurity as a Cruiser Division commander to lead the American carrier force at the battle of Midway when Halsey was confined to a hospital bed in Hawaii with a skin complaint. The self-effacing and introverted Spruance was to lead every amphibious assault from Tarawa to the final battle at Okinawa.

The 5th Amphibious Corps (VAC), composed of the 3rd, 4th and 5th Marine Divisions, was to mount the attack on Iwo Jima. The Marine force was under the overall command of Lt.-Gen. Holland M. Smith – affectionately known to his men as

'Howlin' Mad' Smith. The irascible 58-year-old was facing his last assignment, since a combination of age and political back-stabbing had hastened the end of his career. In the United States, a clique of powerful publishing barons, all of whom had been key figures in the pre-Pearl Harbor isolationist lobby, were now running a vitriolic campaign against Nimitz and his Marine generals in favour of Gen. Douglas MacArthur. Robert R. McCormick, publisher of the *Chicago Tribune*, had described Smith as a 'cold blooded murderer – indiscriminate waster of human life', while William Randolph Hearst, owner of the massive Hearst publishing empire, who had recently been lampooned by Orson Welles in his film *Citizen Kane*, lent his support to MacArthur in his papers. To add to his problems, the US Army, smarting from the humiliation of having two of its generals relieved of command by Smith for 'lack of aggressiveness', also had their daggers at the ready.

Smith was content to take a relatively low-key approach to his position at Iwo Jima in favour of Maj.-Gen. Harry Schmidt, the VAC Commander. 'I think they asked me along in case anything happened to Harry Schmidt,' he was to say later.

Totalling over 70,000 men, the three Divisions were largely made up of seasoned veterans of the Pacific campaigns. The 3rd Division, which had battle experience ranging from Bougainville to the Solomons and Guam, was commanded by Maj.-Gen. Graves B. Erskine, at forty-seven, one of the Marine Corps' toughest generals, and a veteran of the First World War. The 4th Division, heading for its fourth battle in twelve months, was under Maj.-Gen. Clifton B. Cates, another First World War campaigner, famous in Marine circles for a message he sent from the front: 'I have no one at my left, and only a few at my right – I will hold.'

Although it had yet to see action, the 5th Division had a hard core of seasoned troops from the former Raider

Battalions and the Marine Paratroopers, both of which units had recently been disbanded. Under Maj.-Gen. Keller E. Rockey, who had distinguished himself at Chateau Thierry in 1918, they were to prove themselves at Iwo Jima.

At Tarawa and other earlier landings, equipment had been at a premium. Now, in the last year of the war, with the American war machine working at full stretch, the planners had the luxury of almost unlimited choice. To accompany the 5th Amphibious Corps, 485 vessels, including 12 aircraft carriers, 8 battleships, 19 cruisers, 44 destroyers and 43 transports, were assembled, and the combined Navy and Marine force would total over a quarter of a million men. 'I was not afraid of the outcome of the battle, I knew we would win – we always did. But contemplating the cost in lives caused me many sleepless nights,' said Smith.

When Holland Smith received his instructions from Adm. Nimitz on 9 October 1944 to prepare for the invasion of Iwo Jima, he outlined his proposals in a letter to Harry Schmidt who was still on Guam with the 3rd Division. Schmidt and his staff immediately flew to Pearl Harbor, and by mid-October, had formulated the basic outline of the invasion.

The plan was relatively simple – from aerial photographs and maps that had been produced following the extensive reconnaissance of the island by B24 Liberator bombers of the 7th Air Force, it was obvious that there were only two stretches of beach upon which the Marines could make a landing. Gen. Kuribayashi had come to the same conclusion many months earlier, and had laid his plans accordingly.

Both of these landing sites stretched northwards from the base of Mt Suribachi, and the 3,500 yd from the volcano to the East Boat Basin, which enjoyed the advantage of the prevailing wind, was obviously the better choice. The isolation of Mt Suribachi, with its commanding view over most of the island, was the primary objective – once this had been achieved, the force would swing north and attack on a broad front.

At one stage, the planners had contemplated the use of gas to neutralize the enemy garrison. Gas shells were to be fired from warships upwind, and after a suitable period, the Marines would come ashore and occupy the island without the loss of a single man. There was considerable support for the idea in Washington, until President Roosevelt came to hear of it and dismissed the idea – not out of sympathy for the Japanese, but more out of apprehension at the possible wave of outrage among the American public at the use of this kind of weapon.

As the plans came to fruition, it was time to assemble the invasion force. The 3rd Division was the nearest to Iwo Jima, having remained on Guam after taking the island in August 1944. Part of its 'training' included digging out the many Japanese troops still holed up in caves, prepared to fight to the death.

The 4th Division was on Maui in the Hawaiian Islands, and on the neighbouring island of Hawaii, the 5th Division, fresh from Camp Pendleton in California, was at Camp Tawara on the huge Parker Ranch – a sprawl of huts and tents which had originally been established to receive the 2nd Division after its savage battle in the Gilbert Islands.

A reinforced Marine Division usually numbered 20,000–25,000 men, predominantly infantry, each Division had three Regiments of 3,000 men, each Regiment had three Battalions of 1,000 men, a Battalion was divided into three Companies of about 250, and was sub-divided into Platoons of 58–60 men.

To ensure that a Division was as self-contained as possible, a whole host of specialized units were required – Artillery, Motor Transport, Amphibious Landing Craft, Engineers,

Communications, Medical, Intelligence, Military Police, Signals – the list was impressive, as was the amount of equipment and stores that was needed to supply them. Supply ships began loading as early as November, over three months before the invasion, and the list was seemingly endless, ranging from essentials such as water, blood, ammunition, gasoline and food to the bizarre – holy water, dog food, toilet paper and, out of sight of the troops, packs of pre-painted white crosses.

The length of the pre-invasion naval bombardment of the island became a subject of bitter controversy. Gen. Schmidt, in his planning programme, had asked for ten continuous days of shelling by battleships and cruisers, Adm. Hill rejected the idea on the grounds that there would be insufficient time to re-arm his ships before D-Day. Schmidt persisted, and on 8 November submitted a revised request for nine days' shelling. This was also turned down – the Navy thought three days would suffice.

In fact, the Navy had an alternative agenda: a major assault was being planned against the Japanese mainland by aircraft of Task Force 58. To Holland Smith, this was a secondary operation to the Iwo Jima invasion: 'I could not forget the sight of Marines dead in the lagoon or lying on the beaches of Tawara – men who died assaulting defences which should have been taken out by Naval gunfire,' he was to write later.

Schmidt made one final appeal for four days' shelling instead of three, and insisted that the request got to Adm. Spruance, but to no avail. Spruance's comments, 'I know your people will get away with it', was to be of little consolation to the Marines who were destined to die for every yard of ground in a few weeks' time.

Ever since September, B24 Liberator bombers of the 7th Air Force had been pounding Iwo Jima on an almost daily basis. As the build-up continued, the attacks were stepped up to thirty or thirty-five sorties a month. The Japanese, now used to these daily attacks, could usually have the Airfield runway repaired and back in service within hours. On 24 December, Cruiser Division 5 arrived off the coast of Iwo Jima to deliver its Christmas presents – 1,500 rounds of 8 in shells. On Christmas Day, the Japanese returned the compliment with an air raid on Saipan in which four B29 Superfortresses were destroyed and eleven more damaged. At half a million dollars each, the bombers were expensive targets.

On 10 February, the ships of Task Force 58 sailed from the lagoon at Ulithi, 100 miles north-east of Yap. Their mission was to attack targets in and around Tokyo. High on the list was the Nakajima Aircraft Company at Ota, forty miles north-west of the capital, and the same company's engine works at Musashino-Tama, less than ten miles from Tokyo city centre.

To emphasize the superiority the US Navy now enjoyed in the Pacific, the Task Force consisted of 16 fleet carriers, 8 battleships, 15 cruisers and 77 destroyers almost all of them built since the attack on Pearl Harbor in 1941. The Task Force commander was Adm. Marc Mitscher, the same commander who had launched the aircraft of Jimmy Doolittle on his famous Tokyo raid in 1942. For the old Texan, this assault on the enemy mainland was the fulfilment of a long-cherished ambition. He had a deep and unrelenting hatred of the Japanese, strikingly highlighted during the attack on Truk, when one of his destroyer captains signalled that he had picked up a downed Japanese pilot. Mitscher's terse reply was: 'Why?'

Adm. Spruance was also with the Task Force in his flagship, the USS *Indianapolis*, and on 15 February they topped up their fuel ready for the last leg of their trip. Despite worsening weather, with low clouds and occasional snow flurries, the carriers launched their aircraft at 6.00 a.m. against the Nakajima plant at Ota, completely destroying it – something the

Superfortresses had failed to do in a series of raids. The following day, the planes attacked the Musashino-Tama engine works, causing severe damage. To Mitscher's intense disappointment, the worsening weather caused the cancellation of a proposed third strike, and the Task Force turned around and headed for Iwo Jima.

In late December, the 4th and 5th Divisions were ordered to leave their camps and assemble at Pearl Harbor. The 4th Division left Camp Maui a few days after Christmas, the 5th was on its transports by 4 January, and by 27 January they were all on their way to the Marianas.

Once the convoys were under way, the target was revealed to one and all – as aerial photographs and models of Iwo Jima were displayed and studied. To some, the target came as no surprise. A few weeks earlier, a photograph in the leading newspaper on Hawaii had shown a graphic picture of a B24 bomber unloading its bombs onto a conical-shaped island with a prominent volcano at its base, so any Marine with a knowledge of geography would already know where he was probably going.

By early February, the convoy had reached Eniwetok in the Marshall Islands, where they took a couple of days for refuelling, and finally arrived at Saipan on 11 February. To the Marines of the 4th Division, there was a feeling of *déjà vu*: it was only eight months since they had been fighting alongside the 3rd Division in the same hills that now formed the background.

It was not long before the final rehearsals for the invasion got under away. Amphibious tractors (LVTs) full of Marines in full kit disgorged from the low doors of the transport landing ships (LSTs) and into the churning sea. Tinian took on the role of Iwo Jima, and the rows of Amtracs headed for the coast, only to veer away at the last moment – it was not considered necessary to make the actual landing. Ships shelled the coast, and fighter-bombers swept in low to unload bombs and napalm canisters.

The departure from Saipan for Iwo Jima on 15 February was a well-orchestrated affair. First came the LSTs carrying the Marines of the 4th and 5th Divisions, who were to spearhead the invasion. The following day came the troop transports with the remainder of the 4th and 5th and a Regiment of the 3rd Division, who had moved up from their base in Guam. On the last day came the remainder of the 3rd Division and its attached units. A Japanese naval patrol aircraft reported the departures to Gen. Kuribayashi within hours, and all Japanese troops on Iwo Jima and the Bonin Islands went to immediate alert.

The US Navy was already assembling off Iwo Jima, and Adm. Blandy's force was preparing for the bombardment to soften up the invasion beaches and other enemy strongpoints. Ideally suited for this purpose were the old battleships of the fleet. Three of them had been salvaged from the mud of Pearl Harbor after the attack of November 1941, and others, too slow for the Task Forces, still packed a mighty punch with their 16-in guns. The USS *Arkansas*, dating from 1912, had taken part in the Normandy invasion, as had the *Texas* and the *Nevada*. The veterans *New York*, *Tennessee* and *Idaho* were also there. This was to be the swansong for these old ladies, who would be consigned to the breakers' yard in a matter of months.

The island was divided into target areas on a huge map kept in Adm. Blandy's flagship, the USS *Estes*. As a target was destroyed, the area was marked. Minesweepers moved to within three miles of the shore, and as yet, received no gunfire. At 7.00 a.m., the bombardment commenced, but poor visibility hampered the gunners, and the results were inconclusive. B24s arrived from the Marianas, but were unable to find their targets, and returned to base with their bomb loads. At dusk, the fleet withdrew for the day. Few of the targets on Blandy's map were accounted for, and the first day of the three-day bombardment had been a bitter disappointment. 'Howlin' Mad' Smith was not a happy man.

If the first day of the 'softening up' had been disappointing, the following day was to prove disastrous. Saturday 17 of February dawned bright and sunny with almost unlimited visibility. The old battleships opened the day's proceedings with a rolling barrage across the island, and at 8.00 a.m., twelve minesweepers made a run parallel to the invasion beaches, getting within 750 yd of the shore. No mines were found, and the ships retired.

To provide close support, the cruiser USS *Pensacola* had come forward and was now dangerously close to the enemy gun positions on the slopes of Mt Suribachi. Although Gen. Kuribayashi had given strict instructions that no gun was to be fired without his orders, the temptation proved to be too much for one gun crew, who opened up rapid fire. Within three minutes, the *Pensacola* had been hit six times, ammunition boxes on the deck exploded, the Kingfisher spotter plane was hit and burst into flames, and she was holed near the waterline. The cruiser turned rapidly seaward, and retired at speed: seventeen of her crew, including the Executive Officer, Cdr. Austin Behan, lay dead, and 120 other crewmen were wounded.

For the Japanese gun crew there was the frustration of having their gun dislodge itself from its tracks and become unserviceable. They could only fume and wonder how much more they could have achieved with such an easy target.

It was now time for the underwater demolition teams (UDTs, or 'frogmen' as they were popularly known), to scour the invasion beaches for mines and underwater obstructions. These frogmen had earlier performed the vital task of clearing the beaches at Saipan in daylight under heavy fire, enabling the

Marines to make an easier landing. At 10.30 a.m., the teams, totalling over a hundred men, boarded their small fast boats (LCPRs) on the seven destroyers that had lined up parallel to the shore, and headed for the island. The bravery of these men – referred to by the Navy as 'half fish, half nuts' – is difficult to measure.

Although there had been extensive reconnaissance of Iwo Jima by B24 bombers from the Marianas, it had not been possible to determine what, if any, underwater obstacles had been prepared at the invasion beaches. There was speculation and rumour that gasoline had been piped to the water's edge, and that the first waves of troops would be engulfed in a sea of fire. (It is interesting that the same rumours abounded in 1940 when the Germans were poised to invade the south coast of England.)

As the frogmen prepared for their dangerous task, twelve gunboats (LCIs) approached to within 1,000 yd of the shore to cover the operation. Armed with rockets and 40 mm and 20 mm guns, the fragile vessels, originally intended as troop landing craft and constructed largely of timber, were a tempting target.

Gen. Kuribayashi was puzzled: was this the main invasion, or a diversionary move? He recognized the LCIs were troop carriers, and that over 1,500 Marines could be aboard. Erring on the side of caution, he ordered his guns to open fire. With distances worked out to the nearest yard from months of practice, the Japanese artillery opened up from Mt Surubachi and The Quarry area at 10.35 a.m., and within minutes, all twelve gunboats had been hit.

There ensued a frantic scramble to escape from the coast and out of the range of the enemy guns. Nine of the LCIs had been seriously damaged and were out of action, one was floundering, and the remainder were scurrying away at best speed. Smoke shells were fired in an attempt to cover the evacuation, and eventually the survivors were able to retire.

It was during this operation that the first of Iwo Jima's Medal of Honor awards was won when 25-year-old Lt. Rufus Herring, commander of Gunboat 449 (the ships were too small to have names), directed his stricken craft to the destroyer USS *Terror*, supervised the evacuation of his crew, many of them wounded, and although badly wounded himself, refused to leave until everyone was aboard the destroyer.

The destroyer USS *Leutze* had also received a direct hit, killing 7 of her crew and wounding another 33, before the flotilla could join the battleships offshore. It had been a costly morning so far, with 43 dead and 153 wounded, and of the 12 gunships committed, only 4 were able to return to Saipan under their own power. However, the frogmen completed their hazardous task, and could report that there were no obstacles to impede the invasion scheduled for the following Monday. Amazingly, only one frogman was lost, and this was not thought to be due to enemy action.

The only other good news for the Americans was that in firing on the gunboats, the Japanese had revealed the position of some of their guns around Mt Suribachi, near the Quarry and the East Boat Basin, and on the plateau around Airfield No. 1.

At a gloomy meeting aboard Adm. Blandy's flagship that evening, it was concluded that the Japanese positions overlooking the invasion beaches had not been silenced, and that practically all the artillery in the north of the island was untouched. That night, Radio Tokyo announced: 'On 17 February, enemy troops tried to land on Iwo Jima. The Japanese garrison at once attacked these troops and repelled them into the sea.'

The final day of Adm. Blandy's pre-invasion bombardment, Sunday 18 February, was blighted by poor weather. Rain squalls and poor visibility hampered the gunners. Nevertheless, at 4.45 a.m. the 'old ladies' of the fleet, *Nevada*, *New York* and *Tennessee*, opened fire with their 16 in guns, concentrating on positions overlooking the invasion beaches.

The B24s of the 7th Air Force returned, but were unable to bomb through the murk, and flew back to the Marianas with their bomb loads. Carrier planes flew twenty-eight sorties around the two airfields, with only limited success, many of their napalm bombs failing to explode. By afternoon, Blandy withdrew his force and sent a message to Adm. Turner: 'I believe landings can be accomplished tomorrow.' His optimism was not shared by 'Howlin' Mad' Smith, who for the rest of his life spoke with bitterness of the Navy's inability to successfully destroy enemy gun emplacements at Tarawa and Iwo Jima, and particularly of the fact that Blandy's ships retired on D minus 1 with their magazines well stocked with unexpended ammunition.

Blandy had permission from Adm. Spruance to add another day to his schedule if he thought it necessary, but he declined. Holland Smith had reluctantly agreed – he did not want the invasion put back, he would rather have had the bombardment started much earlier. 'We got about thirteen hours' worth of fire support during the thirty-four hours of available daylight,' Gen. Schmidt's chief of staff was to complain.

On the USS *Estes* that night, many of the crew carried a card distributed by the ship's captain. It was a copy of a prayer written three hundred years earlier, in 1645, by one of Oliver Cromwell's generals prior to a battle in the English Civil War: 'Lord, I shall be verie busy this day. I may forget Thee, but do not Thou forget me.'

Four

'Our Most Redoubtable Adversary'

Let's hope the Japs don't have any more like him.
(Aide to Lt.-Gen. Holland M. Smith)

Viewed in retrospect, the decision to appoint Gen. Tadamichi Kuribayashi as the Commander-in-Chief of Iwo Jima proved to be a stroke of genius. At that stage of the war, there were many officers of more senior rank and with more wartime experience, so how did the appointment come about? Certainly, Kuribayashi's credentials were sound – the descendant of a long line of Samurai, the Japanese warrior class whose origins dated back to the middle ages, he was a professional soldier with thirty years' service.

The Samurai caste followed the code of *Bushido*, which extolled courage, honour, loyalty to the Emperor, sacrifice, and a contempt for death. As a Samurai, the ultimate disgrace would be to allow oneself to be taken prisoner by the enemy – it would be a far more honourable fate to choose death.

At the time of his appointment, Gen. Kuribayashi was in his early fifties, and tall for a Japanese at 5 ft 9 in. He could look back on a solid if somewhat mundane career in the Army. In the 1920s, he had served as a deputy attaché in Washington DC, and had used his time well, making an extensive tour by car of Canada and the United States:

I was in the United States for three years when I was a captain. I was taught how to drive by some American officers, and I bought a car. I went around the States, and I knew the close connection between the military and industry. I saw the plant area of Detroit too. By one button push, all the industries will be mobilized for military business.

The General's son, Taro, recalls:

From 1928 to July 1930, my father stayed in the United States as an exchange officer. In those days he often gave me, a grammar-school boy, printed letters. He always composed easy letters, in order to let me read them without any help from others. He used to enclose some sketches with the letters. I have made a book of these picture letters.

In the letters are so many scenes – while visiting Boston, he was lying sprawled in the gardens of Harvard University watching a clock tower, in another he is taking a walk in Buffalo, in another, playing with some American children, and being invited to the house of Medical Doctor Furukohchi, etc. Throughout his letters, it is clear that my father used to drive in many directions in the United States, studied very hard late at night, and tried to be a gentleman. Also, he used to have many friends in foreign countries.

It was during his time in America that he came to fully appreciate the vast industrial potential of that country: 'The United States is the last country in the world that Japan should fight,' he wrote in one of his frequent letters to his wife, Yoshii.

On his return to Japan, he served in the cavalry and saw action in China. At the time of the attack on Pearl Harbor, he had attained the rank of General, and was serving as Chief of Staff to the 23rd Army in Hong Kong. In 1943, he took command of the Tokyo Guard, a responsibility that included the protection of the Imperial Palace and the Emperor. To what extent this appointment influenced his selection as Commander of Iwo Jima is uncertain, but as Commander of the Guard, he was known to Emperor Hirohito, and had been granted an audience – a unique honour bestowed by one of divine origin.

In May 1944, Kuribayashi was summoned to the office of the Japanese Prime Minister, Hideki Tojo, and told of his appointment. It is not difficult to imagine his feelings at the news. Having carefully studied the progress of the war, he was very much aware of the strategic and patriotic significance of Iwo Jima. He would also have known that a successful defence of the island was impossible. Through the military grapevine, he had heard that another distinguished staff officer had been offered the position, but had talked his way out of it.

As a Samurai and a loyal subject of the Emperor, such a course was out of the question, but attempting to hold an undefendable island against the full force of the US Marine Corps (USMC) was a daunting prospect. Aware of the two certainties of the appointment – that Iwo Jima would ultimately fall to the Americans, and that he and his garrison would all perish, Kuribayashi began to work out his strategy.

He was familiar with the methods of the USMC, from their early struggles on Guadalcanal to their pioneering assault on Tarawa and the invasion of Peleliu. He knew that the USA now had the largest navy in the world, almost unchallenged air superiority, and a seemingly unlimited source of men and equipment. He rejected the traditional Japanese defence ethos of halting amphibious landings on the beachhead as futile, and regarded the traditional *Banzai* attack outdated and wasteful.

The seeds of the defence strategy for Iwo Jima were sown in the hills of Peleliu, where the Japanese commander, Lt.-Gen. Inoue, heavily influenced by the thinking of Col. Tokechi Tada, acknowledged as one of the most original strategists in the Imperial Army, had abandoned the standard Japanese defence tactics and concentrated on attrition, wearing down the enemy, as the principal method of defence. 'Victory depends on the officers and men of the entire Army concentrating on recent battle lessons, the ultimate goal is to take advantage of the fact that their equipment is not yet fully consolidated, to destroy their bridgehead at one blow, take advantage of the terrain and carry out strong counter-attacks from previously planned and prepared positions – there will be no rapid exhaustion of battle strength if we pay careful attention to these details,' wrote Col. Tada in a chilling preview of the methods that were to be adopted by Gen. Kuribayashi.

Arriving on Iwo Jima in early June 1944, he was pleased to be greeted by cheering and flag-waving children in the principal town of Motoyama, near the centre of the island. A subsequent tour of Iwo Jima's defences soon changed his mood to one of dismay. The previous commander had been Capt. Tsuenzo Wachi of the Imperial Navy (Wachi survived the war, and later became a Buddhist, priest, spending many years recovering and returning to Japan the remains of the garrison of Iwo Jima). In early May, Wachi had warned of dissent between Army and Navy units on the island, and Gen. Kuribayashi was soon to become aware of these intrigues, which eventually resulted in him replacing eighteen officers who were considered to be disruptive and unsympathetic to his views on how the battle should be conducted.

Setting up his HQ in the north of Iwo Jima, an area he felt would be the last to fall to the enemy, Kuribayashi set about reshaping the defences. During June, the Americans sent a carrier Task Force under Rear-Adm. Joseph Clark to soften up the island and to take reconnaissance photographs: this was to be the forerunner of a series of air attacks by both naval aircraft and B24 Liberator bombers of the 7th Air Force operating out of the Marianas. Many Japanese fighters were lost during these attacks, but Kuribayashi was not unduly concerned at the decimation of his air forces. His prime concern was with the forthcoming land assault, during which he knew that American air superiority would be guaranteed.

Upon his appointment, he had been given *carte blanche* in his options for the defence of the island. He soon realized that the two beaches stretching away from Mt Suribachi to the north and north-east were the only possible sites for the Marine landing, and that the north-east stretch was by far the most suitable because of the prevailing onshore winds.

In June, Maj. Yoshitaka Horie arrived from Japan to act as a member of Kuribayashi's staff (Horie survived the war, and has become important as possibly the only chronicler of Kuribayashi's time on Iwo Jima). 'General Kuribayashi came to Iwo Jima on 13th June 1944, and said, "Let me borrow your house until our office can be built."'

It was Horie who told Kuribayashi of the battle of the Philippines Sea, which effectively destroyed the Imperial Navy. The General was incredulous: 'I did not know of these things,' he said. Horie recalls going with Kuribayashi to inspect the north-east beaches. He measured distances, and flung himself down as if he had just disembarked from a landing craft. 'The enemy must come here,' he said, 'there will be no alternative,' and he pointed his cane as if it were a rifle.

In August, Maj.-Gen. Joichiro Sanada, the Operations Chief of the Army General Staff, made an inspection of Iwo Jima and was dismayed with what he saw. Kuribayashi warned him that if an enemy task force of the size of that of 4 July were to return with one-and-a-half Divisions of Marines, he would only be able to sustain his defence for a week to ten days (it is unfortunate that the US High Command was not aware of this situation, and was unable to update its invasion plans accordingly).

Sanada informed Tokyo of Kuribayashi's misgivings, and the supply of essential materials continued unhindered from that time on. Maj. Horie was transferred to Chichi Jima on 1 July to oversee the transportation of supplies from the harbour there onward to Iwo Jima. He flew in a plane carrying two bombs for anti-submarine operations which made a wheels-up landing when the undercarriage failed to operate.

He at once started organizing the garrison for the vital task of supplying Iwo Jima: 'I gathered some officers of the Chichi Shipping Branch, and told them: "A big transportation will begin in a moment. We may have to work without any sleep and rest, any and all sailing boats and fishing boats will be used. I wish your co-operation." Thousands of bags of cement and tons of reinforcement steel rods for fortifications flowed from Chichi Jima to Iwo Jima as the build-up of the defences got under way.

Work progressed at a furious pace as Kuribayashi, a stern disciplinarian, oversaw the construction of dozens of surface blockhouses and bunkers and an amazing labyrinth of underground fortifications the likes of which had never been seen before in the history of warfare. A total of 15,000 men worked around the clock constructing a maze of underground chambers capable of housing dozens of men. Elsewhere, huge areas were excavated to hold tons of ammunition, water and supplies. Hospitals with operating theatres were located in the north of the island, and the whole system was equipped with lighting – electric, oil or candles. The soft, pumice-like sub-surface was easy to remove, and when mixed with cement, formed an excellent concrete for the surface defences.

The principal drawback to the underground work was the intense heat and the fumes from the sulphur fissures. In some areas, gas masks were essential, and the heat restricted work to only a few hours at any one time. Maj. Horie made occasional trips back to Iwo Jima to liaise with Kuribayashi. On one occasion, he briefly joined in the digging: 'I joined the digging work on Kuribayashi's caves. Using an Army pick, I continued digging the rock, and I found that an average person could not continue work for ten minutes.' The sulphur fumes soon made him feel dizzy, so he tried working with a gas mask, but found it too hot and had difficulty in breathing. He saw passages being dug to a depth of 20–30 metres, with side rooms for sleeping, dining and rest.

One of the first decisions Kuribayashi made was to evacuate the entire civilian population of the island. Food and water were going to be in short supply as the battle progressed, and over a thousand civilians would be an intolerable burden. He soon cut the water ration, and showed a good example by restricting his personal toilet requirements to one cup per day. Maj. Horie was impressed with his single-mindedness: 'I don't know why he had that strong will. It might have come from the blood of the Kuribayashi family.' He was known to express his opinions flatly before his officers and men, and would not then concede on anything. After the war, Horie had the opportunity to speak to Vice-Adm. Kaneko, who had been a classmate of Kuribayashi at Nagano High School in their youth: 'Ah. Kuribayashi!' he said, 'He once organized a strike against the school authorities. He just escaped expulsion by a hair. In those days, he was already good in poetry-writing, composition and speech-making. He was a young literary enthusiast.'

Kuribayashi had anticipated the loss of Mt Suribachi in the early stages of the battle, but was bitterly disappointed that it fell as soon as it did since he had made it an independent command under the control of Col. Atsuchi, with a strength of over 2,000 men. Kuribayashi's strategy of allowing the enemy to land without any major opposition and establish a crowded beachhead before launching his main attack was a success, as testified by the appalling casualties suffered by the Marines on the beaches on D-Day. The loss of Mt Suribachi so early in the battle was a blow he had not anticipated, but the bloody hand-to-hand fighting that continued in the north of the island for so long after the American deadline shows that his plan of attrition was largely successful.

In one of his memos, Kuribayashi wrote: 'Iwo Jima garrison will place some troops around Mount Suribachi, but place the main power in depth. Once the enemy invades the island, everyone will resist until the last moment, making his position his tomb.' Maj. Horie recalls that Rear-Adm. Ichimaru had requested that his Navy troops should be placed together in one place to fight, since the Navy had a custom of wanting to die together. Kuribayashi accepted the request, and the Navy personnel were placed between the east and south sectors, under Ichimaru.

'There were five sectors on Iwo,' Horie reports, 'north, south, east, west and Mount Suribachi sectors. In the case of Mount Suribachi, Colonel Atsuchi was ordered to control everything, but the other sector commanders were responsible only for watch and reconnaissance, liaison and co-operation. Kuribayashi kept overall control.' Maj. Horie transferred his headquarters on Chichi Jima from the coast to the centre of the island, because of the bombing. In a pleasant area surrounded by mountains and near a small river, he set about his duties of sea transportation, communications and assisting the Commander of the 1st Mixed Brigade in tactics.

It was Horie who advocated the use of anti-aircraft guns for ground defence: 'From the lessons learned at Saipan, Tinian and Guam, I said that our anti-aircraft guns would not last five minutes.' Eventually, 50 per cent of Iwo Jima's anti-aircraft guns were used for ground defence by Gen. Kuribayashi. Meanwhile, the rather bizarre suggestion that Iwo Jima, or large sections of it, should be blown up and sunk into the Pacific was being taken seriously in Japan as late as August 1944. At a meeting of the Army Department and the

General Staff on 13 August, which Horie attended, he reported that serious consideration was given to 'the possibility of blowing up most of Iwo Jima', but it was finally considered impracticable. At the same meeting, he was successful in obtaining large quantities of Type 41 dynamite and some mountain artillery for the island's garrison.

On the airfield on his return, he met Col. Nishi, who told him that he had obtained twenty-three extra tanks to make up for those lost in the sinking of a transport. Later, on Iwo Jima, he again brought up the subject of blowing up the island: 'We went to Airfield No. 1 to discuss the subject, but Kuribayashi said: "Can you calculate the amount of dynamite we would need? It is impossible."'

That was Horie's last visit to the island. Around mid-November, he received a telegraph from Iwo Jima informing him that the shortage of food on the island was serious, and emphasizing that priority should be given to food supplies. When the Marines invaded, there was a two-month supply for the defenders.

Thirteen days into the battle, Kuribayashi indicated to Horie that he thought things were entering the final stages: 'Our strongpoints may be able to fight delaying actions for several more days,' he announced. 'Even when they fall, the survivors will continue to fight to the end. Although my own death is near, I calmly pray to God for a good future for my mother country.' Soon after this, schoolchildren in Tokyo sang on the radio the 'Song of Iwo Jima'. Gen. Kuribayashi and his officers and men wept as they heard the piping voices singing:

> When dark tides billow on the ocean,
> A wink-shaped isle of mighty fame,
> Guards the gateway to our Empire,
> Iwo Jima is its name.

Towards the end of the battle, Maj. Horie had occasion to interrogate two US Navy fliers who had been captured and brought to Chichi Jima. He describes one as a Marine captain and the other as an ensign. As Horie had a passing acquaintance with the English language, he was given the job of talking to them. He found that they were from the carrier *Hornet*, and they told him that the Marines involved in the landings were from the 1st, 2nd and 3rd Divisions. This false information was immediately passed to Iwo Jima and Tokyo.

Horie was struck by the nonchalant attitude of the fliers, who informed him that as soon as US troops landed on Kyushu, the war would be over. When they returned home, they said that they would be treated as heroes, and would use their accumulated pay to get married and pay for their honeymoons. They joked and hummed songs, and even wanted to teach Horie how to dance. 'Nothing has ever surprised me more than the psychology of the war prisoners of the democratic countries. It is diametrically different from that of the Japanese soldier,' he said in amazement.

As the battle progressed, Kuribayashi spent most of his time in the numerous underground command posts and headquarters that had been established before the February invasion, gradually moving north and west until he finally ended up in the area known to the Marines as 'Bloody Gorge'. His death has always been shrouded in mystery. Various sources have offered conflicting reports of his end. One account insists that he committed *hara-kiri* in his headquarters in The Gorge as the Marines approached to within yards of the entrance on 25 March. Others say that he died leading an attack against the enemy near Airfield No. 2 at dawn on 26 March.

His son, Taro, offers the following version:

It seems that it was after sunset on 25 March to the dawn of the 26th that surviving Imperial Japanese forces were obliged to stand still under the US onslaught and showering shells. Under such circumstances, he had his sword in his left hand and ordered the chief staff officer, Colonel Takaishi, who was beside him, 'Send snipers to shoot' [Sgt. Oyama heard the order]. Sergeant Oyama, who was seriously wounded in the last combat, fell unconscious, hospitalized by the US, and after having served as a POW, came back and testified the dreadful account of the night to me. My father had believed it shameful to have his body discovered by the enemy even after death, so he had previously asked his two soldiers to come along with him, one in front and the other behind, with a shovel in hand. In case of his death, he had wanted them to bury his body there and then. It seems that my father and the soldiers were killed by shells, and he was buried at the foot of a tree in Chidori village, along the beach near Osaka Mountain. Afterwards, General Smith spent a whole day looking for his body to pay respect accordingly and to perform a burial, but in vain.

The epic defence of Iwo Jima confirmed him as one of Japan's greatest generals. It is significant that a senior Marine officer was heard to call him: 'the best damn general on this stinking island'.

If the planned invasion of the Japanese mainland had gone ahead, there can be little doubt that the kind of fanatical opposition the Marines encountered on Iwo Jima would have been repeated in every city, town and village, and would have resulted in a bloodbath of incalculable proportions. A Marine fresh from fighting in the battle from start to finish comments: 'We were brutalized beyond belief. If we had landed in Japan, we would have shot everything that moved – men, women, children, chickens – anything.' Perhaps the postwar pacifists who are so liberal with their condemnation of the use of the A-bombs to end the war should study their history and reflect on the alternative scenario.

Kuribayashi and his wife, Yoshii, had three children: Taro and their daughters, Yohko and Takako. Takako was a grammar-school girl, and had been evacuated to a village in Nagano prefecture: Yohko died of typhoid fever shortly before the end of the war.

During, and even before the battle, Kuribayashi kept up an interesting correspondence with his wife that reveals much about his attitude as a soldier and his concerns as a father. On 2 August 1994, he wrote:

After my death, my belongings left behind may not return to Japan I believe, so I will keep only necessities with me, and I will send the rest of them back while I am alive. Everyone has a gloomy face and no smiling. The other night, I dreamed of my return home. At the time you and Takako were very much pleased, but when I told them that I only returned home to write my will and I had to go back to the battlefield, Takako looked very sad.

In September 1944, he wrote to Yoshii expressing his concern for her and the children:

Our officers and men know death very well. I am sorry to close my life here, fighting the United States of America, but I want to defend this island as long as possible, and to delay the enemy air raids against Tokyo. Ah, you have worked well for a long time as my wife and as a mother of three children. Your life will become harder and more serious. Be careful of your health, and live long. [At the time of writing – 1998 – Yoshii is still alive in Japan.] The future of our children will not be easy too. Please take care of them after my death.

To his children, Taro and Yohko, two weeks later he wrote:

Tokyo has not suffered from the enemy air raids, but once the island your father is now defending is captured, Tokyo will be raided day and night. The lurid scenes, heavy damage, confusion, etc. resulting from the air raids are beyond words. Those who live idly in Tokyo can never even imagine. If Tokyo is raided, it means that this island has been taken by the enemy – it means the death of your father. You, fatherless brother and sister, must live depending on your mother – you must help mother.

As the battle drew to a close, he wrote:

The battle is approaching the end. Since the landings, the bravery of the officers and men under my command will make even the gods weep. However, my men die one after another, and I am very sorry that I have let the enemy occupy one part of Japanese territory.

After the war was over, Maj. Horie was employed at the US Air Force base at Tachikawa as an interpretor. He suggested to Gen. Ruestow that some stones from Iwo Jima should be distributed to some of the families of those killed on the island:

A pilot flew to Iwo Jima and brought back one big stone unofficially. General Huddnell invited wives of the late

General Kuribayashi, Colonel Takaishi, Lieutenant-Colonel Nakane, Lieutenant-Colonel Nishi, Major Yamanouchi and my wife. At the same time, Mr Nakajima, Mayor of Tachikawa City was invited. These pieces of stone were presented to the wives by Mr Nakajima.

Horie was later instrumental in securing Taro a position at the Air Force base as an architect.

The name of Gen. Kuribayashi has been accorded a place of honour in Japanese postwar history alongside that other outstanding commander, Adm. Yamamoto. In his autobiography, *Coral and Brass*, Lt.-Gen. Holland 'Howlin' Mad' Smith paid him one of his highest tributes: 'Of all of our adversaries in the Pacific, Kuribayashi was the most redoubtable.'

Five

'A Great Day to Die'
(D-Day)

Adm. Harry Hill couldn't have picked a better day to put the Marines ashore. The rain squalls and gloomy skies of the previous days had cleared, and Monday 19 February dawned bright and sunny, with only a brisk 8 kt wind blowing from the north, and blue skies giving unlimited visibility. The sea, although choppy enough to make some Marines seasick, was reasonably calm, with a three-foot surf on the landing beaches. One hard-nosed sergeant surveying his men from the front of their landing craft announced: 'A great day to die, fellers.'

In the pre-dawn gloom, those Marines who had been unable to sleep were the first in line for the customary pre-battle breakfast of steak and eggs. This ritual was frowned on by the doctors and surgeons of the Navy, who knew that they would be treating many stomach wounds before the end of the day, but the veterans of previous battles were aware that this would probably be the last decent meal they would get for days, or even weeks.

During the night, Adm. Spruance, aboard his flagship, USS *Indianapolis*, had arrived with Mitscher's Task Force 58 fresh from their highly successful assault on the Japanese mainland. Adm. Turner, dressed in his customary bathrobe, had come topside to see how the weather was. The previous night, he had listened to a Japanese radio broadcaster warning him that he would never leave Iwo Jima alive. 'Maybe you'd better come and rescue me,' he had radioed to Spruance.

At 6.30 a.m., Turner issued the order, 'Land the landing force', and the curtain rose on the greatest battle in Marine Corps history. As the transports and landing craft prepared for the mammoth task of ferrying thousands of troops to the island, at 6.40 a.m. the Navy commenced the final bombardment, and seven battleships, four cruisers, three light cruisers and an armada of destroyers began the systematic pounding of the slopes of Mt Suribachi, the landing beaches, Airfield No. 1 and the area around the Quarry and East Boat Basin at the northern limit of the beaches. To this day, the slopes of Mt Suribachi are flecked with deep-red rust patches as a reminder of the thousands of tons of steel hurled at the volcano over half a century ago.

At 6.45 a.m., a flotilla of nine rocket-firing gunboats approached to within 250 yd of the shore and blasted the invasion beaches from the Boat Basin to the edge of Suribachi. A massive air strike by planes of Task Force 58 had been arranged, and during a lull in the naval bombardment, Dauntless, Hellcat and Corsair bombers and fighters blasted and strafed the southern end of the island. As the planes wheeled away to return to their carriers, twenty-four Corsairs of the Marine Corps squadrons dropped dozens of napalm canisters and blasted the Japanese positions around Airfield No. 1 in a daring low-level sortie that brought roars of approval from the Marines offshore. Once the aircraft had cleared the island at around 8.25 a.m., the Navy resumed its pounding.

The invasion beaches lay on the south-east of Iwo Jima, between Mt Suribachi and the East Boat Basin, a distance of just over two miles, and were divided into seven sections of 500 yd each.

Directly under the shadow of Mt Suribachi lay Green Beach, flanked on the right by Red Beaches 1 and 2, Yellow Beaches 1 and 2, and Blue Beaches 1 and 2. To spearhead the attack were the 28th Regiment of the 5th Division under Col. Harry Liversedge (Green Beach) and the 27th Regiment of the 5th Division under Col. Thomas Wornham (Red Beaches 1 and 2). The 23rd Regiment of the 4th Division under Col. Walter Wensinger was allocated Yellow Beaches 1 and 2, and the 25th Regiment of the 4th Division under Col. John Lanigan completed the line-up on Blue Beaches 1 and 2.

On paper, the plan was deceptively straightforward. Col. Liversedge's 28th Regiment would attack straight across the neck of the island to the opposite coast, swing to the left, and isolate and then secure Mt Suribachi. On their immediate right, Col. Wornham with the 27th Regiment would also cross to the opposite coast and swing north. From Yellow Beaches 1 and 2, Col. Wensinger's 23rd Regiment would seize Airfield No. 1 and then thrust northward towards Airfield No. 2. On the extreme right, Col. Lanigan and his 25th Regiment would assist in the assault of Airfield No. 1, and would also swing to their right to neutralize the high ground around The Quarry, overlooking the East Boat Basin.

What the planners had not fully appreciated was the condition of the beaches. Extracts from the Operational Plan of the 23rd Regiment reveal that the planners were not aware of what lay ahead for the first wave of Marines: 'There are from two to five wave-cut terraces inland from the water's edge and small boats should have little difficulty in pushing well up onto the beach . . . Troops should have no difficulty in getting off the beach at any point . . . The isthmus provides excellent landing beaches . . . Sand and silt have been deposited at the base of the terraces and form an easy approach inland.' It is fortunate for these deskbound planners that they were not required to land on D-Day to verify their conclusions.

Violent storms and constant onshore wave action had indeed terraced this stretch of beach, but a wide strip of black volcanic ash at the water's edge led to a steep slope some 15 ft high, and beyond this were further terraces before the Motoyama plateau was reached. Chuck Tatum, an eighteen-year-old member of a machine gun squad with the 27th Regiment, recalls: 'Looking inland, all I could see was a mountain of black sand – did intelligence know about them? Were they surprised?'

Meanwhile, the task of disembarking thousands of Marines from troopships and LVTs was gathering momentum. The logistics were daunting – co-ordinating hundreds of landing craft, getting them into sequence and onto the right beach at the right time was in itself a monumental task. Added to this was the timing of air strikes and the bombardment by battleships and cruisers, all of which had to be dovetailed into a rigid schedule, and it soon became obvious why Adm. Kelly Turner's expertise was held in such esteem in the Pacific campaign.

On the LSTs, the Marines received their orders to go below and board their Amtracs. As they descended into the hold, they were immediately gripped by the overpowering stench of diesel smoke. The noise of Amtracs with their engines throbbing reverberated around the cavernous interior, and all heaved a sigh of relief when the bow doors opened and a wave of clean air surged into the dim interior.

As the orders were received, the Amtracs nudged forward towards the daylight, their tracks clanking on the bare steel decking, until they reached the ramp. Then there was a sharp upward tilt and a forward plunge into the sea as the Marines desperately fought to keep their balance. Al Kirtley was a sailor aboard the USS *Bolivar* (APA 34), an attack transport lying offshore. One of his duties was as a motor mechanic on a LCVP (Landing Craft Vehicle Personnel) ferrying Marines to and from the invasion beaches. He had been at battle stations since dawn, and after a hurried breakfast, manned his craft, No. 24. The *Bolivar* was carrying Marines of the 21st Regiment of the 3rd Division – reserves, but still embarked on D-Day:

As daylight broke we could see some of the 500 ships in our fleet off the southern tip of Iwo Jima. With Mount Suribachi in view, our squadron moved slowly now into place off the south-eastern coast, where our greater assault strength would hit. By 7.30 a.m., the line of departure was set at two miles off the beach. Anchor chains began a thunderous rattling to the bottom as our transports reached their assigned stations. It was somewhat choppy that morning. The twenty-four boats loaded Marines from eight cargo nets, one at each of our hatches, as one port and one starboard. Earlier, it had been overcast, but the sun came out as the morning wore on.

The Task Force battlewagons and cruisers were laying in a last bombardment along the beaches just before the first wave was to land. At about 8.30 a.m., the flagship dipped her pennant and the first waves of the 4th and 5th Divisions were off and running. Ahead, close to the beaches, LCIs moved in quickly before those waves to release a 20,000-round crack of rockets just above the beach. It all went as planned: there would be 9,000 men ashore in less than an hour. We circled our boats for about six hours on D-Day. At noon, they signalled us to pull alongside for boxes of sandwiches, rations and hot drinks. The food gave us a better feeling, and we went back to circling.

To try to cheer up the Marines, Al told them that they wouldn't land until his birthday, 21 February. His forecast was prophetic, for after spending all day Tuesday in the craft, incessantly circling, Wednesday was indeed the day:

We circled until mid-morning, and some began to have doubts. The beach crews were having a tough time getting supplies and ammo in and off the beach while under heavy gunfire. The pennant went down about 10.30 a.m. Our boats fell into line side by side and headed for the beach. The coxswain throttled to full speed, and we spread out in order to be a harder target to hit. With twenty-four boats taking 25 to 30 men per load, each boat would make three trips for the Marines, and extra trips for ammo, Jeeps, water trailers, etc. Boats returning would bring wounded.

On the first approach to the beach, we were getting more nervous the closer we came. When we were about an eighth of a mile from the beach, another boat cut sharply across our course as he came out from the landing zone. When he was directly in front of us, a mortar caught him. I ducked momentarily as I saw the explosion, and heard the shrapnel rattle across our ramp. Our coxswain slowed and swerved, and as I looked again, nothing could be seen. We roared in, and as our bow scraped the bottom, the deck hand dropped the ramp. The Marines charged out across the beach.

As the LCVP attempted to raise the ramp to leave, it became jammed. The black volcanic ash was packed into the hinges, and Al had to use a sweeping brush to clear them: 'I later thought that I must have appeared ridiculous standing in the middle of the open ramp sweeping under fire.'

To spearhead the landing, sixty-eight LVT(A)s (armoured amphibious tractors with a 75-mm howitzer and three machine guns) were to form a ring of fire some 50 yd into the beachhead to cover the first wave of Marines. Leaving the line of departure at 8.30 a.m., they arrived on the beaches a few minutes after 9.00 a.m. only to encounter the 15 ft-high terraces of soft ash. Some of the tractors managed to find a way around the obstacle and pushed forward, but for many the task was impossible, and they were compelled to return to the water and attempt to engage the enemy from offshore positions.

Shortly before the LVT(A)s were due to hit the beaches, the Marine Corps Corsairs returned to strafe the area for the last time. Roaring in from the south, they skirted Mt Suribachi, and bombed and blasted the whole area up to the East Boat Basin with napalm and machine guns before wheeling away to join the USS *Essex*. At this time, Maj. Raymond Dollins, the air observer for the 5th Division, was circling the volcano. Over his radio frequency, many seamen smiled as he sang:

> Oh what a beautiful morning,
> Oh what a beautiful day,
> I've got a terrible feeling
> Everything's coming my way.

Within minutes, Dollin's plane, trailing flames and smoke, crashed into the sea near to a wave of assault tractors. One picked up the bodies of Dollins and his pilot.

Within a few minutes, the first of the troop-carrying LVTs arrived, and as the ramps were lowered, the Marines hit the beach at a fast run, which rapidly deteriorated to a slow trudge as they sank deep into the ash. 'Just as I left the Amtrac, running at high port I saw a Marine on my left flank blown up, and he turned into a large ball of fire, killing him instantly,' recalls Pfc James Justice of the 27th Regiment, who was among the first on Red Beach 2. 'The only thing left of him was about thirty feet of intestines which were strewn over the beach in front of me, and I almost slipped down running over them. I later learned that he was a flamethrower with his tanks full of fuel, and he had received a direct hit from a Japanese shell, igniting everything, including himself.'

As yet, the Japanese were content to let the build-up continue. For months, the artillery positions on the slopes of Mt Suribachi and on the heights overlooking the East Boat Basin had fine-honed their target areas and ranges. All they now awaited was the command from Gen. Kuribayashi.

As the first Marines attempted to move forward, successive waves of Marines arrived at intervals of around five minutes, piling up on the beaches, and the situation rapidly deteriorated. Some enemy fire was hitting the landing areas, but the Japanese were biding their time.

From the Green and Red Beaches, Col. Liversedge reported 'Resistance moderate, terrain awful', and Col. Wornham said: 'Light resistance'. From Yellow and Blue Beaches, Col. Wensinger signalled 'Moderate mortar fire', and Col. Lanigan found the situation 'Generally favourable'.

Some of the more optimistic Marines were beginning to think that the Navy had indeed silenced the bulk of the enemy positions. Little did they realize that the Japanese, in even larger numbers than the intelligence reports had surmised, were well dug in among their superbly prepared underground positions, waiting for the rolling barrage to pass over them.

As the waves of Marines hit the beaches – over 6,000 within a few minutes – congestion was now becoming a major problem. Some troops attempted to dig foxholes, but the loose, coarse ash just piled back into the holes as fast as it was dug out – 'Like trying to dig a hole in a mound of corn' was the way one Marine described it. Others attempted to scale the first terrace, but found it hard going, weighed down with scores of pounds of equipment and weapons. The sand and ash came up to mid-calf, and in one section, a Marine found that the only way he could reach the top was by charging diagonally at around 45 per cent to the rim. Earl Dunlap, a corporal with the 25th Regiment, recalls:

We landed at about 9.00 a.m. on Blue Beach. We were under extremely heavy fire coming at us from all sides. The beach was very soft and steep, and it was like climbing a rapidly moving escalator going down – every three steps up you took, you slid down two. We were in a long, large tank trap which the Japs had zoned into. As I was climbing to the top, a large shell or mortar exploded right behind me, blowing me right to the top of the parapet, and in the process blew the pack right off my back, along with my carbine. Fortunately, I wasn't touched, and then moved my squad out as rapidly as possible.

For the vehicles, the situation was even worse. As artillery and jeeps attempted to move inland, they sank up to their hubcaps. 'Steve and I moved inland to the first terrace, which looked like Mount Everest. Volcanic ash sucked at our legs as we climbed. We were slowed to a crawl then halted by exhaustion. It was impossible to continue,' said Chuck Tatum.

For Gen. Kuribayashi, the congestion on the beaches was an added bonus. He had anticipated that the Americans would move inland more rapidly, and that he would be able to lay down his massive artillery barrage as they moved across the plateau towards Airfield No. 1, but as the Marines massed on the beaches and the landing craft and supply ships cluttered the shoreline, he decided that the time was ripe for the first stage of his defensive strategy.

A little after 10.00 a.m., the full fury of the Japanese defence was unleashed on the Marines. From the base of Mt Suribachi to the East Boat Basin, a torrent of artillery shells bracketed the beach and incoming landing craft. Mortars showered down like rain from dozens of well-concealed emplacements. Machine-gun fire shredded the oncoming Marines from elevated positions near the edge of Airfield No. 1, and landmines sown months earlier exploded on the first stretch of level ground beyond the beaches. Landing around this time, Pfc Otis Thomas of the 5th Division recalls:

Our ducks [Amtracs] landed on the right of a wrecked LCM, shielding us from machine gun fire from the caves for a moment. Pte. Parent made one step on the beach, and took a bullet through the right chest. He was loaded back on the landing craft and sent out to the ship. Looking up at the caves, we could see flashes of fire in the darkness, and we realized that we were looking down the Japanese machine gun barrels. The beach was covered with bodies. Every shell lifted more bodies up in pieces. The waves floated our dead in, and then out, and back again.

I saw the beaches covered in Valentine cards, so out of place scattered among the dead. (We had received our last mail call on St Valentine's Day, and the fellows had stuck them in their pockets to read again.) Going in, the 'Big Swede' had told me that he was going to stick with me. On the beach, I dropped to my knees and started scooping sand to get down below the surface so the concussion and shrapnel would fly above me. 'Big Swede' ran away from every shell burst, dashing by me, shouting 'Run for it.' I finally pulled him down, saying 'Get below the shrapnel. Help me hollow out a hole. It will take a direct hit to get us.'

'You'll never hear the one that gets you,' so they joke. I heard a thud, looked around, and saw a 90 mm round buried about two-thirds in the sand two feet behind me. The spinner on the tip that helps guide the missile in flight was still spinning. It was a dud – my luck was holding.

Kuribayashi's pre-arranged strategy was now paying dividends. With the beaches crowded, and becoming more so by the minute, he hoped to slaughter hundreds at the water's edge and halt the waves of reinforcements.

Messages flashed to the control ship *Eldorado* at 10.36 a.m. from the 25th Regiment on the Blue Beaches: 'Catching all hell from The Quarry. Heavy mortar and machine gun fire. Troops inland 200 yards pinned down.' At 10.39 a.m. the 23rd Regiment on the Yellow Beaches signalled: 'Taking heavy casualties and can't move for the moment. Mortars killing us.' At 10.42 a.m., the 27th Regiment radioed from the Red Beaches: 'All units pinned down by artillery and mortars. Casualties heavy. Need tank support fast to move anywhere.' And in the shadow of Mt Suribachi, the 28th Regiment reported at 10.46 a.m.: 'Nearly across the neck, but taking heavy fire and forward movement stopped. Machine gun and artillery fire heaviest ever seen.'

By now, Harry Hill had got 6,000 men ashore, a few bulldozers that had arrived in an early wave were hacking at the terraces in an attempt to clear a lane for the tanks and transport, and the artillery were gradually getting into a position where they could return the enemy fire.

From concealed positions that had withstood everything the Navy could throw at them, a torrent of devastatingly accurate fire rained down on the Marines. The 'superb Japanese artillerymen', as one Marine colonel described them, raked the beaches from one end to the other, delivering the inferno that they had spent months planning. As the Marines clambered and crawled their way over the terraces and onto solid ground, they encountered the minefields and direct machine gun fire that had so far remained silent.

Gen. Kuribayashi had foreseen the vulnerability of Mt Suribachi at an early stage of his planning. With less than half a mile of land at its base, he realized that the volcano would rapidly become isolated, and had decided that it should be an independent bastion that would hold down large numbers of the enemy for a long period.

Col. Kanehiko Atsuchi was in command, with over 2,000 men under him, and the main defensive ring of artillery and mortars had been dug in around the base, although there was still a mass of tunnels and caves all the way to the summit.

Col. Harry Liversedge's 28th Regiment began disembarking on Green Beach shortly after 9.00 a.m. Lt.-Col. Jackson Butterfield's 1st Battalion, with 'B' and 'C' Companies abreast, were to clear a path for Lt.-Col. Chandler Johnson's 2nd Battalion to follow and turn towards Suribachi.

Getting off the beach proved a mammoth task in itself. Lt. John Keith Wells recalls:

Our small platoon would land on the extreme left flank of the entire landing force directly under the high ground surrounding Suribachi. Japanese in their caves and gun positions looked down on us from the mountain. At this point 70 per cent, possibly 80 per cent of the landed Marines remained on or near the beach.

The battle itself raged only a few yards from shore. Marine landing craft found it hard to get ashore without coming over men and equipment. The wounded Marines lying flat on the ground and away from the unloading area remained reasonably safe from incoming tanks and the firepower of the Japanese. Nothing could be done for the seriously wounded Marines – they just died.

The off-beach sand that we were forced to travel through was made from volcanic ash. Walking in it was much the same as walking in a barrel of marbles or oozing mud – we could sink almost to our knees with every step.

The only big problem the Japanese had at this time was choosing targets. Dead Marines were already a common sight. This did not bother me as much as a man's leg lying beside me, oozing blood into the sand. The foot had a Marine boot on it. This feeling for slaughtered human beings did not last long. It would surprise most people to know how fast the human race can degenerate to the basic primitive state.

The 1st Battalion, ignoring Suribachi on their left, were under constant heavy fire as they pressed towards the far shore. Their right flank, which no Marine force had as yet penetrated, was also vulnerable, and came under fire.

The main Japanese defence, Capt. Osada's 312th Independent Infantry Battalion, was encountered near the centre of the isthmus, and fierce battles erupted around a series of pillboxes and bunkers. Some were destroyed, others by-passed in the relentless push across the island. The dead were left where they lay, and the wounded were attended to by Corpsmen, who, as usual, were there in the thick of the action.

It was during this stage of the 1st Battalion's advance that the first Marine Corps Medal of Honor of the battle was won. Cpl. Tony Stein, a 24-year-old veteran of Guadalcanal and Bougainville, and a toolmaker before the war, had fashioned himself a highly individual weapon which he called his 'stinger'. Basically, it was a .50 machine gun from a Navy fighter which had crashed in Hawaii, which he had adapted into a hand-held weapon.

Disregarding heavy enemy machine gun fire, he attacked one pillbox after another until they fell silent. Each time he ran out of ammunition, he made forays back to the beach minus his helmet and boots, and returned to continue his private battle until nine enemy positions were wiped out and at least twenty of the enemy lay dead.

Twice he had his 'stinger' shot from his hands, and he was wounded in the shoulder by a chunk of shrapnel. Although ordered back to the beach for medical treatment and evacuation, he managed to talk his CO, Capt. Wilkins, into allowing him to stay in the front line. Stein was to die later in the battle without knowing of his award.

At 10.35 a.m., the first Marines, six men of 'B' company under Lt. Frank Wright, hit the west coast, soon to be joined by the remnants of 'C' Company with Lt. Wesley Bates. Mt Suribachi had been isolated in 90 minutes of savage and bloody fighting. By-passed pockets of Japanese infantry continued to offer fierce resistance, and 'A' Company, which had landed in reserve, joined with the remnants of the 1st Battalion in mopping up.

Meanwhile, the 2nd Battalion had landed among a fusillade of mortar and artillery fire. The Marines immediately dived for the nearest cover – the terraces, or a handy shell hole. It was imperative that they move forward from the crowded beaches, and Lt.-Col. Johnson, their CO, was seen marching up and down the beachhead, kicking backsides and yelling: 'OK, you bastards – let's get the hell off this beach.'

The 2nd Battalion, whose main purpose was to support the 1st and participate in the attack on Suribachi, had landed on the extreme right of Green Beach, almost alongside the mountain, and were in a very exposed position. Lt. Keith Wells and his 3rd Platoon had to move rapidly northwards to join the others at the assembly point, and came under fire from the mountain. Wells was on his feet, urging his men forward, when he was felled by one of his corporals just in time to avoid a large metal fragment which whistled over his head: 'Cpl. Harold Keller jerked me violently down the slope to avoid my being cut in half by that large piece of flying metal. He saved me from death,' said Wells.

'Easy' Company eventually reached their assembly area, which was not far from the 28th Regiment command post, where the CO, Harry Liversedge ('Harry the Horse' to his Marines) was busy organizing his men for an expected enemy counter-attack. By this time, the tanks were beginning to get ashore, but not without great difficulty. The crowded beaches – littered with bogged-down transports, stranded and abandoned landing craft, wounded awaiting evacuation, and sheltering troops who were constantly arriving from the point of departure – made for hard going. When they hit the beach, they were confronted by the terraces, and had to start to look for the access roads that had been hurriedly carved out by the Seabee caterpillars.

The principal Marine Corps Tank of the Pacific campaign was the Sherman. At 32 tons, and with a maximum speed of 24 m.p.h., it outclassed the Japanese 'Ha Go' 10 ton tank in all respects. Its 75 mm gun proved to be ideal for reducing enemy pillboxes and strongpoints, and the flamethrower variant (nicknamed the 'Ronson' or 'Zippo' by the Marines) was vital in the later stages of the battle, when the Japanese increasingly resorted to fighting from caves and hillside bunkers. In the European theatre, however, both the Sherman and its British equivalent, the Churchill, were no match for the German Panther or Tiger tanks with their superior guns and armour.

Fourteen Shermans plus two flamethrowers, one bulldozer tank and one Retriever of the 5th Tank Battalion had been scheduled to land on Red Beach No. 1, but reports indicated that this area was inaccessible. After arguments between the Battalion commander and the Navy control vessels, the tanks eventually landed at 11.30 a.m., and had to make a long northern detour to find an exit point from the beaches, losing one tank in the process.

Company 'C' tanks crossed the neck below Suribachi around 2.00 p.m., and provided vital assistance to the harassed

Marines, who were becoming increasingly bogged down by the fire from a complex of blockhouses. Threading their way through enemy minefields and under heavy anti-tank gunfire, four Shermans received direct hits to their turrets before suppressing the opposition.

Bert Clayton's arrival on the D-Day beaches was memorable:

We gathered at our assigned disembarkation stations. It's 9.00 a.m., the first infantry troops are hitting the beaches right about now. We're in the ADC [Assistant Division Commander] Group. They've scheduled us to hit the beach about 11.15 a.m. It'll still be 'hot' by then. In the distance, we can see the effects of the Navy's long 'rifles' – the big 11 in, 14 in and 16 in shells walk up and down the island, raising gigantic plumes of dust and volcanic ash.

Each man is lost in his own thoughts. Few express them aloud, but Al Drobnick laughs and says to no one in particular: 'I'm too young to die.' He means it to sound like a joke, but no one doubts he means it. Then he adds: 'It's not the bullet that has my name on it that worries me, it's the one that says "To whom it may concern."'

We're loaded now, and the Coxswain guns his engine. We pull away from the *Deuel* [APA 160], heading for our area of rendezvous, where we'll meet the other landing craft and dance in circles endlessly, awaiting the signal for us to form our line and head for the beach.

The action heats up on the island. Carrier aircraft are pounding the living hell out of Suribachi with machine gun fire, bombs and rockets. It looks like what we're used to seeing in the movies and in combat films. Something happens. The Coxswain gives his craft full throttle, and we join the other LCVPs in a sudden mad rush for the beach.

Oddly enough, I'm not afraid, just fascinated – too damn

dumb to be afraid, I guess. We're maybe 500 yards from shore, and we can see figures struggling up the terraces. Some type of enemy fire is hitting the water in the midst of the boats ahead of us – someone yells 'Dammit Clayton, put your helmet on!' Yeah, he's right. I put my steel pot on.

We're very near the beach now, and the sound of artillery and mortar fire explosions grows much louder. It's a lot like our mock assaults on San Clemente Island, but a lot noisier, just like the movies.

The LCVP runs aground, and the ramp drops abruptly, sending up a shower of salt spray. Mortar fire seems to be falling all around us now. There are maybe ten or twelve of us in our cargo compartment along with the radio Jeep. 'Let's go!' someone yells. We move up towards the front, but the Jeep driver is having trouble getting started, and we're being held up.

'Go! Go! Dammit, get the hell off!' screams the Coxswain. He probably doesn't want to get marooned in this hell hole. Can't say that I blame him. I move to the ramp and jump off, figuring I'll sink knee-deep. Instead, I go up to my hips. I scramble to the first terrace and crouch down next to a guy lying prone in the volcanic sand. I start to ask him what the hell's going on, but I noticed that his right leg is askew. Looking closer, I see that his right foot is clear up around his helmet. Something's wrong, he's not moving. Then I realize that he is dead – the first corpse that I'd ever seen.

I jump up and start climbing the terrace, heading for where our CP is supposed to be setting up at the southern end of Airfield No. 1. Suddenly, it's all too real. It's not like the movies any more.

Gen. Kuribayashi's counter-attack was inflicting grievous losses on the invaders, but he had made what was probably his only serious mistake of the battle – he had waited too long to counter-attack.

As the morning passed, more and more Marines were advancing towards their objectives. Determined, superbly trained and disciplined, more than 6,000 were now making inroads into the Japanese defence lines. Casualties were appalling, but there could be no retreat – not that anyone considered it. The objectives were ahead, and that was the only way the Marines intended to go.

While the 28th Regiment were busy at the foot of Mt Suribachi, the 27th, on Red Beaches 1 and 2, were having their own problems. Maj. John Antonelli's 2nd Battalion on Red 1 hastily assembled and advanced alongside Lt.-Col. John Butler's 1st Battalion on Red 2, both hoping to head towards the southern end of Airfield No. 1, but there was little forward movement. Everywhere, the picture was the same: a fusillade of mortar and artillery fire kept the troops pinned down on the terraces. Casualties crowded the beaches, and were mounting by the minute.

Tanks desperately clattered along the shore, looking for the elusive gaps in the terraces, and more and more landing craft ground ashore onto the already crammed beaches. On Red Beach 2, a Marine legend, Gunnery Sgt. John Basilone, was urging his machine gun platoon up from the beaches. As they advanced towards the perimeter of Airfield No. 1, a mortar shell exploded, and five men were killed instantly, Basilone among them.

'Manila Joe' Basilone had been the first enlisted Marine to win the Medal of Honor in the Second World War, in October 1942. During a night-time *banzai* attack in the bitter campaign on the island of Guadalcanal, he single-handedly stemmed a tidal wave of enemy troops bent on overrunning the Marine positions. When dawn broke, thirty-eight bodies, the remains of a Japanese company, lay before the American perimeter.

Sent back to the United States, he had been feted by Hollywood stars and paraded for War Bond drives throughout the country. Declining a 2nd Lieutenant's bars, he returned to the war with the 5th Division. 'Staying behind would be like being a museum piece,' he declared.

Chuck Tatum knew 'Manila Joe', and was nearby at the time:

Now we were halfway across the island, but caught in our own trap, exposed to artillery and mortar fire in a big, open pit, but Basilone told us to stay, and we were doing it. I gingerly peered from our position towards the landing beach. A group of Marines was advancing towards the runway with Basilone in the lead. I felt momentary elation – 'Gunny' Basilone was coming back with more men. I heard Jap rounds impact on the men 75 yards from the 'safety' of our shell hole. I watched in horror as the explosion tore the troops apart. It was awful. It looked like Sergeant Basilone was down – nobody moved, the bombardment was creeping towards us, and I ducked for cover. I don't remember when, but some time that afternoon, the word came: Basilone was dead.

Walter O'Malley, of E-2-27th Regiment, tells of another case of bad luck:

We were about halfway across the island when Ralph Lancaster took a round in the calf of the leg. He didn't even realize it at first, probably because of the adrenalin. He soon became aware, though, and was helped back to the beach. Probably delighted at receiving a non-crippling 'million-dollar' wound, he trumpeted: 'This is my ticket out of here!'

But while he was waiting to be evacuated, an artillery shell landed nearby, and he was killed.

After the war, Roy Felty from Kentucky, one of Lancaster's buddies, travelled to Toledo to visit Ralph's fiancée, and ended up marrying her.

By 11.30 a.m., the southern end of the airfield had been reached, and a message was flashed from Gen. Schmidt for the 27th Regiment to exploit any weak spots, Schmidt was anxious to get the Marines off the beaches and on to the southern plateau. Things were not moving fast enough for him, and it was becoming obvious that the D-Day objective – a line roughly from The Quarry near the East Boat Basin across the centre of Airfield No. 2 and over to the west coast – was not going to be achieved. But then the high command's prediction of a 'ten-day battle' was always an unrealistic target.

There were now two distinct phases to the battle – the advancing Marines desperately moving towards Airfield No. 1 through a maze of pillboxes, machine gun emplacements, trenches and tank traps, and the men on the beaches attempting to survive the concentrated fury of the Japanese bombardment.

Kuribayashi's strategy – let the enemy concentrate on the beaches, then annihilate them with artillery and mortars – was having only a limited effect. He had underestimated the capacity of the Marines to re-group and advance regardless of casualties and lack of tank and artillery support.

To say that the troops on the beaches felt vulnerable would be the understatement of the century. In virtually every shell hole there was at least one dead Marine. At the base of the terraces, the wounded lay waiting for evacuation by the landing craft that were running the gauntlet of the shredding barrage.

Second Lt. Benjamin Roselle, one of a six-man Naval gunfire liaison team, had managed to reach the second row of terraces, only to be pinned down by heavy artillery fire. As they attempted to move forward, one of his men fell wounded only feet away. Roselle strapped the man's radio equipment to his back and moved on.

Within minutes, a mortar shell exploded among the group, and Roselle and two others went down. The two struggled to their feet, but Roselle could not – his left foot and ankle hung from his leg, held by only a ribbon of flesh. He ordered the wounded back to the beach as someone applied a tourniquet to his leg. Pinned down, with no hope of advancing, the men dug in and sweated out the barrage. Within a few minutes, a mortar shell made an almost direct hit among them, and fragments tore into Roselle's other leg.

Those Marines that were able, crawled back to the beach in search of a Corpsman, while Roselle and the remains of his group crowded into a shell hole. For nearly an hour they lay, trying to anticipate where the next shell would land. They were soon to find out. An artillery shell burst almost on top of them, tearing off one man's leg and wounding Roselle for the third time, in the right shoulder.

The wounded Marine dragged himself away on his elbows, and Roselle found himself with only the dead and a grisly assortment of body parts for company. But his ordeal was not yet over. A fourth hit bounced him several feet into the air, and hot steel ripped into both thighs. For some odd reason, he wondered what time it was. As he lifted his arm to look at his watch, a mortar shell exploded only feet away, blasting the watch from his wrist and tearing a jagged hole in his forearm: 'I was beginning to know what it must be like to be crucified,' Roselle later said. Soon, a medical party arrived, set his fractured arm, and carried him to the beach.

He was eventually taken to an LST hospital ship, where his foot was amputated.

By early afternoon, the Marines from Red Beaches 1 and 2 were beginning to reach the approaches to Airfield No. 1. The airfield was on a plateau, and the perimeters rose steeply on the eastern side. Hundreds of the enemy had been killed, and the remainder now fought with their backs to the main south-west–north-west runway.

As the Marines and the Shermans that had escaped from the log jam on the beaches reached the 20 ft-high slopes, the Japanese disappeared into the airfield drainage pipes and over the runway. At twenty-three, Ross Doll was the old man of his company. He saw his first Japanese on the skyline on D-Day: 'I took aim, but my gun misfired.' Ross soon learned that it was not a good idea to try to use a tank as a shield: 'They knew that where there was a tank, there would be troops nearby, so they would home in on them. You had to dig in, and afterwards repair the communication lines that they had chewed up.'

Among the chaos on the beaches, the Seabees, the Naval Construction Battalions, were performing miracles. Landing with the early waves of assault troops, they were desperately trying to get the tanks, artillery and transports off the beaches and into action. With their bulldozers, they attacked the terraces, carving passages through the 15 ft-high walls of volcanic ash and sand to allow the tanks and transports access to the island. On the beaches, their cranes unloaded vital supplies – ammunition, water, food, fuel and medical supplies – while the tractors attempted to pull clear the transports that lay bogged down, axle-deep in the sand.

The Seabees were a comparatively new addition to the US forces. Formed shortly after the attack on Pearl Harbor, they were largely recruited from the construction industry.

Their job was to build whatever the forces needed – bridges, airfields, roads, accommodation, storage tanks – the Seabees would find a way of doing it. On Iwo Jima, specially trained parties of Seabees cleared minefields. Others demolished obstructions and towed away damaged and wrecked tanks and vehicles with their caterpillar tractors, dug shelters for ammunition and supplies, and unloaded the never-ending stream of amphibious craft.

To find a young Seabee was a novelty. The majority were volunteers in their forties or even fifties – 'Protect your Seabees: one of them could be your dad' was a familiar joke. At Iwo Jima, their casualty figures were high. One unit lost seven men to a mortar barrage before they got twenty yards from their landing craft, and throughout the battle they worked and sometimes fought alongside the Marines – the Japanese shells and mortars were not selective as to whom they killed.

The 9th Naval Construction Brigade was composed of two regiments – the 8th and the 41st – and there were three Naval Construction Battalions, the 31st, 62nd and 133rd, in the 41st Regiment. The 133rd was the only battalion to get all its men ashore on D-Day, with the 62nd arriving five days later.

These recruits from America's road-, bridge- and dam-building industries were the men who transformed the island as fast as the Marines cleared it. They built a giant airfield on the central plateau on the site of Airfield No. 2, with a main runway 10,000 ft in length, and paved over fifty-five miles of road on the island. The 133rd alone lost 2 Officers, had 37 men killed and 137 wounded on D-Day alone. At the end of the battle, they had 200 Purple Hearts and 10 Bronze Stars.

As news of the congestion on the beaches was relayed back to the *Eldorado*, Adm. Kelly Turner decided that it was unwise to add to the log jam, and closed the beaches for two hours.

From 1.00 p.m. to 2.58 p.m., the seaborne traffic came to a halt while Seabees and Marines desperately struggled to clear a passage through the terraces and unload the masses of supply craft that stood in rows across the invasion beaches.

At the extreme right of the landing area lay Blue Beaches 1 and 2, and beyond them the East Boat Basin, overlooked by a row of cliffs and The Quarry. Before the assault troops had even left the point of departure, Gen. Cates, Commander of the 4th Division, had scanned the area through his binoculars from the bridge of his ship and declared: 'If I knew the name of the man on the extreme right of the right-hand squad of the right-hand Company of 3/25, I'd recommend him for a medal right now.'

Because of the obvious danger presented by the high ground dominating this area, Col. Lanigan landed both the 1st and 3rd Battalions of the 25th Regiment on Blue Beach 1, from where they made a two-pronged attack – the 1st Battalion moved straight ahead, and the 3rd swung to the right to clear Blue Beach 2 and assault the cliffs and The Quarry.

Although the Japanese gunners on the cliffs had the range down to the nearest foot, remarkably little fire was encountered by the first wave of Marines, and by 11.30 a.m. the 1st Battalion under Col. Hollis Mustain had advanced to within 600 yd of the north end of the main runway of Airfield No. 1.

The tanks of the 4th Tank Battalion had begun landing on Blue Beach 1 at around 10.20 a.m., and immediately drew very heavy fire from the enemy artillery. All three Tank Landing Vessels were soon hit, but succeeded in withdrawing after unloading, and the Shermans desperately searched for an exit point from the beach. One tankdozer (a Sherman fitted with a bulldozer-type shovel) scooped a passage through the first terrace, but was disabled when it struck a horned mine. Once it had ground to a halt, the Japanese artillery pounded it into a twisted mass of useless metal.

The remaining tanks advanced in single file until they reached the edge of a minefield. From there, they engaged the enemy bunkers with their 75 mm guns until engineers were able to approach to clear the minefield. The Japanese gunners soon received clearance from Gen. Kuribayashi's HQ, however, and a ferocious barrage rained down on both Blue and Yellow Beaches. From the cliffs and from the front, the Japanese poured everything that they had upon the 4th Division Marines.

At 2.00 p.m., the 25th Regiment made a co-ordinated attack, while the 1st Battalion continued with their attempt to move forward, making an advance of about 100 yd before being pinned down by intense fire from pillboxes. The 3rd Battalion, under their commander, Col. 'Jumpin' Joe' Chambers, pressed across Blue Beach 2, and against unremitting fire, began to scale the cliffs around The Quarry. From a landing force of 900 men, 3rd Battalion were now down to 150, and 19 officers were out of action.

As the day drew on, 3rd Battalion were given orders to withdraw 100 yd for temporary respite, as relief from the 2nd Battalion, which had landed in reserve at 12.50 a.m. on Blue Beach 1, moved into forward positions that had been laboriously secured.

On Yellow Beaches 1 and 2, at the centre of the landing area, a relatively quiet landing was soon violently interrupted by a withering barrage of mortar and machine gun fire. Directly to the front of the 23rd Regiment were two large blockhouses and a number of pillboxes. Behind Yellow Beach 1, the Marines were faced by Maj. Matsushita's 10th Independent Anti-tank Battalion, while Yellow Beach 2 was held by Capt. Awatsu's 309th Infantry Battalion. The blockhouses had been severely damaged by naval gunfire, but were both still operational and offering fierce resistance.

The CO of the 1st Battalion, Lt.-Col. Ralph Haas (who was

to be killed in action the next day) made an urgent call for artillery and tank support, but one of his men, Sgt. Darrell Cole, decided that there was no time to waste waiting for reinforcements. Armed with only grenades and a pistol, he single-handedly silenced five enemy pillboxes before being killed by a grenade that landed at his feet. Cole was to be awarded a posthumous Medal of Honor.

On Yellow Beach 1, Capt. Kalen led his men from the beaches into a hail of fire as they approached Airfield No. 1. Within minutes, his radio man was hit. Kalen crawled towards him, but was himself wounded. His squad, pinned down by murderous fire for over forty minutes, could only watch in desperation as Kalen bled to death. Offshore, the gunnery officer of the cruiser USS *Chester*, Lt.-Cdr. Robert Kalen, was not to know of his brother's death for over a month.

At the base of Mt Suribachi, mopping-up operations were in full swing in the wake of the 1st Battalion. Many enemy positions had been by-passed, but were being reoccupied as soon as the Marines advanced. Lt. Keith Wells of 'Easy' Company witnessed the struggle:

Quickly, I looked back at the 1st Battalion men crossing the island. Each consecutive wave repeated almost the same battle as the one before as knocked-out Japaneses positions were re-manned. We watched as two new enemy positions began firing. The first wave of Marines had by-passed these positions because they were inactive.

Marines were being shot in the back by by-passed well and wounded Japanese that were pretending to be dead. Word was passed, and the dead Japanese on top of the ground were targeted time and again as each new group passed over. We watched as each new group would shoot the same dead

Japanese so many times that only their clothes held them together. Soon, a mixture of dead, wounded and live Japanese and Marines lay scattered across the island. The situation was a hodgpodge of death, destruction and confusion for those who followed.

Lt. Wells' 3rd Platoon was ordered to cross the island at the foot of Mt Suribachi to join up with and support the 1st Platoon Marines, who were already on the far side of the isthmus, and who had radioed back they had many wounded and no Corpsman.

The platoon set off at a run in a chain of four squads, drawing a hail of fire as they went. After a while, they came across a stretcher-bearing party heading back to the beach, and stood aside to let them pass. On the stretcher was Capt. Mears, an old friend of Lt. Wells. As they resumed their advance, they heard loud explosions to their rear: 'It caused me to turn and see what I already knew. Mears and his stretcher-bearers were blown to bits by one or more large shells.'

Moving through a mass of ridges and anti-tank ditches, the platoon came across many unattended wounded Marines. Some asked for help as they passed, but they had to press forward to the other side of the island. A heavily fortified area lay ahead, and the enemy gunners were directing their fire at Wells and his group. 'The enemy loved to kill leaders,' he said. Wells dived for a small hole, and landed on top of a dead Japanese: 'My right knee landed in the open stomach of a dead Jap. The odour was more than I could stand. I stayed there with the body until the bullets and sand quit flying over me.'

Two tanks were coming to the Battalion's rescue, but were attracting very heavy fire from the enemy's guns. The tanks acted quickly, and destroyed many pillboxes. After by-passing a large concrete blockhouse, the platoon finally reached the

1st Platoon HQ, and as it was now getting late in the day, they helped set up a defensive perimeter.

Evening was now approaching, and the Marines prepared to consolidate their tenuous hold on the island. Night-fighting was not favoured by the Marine Corps, and there were few times during the Pacific campaign when they volunteered to engage the enemy during the hours of darkness.

The Japanese, on the other hand, were very adept at night-time *banzai* attacks, infiltration and forays for food and water. The Marines always kept a good watch on the nocturnal activities of the Japanese – it would be the height of folly not to.

The temperatures dropped dramatically. To many Marines, used to fighting in the tropical climes of Guadalcanal, Bougainville and the Marianas, the chill came as a shock. Their thin clothing offered little protection against the unaccustomed cold, and most had had little if anything to eat or drink since leaving their transports at the crack of dawn. Sgt. Harold Best, with the 2nd Battalion of the 26th Regiment, recalls that first night:

I formed our platoon into a triangle, one squad facing the beach, the second facing Suribachi, and the third facing north. Jap artillery and mortar fire continued. Some time in the night, an enemy plane got through our Navy screen. His bombs fell in Jap-held areas, to our delight. The sky lightened up with AA fire as all the ships opened up. I lay in my hole, enraptured by all the fireworks. Off in the distance, I could hear an occasional call for a Corpsman as somebody would be hit. David Stewart, a friend, was holed up in a small hole with a buddy. A Jap tossed a grenade. It rolled under their packs and exploded. It threw David and friend backwards. As the Jap charged and thrust his bayonet into

David, it penetrated his thigh and stomach. The Jap disappeared into the darkness.

Pfc Thomas also had a rough day and night:

Crawling forward through the rocks, we came under heavy artillery fire. Casualties mounted as flying fragments hit everywhere. We dropped to our knees, rifles ready for the counter-attack we felt would follow, paying no attention to anything, but looking through the cloud of dirt and debris for the charge.

Something hit me in the back and knocked me flat. I couldn't move, could hardly breathe, and felt numb all over. As feelings came back, I found a shrapnel fragment as big as my hand. I flicked it up, and it was too hot to hold. My pack was torn and ripped, but my luck had held – a little higher or lower would have been fatal. We lost four from that shell. Three we couldn't identify, the other poor soul had only a leg sticking out of his shoe, while the rest plastered the rocks.

No one slept. We kept watch all night, one hour on and one hour to cat nap, two men in a hole. Japs came along every night, probing our lines, rolling grenades into holes, always shortly after dark or a few minutes before daylight. We ate very little, a few 'C' rations at night to keep our strength up.

At sea, the large vessels retired to their night-time stations further away from the coast, while gunboats and destroyers patrolled offshore, occasionally firing at the high ground above the 4th Division positions and at the slopes of Mt Suribachi.

Throughout the night the destroyers maintained a display of flares to illuminate the front line. Slowly descending under silk parachutes, the pyrotechnics added to an eerie sense of unease as every rock, hillock and bush took on the appearance of a possible enemy.

The Japanese soon started what was to become a regular night-time occupation: firing large and very inaccurate mortars and rockets. The 320 and 675 lb spigot mortars, with their distinctive shriek, launched from crude wooden ramps, sailed over the American lines in a wild and unpredictable trajectory, since the range was determined by the amount of powder in the charge. Some fell among the Marines, while others sailed around the sides of Suribachi and plopped harmlessly into the sea. 'You could see it coming, but you never knew where the hell it was going to come down,' said Lt.-Col. Robert Cushman.

The Japanese kept up their artillery and mortar fire throughout the hours of darkness. A direct hit on the command post of the 1st Battalion of the 23rd Regiment killed the CO, Lt.-Col. Ralph Haas, and his operations officer, Capt. Eberhardt. The beaches, where a shuttle service was bringing in supplies and evacuating wounded, came in for such a battering that Yellow and Blue Beaches were closed down from 11.00 p.m. onwards. To add to the confusion, small parties of Japanese infiltrators were getting through to the beaches. One such group set fire to a dump of ammunition, gasoline and flamethrower fuel belonging to the 4th Division, which caused a spectacular fire that could be seen all over Iwo Jima.

Marines kept watch on a rota system, one catching a few hours' sleep while others peered into the gloom for the enemy, who made full use of the vast underground tunnel system to pop up in front of or even behind the wary Marines. Thomas Remondino of 'A' Company 5th Engineers had good reason to remember the night of 19 February:

I was caught in a mortar barrage. When the smoke and dust cleared, my first impression was: 'I'm either sitting in a pool of blood, or I shit my pants.' Since that was my first night in the front line, either event could have happened.

I never figured to be flown out with such a minor leg wound. I can still see the serious expressions on the faces of my buddies when I was carried through the bivouac area. They claimed I was grinning from ear to ear. I was just trying to make them feel at ease.

Near the southern end of Airfield No. 1, where the 27th Regiment had a tenuous foothold, over a hundred Japanese charged down the runway, to be met with a hail of machine gun and rifle fire, while on cliffs near the foot of Mt Suribachi, men of the 28th Regiment were amazed to see a barge full of enemy troops round the point and land just short of Green Beach. The Marines soon despatched them with a volley of rifle fire.

Occasionally, these night-time encounters ended in tragedy. In one foxhole, a Marine saw a Japanese infiltrator pass by the side of his position. He leapt from the hole shouting 'Jap! Jap!', and was immediately shot dead by a Marine from a nearby position.

On the slopes of Suribachi, Maj. Subashi Yonomata, an artillery observer, had a grandstand view of the day's activity. His diary, recovered after the mountain had been captured, has many interesting observations:

It is getting dark now [D-Day], and the flashes of our shells exploding make the scene an eerie spectacle. Few, if any, of the Americans will escape its wrath. Our low-level defences in the centre and the north position of the island are now combining their firepower with ours. The Marines of the Yankees are in the midst of a flaming hell.

It was during the hours of darkness that the transport ships arrived with the Marines of the 3rd Division, who were to be held in reserve until the situation on the island could be clarified.

Ashore, a few lucky Marines had discovered the vents of hot sulphur vapours rising from the volcanic sub-surface. Braving the foul smell of rotten eggs, they found that by placing sheets of cardboard, plywood or lengths of wood across the fissures, they could have a hot bed for the night. One Marine recalls looking to his left and right and seeing rows of foxholes filled with Marines, looking for all the world like a row of pans steaming on a stove.

Aboard the command ship *Eldorado*, 'Howlin' Mad' Smith sat and studied the day's reports, and wondered why the Japanese had not attempted a *banzai* charge during the night, as they had on most other battlefields. 'I don't know who he is, but the Japanese general running this show is one smart bastard,' he said to a group of war correspondents. Ashore, another correspondent, Robert Sherrod of *Time-Life*, surveyed the scene and said: 'The first night on Iwo Jima can only be described as a nightmare in hell.'

Six

The Jaws of Hell (D+1–D+2)

Each man should think of his defence position as his graveyard. Fight until the last, and inflict much damage on the enemy. (Lt.-Gen. Kuribayashi)

D+1

After the fine weather of D-Day, Tuesday 20 February dawned cold and miserable. A chill wind swept the island, and the congestion on the beaches was compounded by a four-foot surf.

The Marines had now established a firm pattern of attack. The 28th Regiment, having isolated Mt Suribachi from the rest of the island, faced the daunting task of capturing it, while the remainder of the invasion force moved north. The beaches that had been closed the previous day reopened at 6.00 a.m., but because of the log jam and the constant Japanese artillery and mortar fire, had to be closed again at 9.30 a.m.

A team of underwater demolition men was sent by the Navy to blast some of the smaller craft with TNT, and vessels smaller than 120 ft in length were banned from all beaches. On the shore, bulldozers, tractors, Jeeps and even tanks lay disabled or bogged down, some lying on their side where they had been blasted by enemy artillery. The terraces and the black volcanic beaches were littered with a plethora of boxes, blankets, water bottles, ponchos and abandoned gas masks.

The evacuation of the casualties had by now become a priority. Several Tank Landing Ships (LSTs) were being used as intermediate hospital ships. Lying about 2,000 yd offshore, they handled the casualties from the beaches, and decided priorities – the more serious cases were shipped out to the regular hospital ships lying further offshore, minor wounds were tended there and then, some Marines being allowed back to their units immediately.

At 8.30 a.m., the Marines began a simultaneous attack – the 28th Regiment against Mt Suribachi, and the remainder to the north across Airfield No. 1 and towards Airfield No. 2, with the right flank hinged on the cliffs around the East Boat Basin. James Justice, with the 27th Regiment, was on the move somewhere near Airfield No. 1:

> As we started our advance the morning of 20th February, I recall seeing a Marine from a mortar platoon hit – he had received a direct hit from a Japanese shell, his jaw was blown away exposing his teeth, and his skull was blown open. There was a ball of grey matter, part of his brains, about the size of a golf ball lying on top of his right ear. He was still alive, and was making a motion with his right hand for somebody to shoot him. A Corpsman was on his way to help him.

With daylight came the carrier planes, concentrating on the lower slopes of the volcano with napalm and bombs, while from the coast, the destroyer USS *Mannert L. Abele* shelled the slopes from the west, and the minelayer USS *Thomas E. Fraser* attacked from the east. The tanks were slightly delayed. Eight were available, but ammunition and gasoline had not yet been delivered, and the constant attention of Japanese mortars forced them to keep moving around.

The men of the 28th Regiment were under no illusions about the task ahead of them. The east side of the line faced a long, wide stretch of open, sandy ground, and on the west lay a mass of stunted trees and bushes. Beyond lay a band of rocks and boulders leading to the slopes of the volcano itself, with the main Japanese defence positions concealed in caves and tunnels bristling with artillery pieces, mortars, machine guns and rifles. The enemy were in a perfect defensive position, with unlimited observation of every Marine movement.

Under Col. Atsuchi, 2,000 troops defended Suribachi. His orders from Gen. Kuribayashi were to hold the mountain for as long as possible – all were expected to die at their posts. Although Atsuchi had lost many of his heavy guns to naval gunfire, the defences were still formidable – seventy concrete blockhouses and fifty reinforced positions faced the Marines on the lower slopes alone.

The Marines attacked on a broad front with artillery support, 37 mm guns and 75 mm halftracks, but had gained less than 75 yd by noon. Using demolitions and flamethrowers, they blasted their way forward, and suffered heavy casualties all along the line. The tanks joined the battle at around 11.00 a.m., and provided valuable support, while behind the front line, the 1st Battalion, in reserve, had a hard day mopping up by-passed pockets of resistance and accounting for over seventy-five of the enemy.

Col. Atsuchi and his men offered stiff resistance, but by mid-afternoon he radioed Gen. Kuribayashi: 'Enemy bombardments from the air and sea and their assaults with explosions are very fierce, and if we ever try to stay and defend our present positions, it will lead us to self-destruction. We should rather like to go out of our positions and choose death by *banzai* charge.' Clearly, Atsuchi was wavering, but a *banzai* charge was the last thing Kuribayashi wanted from the defenders of Mt Suribachi – he did not bother to reply.

Capt. Dave Severance, 'E' Company Commander, ordered the 3rd Platoon to replace the 1st Platoon in the front line, a distance of about 200 yd away and over open ground.

Lt. Keith Wells looked out: 'I saw little or nothing to shield us from the enemy's fire power. The men of the platoon would be open targets all the way.' He decided to make a personal reconnaissance and then have the platoon follow in small groups:

I took off running. It was all open ground, every Marine and every Jap could see me, I was a moving target, and unless I stopped, the enemy's small arms fire would need to be lucky to hit me. All I could think of was: 'I'm not hit yet. I'm not hit yet.'

I did not travel far until a small machine gun began firing at me in earnest, and the sand flew around me. Near me was a shallow pothole. A Marine from the 1st Platoon occupied the only safe end of the small shelter. Only his head and shoulders had protection. One very quick glance assured me the Marine was dead. He looked drained of all his blood. I was wrong. When I landed at the far end of the shallow pit, the other man opened his eyes and gently shook his head.

Quickly, I jumped and landed behind a small mound of dirt. I left my poncho in the depression – the Japanese machine gun ripped it to shreds. I looked back and expected a few or possibly a squad from the 3rd Platoon to be heading my way – instead, here came the whole goddamn platoon. They looked like wild animals.

Sgt. Thomas was in the lead. Mad! I was never so mad in all my life – I get mad now thinking about it. We were not attacking, we were setting up a defence for the night, with a planned attack tomorrow. How could anyone be so stupid?

I had a mental picture of the Japanese machine gunner waiting until the platoon stopped and gathered around me. He would have a field day. When the Jap machine gunner did start firing again, one of our machine guns found him. I could hear the familiar series of bursts from one side and then another. They lasted only a few seconds before the Japanese gun went silent.

The men of the 3rd Platoon dug in for the night, but their ordeal was not yet over. As dusk descended, the Japanese artillery commenced a rolling barrage all along the Marine front line:

These explosions were walking up our defence line, every explosion was getting nearer, and I had no place to go. I am not sure who it was, but there were two men in a shallow depression beside me. I laid down next to their spot – I guess I wanted company. With my face down, my helmet pushed back to help cover my head, I covered the rest of my neck with my arms.

The shells continued walking up our lines, exploding only a few feet away, and literally raising the earth into the air. We could hardly breathe, and I opened my mouth to equalize the pressure. Someone told me it would prevent the bursting of our ear drums.

I was sick, sick, sick. The explosions were coming directly up our line with no wasted shells. All I could think about was the great loss of men. There is no way of expressing the horror of this experience. I believe this was the most nerve-racking experience I have ever endured. I just knew they were blowing the men all to pieces, and there was not one thing I could do about it. What made it even more horrifying, it stopped soon after passing through us, and started back again.

My muscles were so tight I thought that they would burst. When the shelling ceased, I was shaking like a leaf. Before this happened, nothing scared me – I did not have time for that luxury. The ear-bursting noise stopped instantly, and the silence seemed just as loud or louder. I got rid of the shakes – there were too many things to think about. It would soon be that time of day when Marines kill anything that moves – friend or enemy.

Although the day's gains were slight, the Marines were now poised for the big assault on the mountain tomorrow.

In the late afternoon, engineers from the 5th Division had found a buried cable of 1½ in diameter and cut it. It was the radio link between Gen. Kuribayashi's HQ and Mt Suribachi – from now on, Col. Atsuchi was alone.

Some time during the night, a group of Japanese troops began to gather near the eastern foot of Suribachi, and the destroyer USS *Henry A. Wiley* closed in to around 200 yd and blasted the area by the glare of searchlights. From the slopes of the volcano, white and amber flares were fired into the American lines which directed artillery fire from the north, but the expected major night-time counter-attack never came.

On the slopes of Suribachi, Maj. Yonomata wrote in his diary:

I am gravely concerned. Despite the effectiveness of our incessant barrage, they have gained the plateau and are even now moving towards the base of our mountain, approaching our minefields and hidden emplacements. Aircraft have returned, and are saturating our fortifications with fire bombs. They are dropping these on the sides of the cliffs, sending rivers of flame running down into our positions. It is night, and our guns continue to rake the beaches and plateau area where the invaders remain. The boldness of their Navy is quite distressing, for, sneaking close in the darkness, they have suddenly commenced a vicious barrage. I can hardly write this as my hand trembles so violently from the continuous concussion. It is becoming so intense that my brain feels numb – I cannot write any more at present.

In the north, the Marines were spread across a 4,000 yd front. From the cliffs above the East Boat Basin, the line ran along the south-east ridge of Airfield No. 1, and across the island to the base of Mt Suribachi.

The attack had started at 8.30 a.m., with the right flank holding at The Quarry, and the left moving north in an attempt to straighten the line. The terrain was relatively clear – bunkers, pillboxes and landmines barred the way across the plateau, but the area was devoid of the hills, ravines and gullies that were to be the Marines' nightmare later in the battle.

By noon, with the aid of tanks, the whole of Airfield No. 1 had been taken. This was a bitter blow to Gen. Kuribayashi, who had not expected the Americans to advance this rapidly. Maj. Horie explains:

On 19 February, American forces landed on the first airfield under cover of their keen bombardments of aircraft and warships. Although their landing direction, strength and fighting methods were same as our judgement, we could not take any countermeasures towards them, and 135 pillboxes we had at the first airfield were trodden down and were occupied only two days after their landing. We shot them bitterly with the artillery we had at Motoyama and Mount Suribachi, but they were immediately destroyed by the enemy's counter-fire. At that time we had opportunities to make counter-offensive attacks against the enemy, but we knew well that if we did so, we would suffer much damage from American bombardments of aircraft and vessels, therefore our officers and men waited for the enemy to come closer to their own positions. In fact, this Airfield [No. 1] was trodden by American forces in only two days. If we had infused this great strength, many materials, and three months of labour which was used on the airfield into the defence of Motoyama district and Mount Suribachi, we would have been able to make these areas much stronger.

By mid-afternoon, the brand new battleship USS *Washington* had arrived off the coast of Iwo Jima, and was impatient to display its firepower. With the assistance of an air-spotter, the huge ship blasted away at a cliff line between the southern end of Airfield No. 2 and The Quarry. Its 16 in salvos caused a landslide which blocked a number of enemy caves.

Near the west coast, units of the 26th and 27th Regiments of the 5th Division pressed forward with the help of tanks, and feeling their way through minefields under heavy artillery and mortar fire, advanced 800 yd. The marines now had an almost straight front line across the island just north of Airfield No. 1, but were still short of the 0–1 line, the projected D-Day objective.

The 25th Regiment Marines, advancing from Blue Beach towards Airfield No. 1 and the cliffs west of The Quarry, were to suffer at the hands of both the Japanese and their own forces. At 11.00 a.m., the Japanese scored a direct hit on the battalion command post, killing six Corpsmen and wounding seven others, and at 4.00 a.m., carrier planes attacked Company 'B' of the 1st Battalion of the 24th Regiment with rockets, bombs and machine-gun fire as they positioned themselves on top of The Quarry, despite the fact that yellow panels were being displayed to mark the Marines' front line. Five men were killed and six wounded as a result of this attack. To add insult to injury, as soon as the Navy fighters had left the area, naval gunfire and 'friendly' artillery began to fall among the unfortunate company.

Gen. Schmidt now decided that the situation ashore warranted the embarkation of the 21st Regiment of the 3rd Division – an indication of the top brass's concern at the slow progress of the battle so far. Schmidt knew that the Joint Chiefs of Staff had hoped to keep the 3rd Division out of Iwo Jima altogether, maintaining them intact for the forthcoming invasion of Okinawa.

Shortly before noon, the 21st Regiment began to board their landing craft, but a high sea and rain hampered the operation, and there were a number of casualties as men fell into their craft or into the sea. The situation on the beaches had not improved, and the regiment circled for six hours before Gen. Schmidt ordered them back to their transports. Many of the Marines suffered from seasickness after their long, wet ordeal, and a few landing craft, unable to make it back to the transports, drifted around all night.

Throughout the first and second days, the demand for artillery support was desperate. The 105 mm howitzers of the 14th Regiment of the 4th Division came ashore in amphibious trucks (DUKWs). The 3rd Battalion landed at mid-afternoon, and were operational in prepared positions near Red Beach 2 and Yellow Beach 1 by 5.30 p.m. However, the DUKWs of the 4th Battalion, which were launched from LST 1032, had a disastrous afternoon. The first DUKW to hit the water was swamped by the sea and sank. In rapid succession, seven more DUKWs and their precious cargoes floundered in the heavy sea and were lost, together with twelve officers and men. Only four of the craft made it to the shore to join the 3rd Battalion.

LST 779 reached Red Beach 1 at 4.30 p.m., and tractors hauled four 2½ ton 155 mm howitzers across the island to the 5th Division lines near the west coast. Ross Doll vividly recalls a particularly gruesome event:

There was a heavy mortar barrage. About 20 yards away there was a huge crater, about 12 feet deep and 20 feet across, probably made by a 16-inch naval shell. There were six or eight men in there when the barrage started. Nearby, I recognized an old high school friend, Gus. He dived head-first into the shell hole, but while he was still in the air, a mortar shell hit the pack on his back and exploded. There wasn't much left of Gus.

That same afternoon, Woody Schaffer got killed when a mortar shell exploded six or eight feet in front of me. The particles from that shell hit me under the chin. A Corpsman nearby came over and said: 'You've been wounded. Let me wipe the blood off.' He took his pocket knife out, covered the edges of the blade with iodine, and removed several splinters from my chin.

I was offered the Purple Heart, but did not take it. Years later, when I was shaving, the razor would come to an abrupt stop, and I would have to get tweezers and remove pieces of metal from my chin.

The second day on Iwo Jima was coming to an end. The Marines had control of almost a quarter of the island, but the day had cost them dearly, with nearly a thousand dead and wounded. Offshore, gunfire support ships harassed the enemy, while destroyers provided constant illumination with their star shells. A small counter-attack in the 5th Division lines at 8.00 p.m. was easily repulsed, while a hundred Japanese unsuccessfully stormed the 4th Division positions at 4.40 a.m. Throughout the night, both sides maintained a barrage of mortars and rockets.

During the afternoon, it had started to rain, and continued through the night, Marines lay miserably in their foxholes while the rain collapsed the sides of their emplacements.

As they shivered and soaked, the old hands among them recalled the hot jungles of Guadalcanal or the blistering sands of Kwajalein.

Throughout the battle, Dale Worley kept a diary of daily events. This was strictly against orders, as was unofficial photography, but the accounts are a fascinating account of what daily life was like for the front-line Marine:

> Very little sleep last night – cold. Wish I had my blanket roll. Field piece fired at us all day, blew up our ammo dump. We finally got him. Still eating 'Ks' ['K' Rations]. Would like some hot chow. I would give a dollar for a hot cup of joe, [coffee]. Land crabs and bugs bad here.

D+2

> You knew that other guys were going to be killed – not you, other guys. (Anon.)

By Wednesday, the pattern was set. The 28th Regiment was poised at the base of Mt Suribachi, and would begin the assault that morning. The remainder of the Marines would move north on a broad front – in the west, the 26th and 27th Regiments; in the centre, the 23rd, and in the east, the 24th.

During the night, the already bad weather had deteriorated even further. A gale force wind howled down the island from the north-east, rainclouds scurried across a leaden sky, and six-foot waves crashed onto the crowded beaches. Adm. Turner had no option but to close them yet again.

At 7.40 a.m., a massive barrage of artillery, rockets and naval gunfire rained down on the Japanese positions immediately to the front of the Marines' front line, and the Navy sent in sixty-eight of its carrier planes to add rockets and bombs. As the gunfire lifted, the Marines of the 4th and 5th

Divisions moved forward against a mass of well-concealed enemy positions, and casualties soon mounted.

On the far left, near the west coast, the terrain was suitable for tanks, and the 26th and 27th Regiments, supported by Shermans, advanced almost 1,000 yd – a large gain by Iwo Jima standards. Casualties had been heavy, but the troops were now almost at the 0–1 line – the point that an over-optimistic High Command had set as the target for the first day of the invasion.

As a result of this rapid advance, a gap developed between the 27th and 23rd Regiments at the centre of the line, and another company, 'B' of 1-27, was brought forward from the reserve. At this time, Gen. Rockey, Commander of the 5th Division, moved his HQ from the USS *Cecil* offshore to the southern end of Airfield No. 1.

On the eastern side of the line, the 4th Division Marines were unable to make much impression on the enemy. Moving out from their overnight positions, they encountered a number of minefields, all covered by well-placed Japanese strongpoints which had to be cleared by engineers under the cover of tank gunfire. Because of this and the rugged terrain which faced the troops, advances of only 50–300 yd were possible. More reserves were moved forward as the battle developed, and the casualties continued to mount. Col. Wensinger, CO of the 23rd Regiment, brought up a company of 1-23 to bolster the centre. Among the many casualties that day was Lt.-Col. Hollis Mustain, CO of 1-25, killed by enemy artillery at 10.00 a.m. while checking his front line.

Despite the weather, Gen. Schmidt again disembarked the 21st Regiment of the 3rd Division, and they landed throughout the afternoon on Yellow Beaches 1 and 2. Gen. Cates, Commander of the 4th Division, was anxious to come ashore to establish his HQ, but after his assistant commander, Brig.-Gen. Hart, had come ashore at 12.45 p.m. and reported that Blue Beach was still under very heavy enemy fire, and that an exploding ammunition dump was threatening most of Yellow Beach 2, Gen. Cates was advised to stay aboard the USS *Bayfield* until Thursday. Cates decided that the 3rd Division reinforcements should be used the following day to relieve the 23rd Regiment at the centre, and issued orders to that effect at 5.00 p.m.

As the day drew to an end, the Japanese harassing fire continued, and small groups of the enemy infiltrated the Marine positions. At around 9.00 p.m., an undetermined number of the enemy hit both flanks of the 27th Regiment, but were repulsed within the hour – Dale Worley's diary records: 'We broke up a Nip counter-attack last night. Really blew them to pieces. Myers in 'K' Battery got his head blown off by a mortar this morning – I liked him. Rained again today – still cold.'

At about the same time, reports were received that the enemy were attempting a seaborne landing behind the American lines on the west coast. The light cruiser USS *Pasadena* and the destroyer USS *Twiggs* were sent to investigate. Although a radar contact was established, an intense search failed to locate any small-boat activity.

The Japanese continued their disruptive fire throughout the night and into the early morning. At 11.30 p.m., around two hundred enemy troops gathered at the end of Airfield No. 2 and advanced towards the lines of the 23rd Regiment. A combination of artillery and naval gunfire obliterated them before they could leave the end of the runway. At 3.00 a.m., it was reported that an enemy aircraft had dropped three bombs behind Blue Beach.

Theodore Blyshak was a sergeant with 'A' Company of the 1st Battalion, 26th Regiment. To his men, he was 'Captain Bly'. On the transport ship, he recalls that some tactless officer had said: 'Look around you – one in every three of you will not return, but you will make history.' Little did he know how prophetic the first part of that statement would be.

On the third night, the enemy charged his position. Blyshak fired his .45 pistol at a sword-wielding Japanese officer, who spun and sliced off a Marine's ear and slashed his shoulder. He then turned and lunged at Blyshak, plunging his sword through the right side of his chest. Another Marine fired about twenty rounds and killed him. Minutes later, a grenade landed among them. Someone threw his backpack onto it and trampled on it, and the ensuing explosion blew off his foot. Blyshak and the other wounded Marine tried to get away. With his chest bleeding profusely, Blyshak crawled, dragging the other man, and after several close calls, arrived at an aid station. The enemy were still all around, and Blyshak was handed a gun. Soon, he saw a Japanese soldier crawling close to the aid station, and he shot him. That was the last he remembered before he passed out.

Tied to a tank and transported to the beachhead for evacuation, he was hit by shrapnel in the back and shoulder, and received a bullet wound in the calf of his leg. When he awoke, he was being hoisted onto a hospital ship, where he received extensive surgery. Blyshak spent months in hospitals in Hawaii, San Francisco, Chicago and Philadelphia before he was fit to return to duty at Camp Lejeune.

Daybreak saw the arrival of forty carrier planes over Mt Suribachi. For 20 minutes the base of the volcano was pounded by bombs, rockets, napalm and machine-gun fire as a prelude to the assault by the 28th Regiment.

Supported by fire from cruisers and destroyers, the Marines launched their attack at 8.25 a.m. A 2nd Battalion patrol worked their way around the volcano from the east coast, and by afternoon had reached Tobiishi Point, the southernmost point of Iwo Jima.

On the land side, the Marines, as a result of Tuesday's dogged attacks, were now only 200 yd from the Japanese main defence line. The main thrust was to be made by the 2nd Battalion on the left (under Lt.-Col. Chandler Johnson), the 3rd Battalion (under Lt.-Col. Charles Shepard) and the 1st Battalion on the right (under Lt.-Col. Jackson Butterfield).

Again, the tanks were delayed by slow refuelling, and the Marines moved forward under cover of a continuous artillery barrage. The 1st Platoon, near the west coast, made rapid progress as they swung around the base of the mountain at the water's edge, but elsewhere the Japanese resistance was solid. As the Marines edged forward, they saw evidence that the naval and air attacks had not been in vain – shattered blockhouses, cratered trenches and huge tracts denuded by napalm.

Attacking a labyrinth of trenches on the lower slopes, Sgt. Hansen and Pte. Ruhl were blasting away at a group of Japanese troops when a demolition charge landed at their feet. Ruhl dived on top of the charge, absorbing the full blast, and died saving the life of his companion. He was to receive a posthumous Medal of Honor.

The 3rd Platoon in the centre met very heavy opposition, and it was not until the arrival of tanks and halftrack-mounted 75 mm guns that any progress was made. By 2.00 p.m., they had secured the foot of the mountain. By nightfall, the 28th Regiment had formed a semicircle around the north side of Mt Suribachi, and the lines had moved forward 650 yd on the left, 500 yd in the centre, and 1,000 yd on the right.

The enemy continued their harassment all through the night. Men from the 81 mm mortar platoon repulsed an attack and killed sixty of the enemy, and on the western beach, 'C' Company ambushed and killed another twenty-eight men trying to move to the north of the island. Dale Worley's diary records:

Rained all day – had my first hot joe and hot chow since I left ship – it was priceless. Moran was killed. A Nip nambu [machine gun] got him twice in the arm and once in the guts. Am dirty, tired, wet, cold and damn miserable. This is hell.

Lt. Keith Wells of the 3rd Platoon, 'Easy' Company, viewed the menacing slopes of Suribachi with more than a little trepidation:

It looked hopeless. We had little or no protection from the enemy. I have a five-gallon water can in front of me and a white wool blanket wrapped around me. I wondered what in the hell we were going to do and how the hell we were going to do it. My weapons were already clean, but while I was thinking, I cleaned them again.

The artillery and naval gunfire had denuded the ground before them, and huge, blackened patches marked the impact of napalm canisters. Standing starkly to their front, a chain of blockhouses and connecting trenches loomed in the morning light.

Wells decided that a brief reconnoitre of the enemy lines was called for. Leaving his weapons behind, he crawled forward to higher ground and studied the Japanese lines. Not more than sixty yards to his front, a Japanese officer returned the stare. Wells shouted back to his men 'Get that son of a bitch!', but before anyone could act, the officer stood up, gave a broad grin, and disappeared behind a damaged bunker.

Crawling back to his lines, Wells phoned Company HQ and asked what assistance he was likely to get as they moved forward. The reply was that the tanks were still refuelling and topping up on ammunition, and that the only Marine artillery pieces in the area were facing the opposite way. The mortars were out of ammunition (they were not of much use anyway, as most of the enemy were underground), and the heavy Navy ships had not yet returned from their night-time stations many miles offshore. Less than reassured, he was told that an air strike could be arranged. The carrier planes duly arrived and swarmed over the slopes of the volcano, but in their concern not to hit the Marines, who were all in exposed positions, they attacked too far forward, and hardly touched the Japanese lines.

To compound their problem, the Marines now faced rows of barbed wire which they had themselves placed in front of their lines the previous night to prevent Japanese infiltration. It had been assumed that the morning advance would have been spearheaded by Shermans, which would have flattened the wire before them.

The order to attack came through from HQ, and the Marines moved out:

We had nothing to attack with but our hand weapons, and nothing to protect us but the clothes on our back. Our situation looked so hopeless that I could not order the platoon to follow me. I stood up, pointed my tommy gun towards the enemy, and took off running straight towards that grinning officer's bunker – I could think of nothing else to do.

Never did I feel so alone in my life. The attack was unreal, like something out of a movie. Out of the corner of my eye I saw Sgt. Thomas pulling rolls of wire out of the way, and then I saw Hansen and our platoon runner trotting close behind me. The others were coming, I just knew it.

The platoon, for some inexplicable reason, did not come under fire, and reached the Japanese front line:

Ruhl, Hansen, Thomas and I were leading this wild attack. Immediately behind us was a sprinkling of four squads, including a young machine gunner and his helper from 'I' Company. We continued to run straight at the enemy, I could not believe that they were not shooting at us.

I stopped at the far edge of a bomb crater, and quickly looked back across the open ground. 'I' Company were still in their defence positions. The 3rd Platoon's right flank remained exposed. Shells were landing among the last to leave the defence position, but when the dust cleared, I could see some men stand up and continue running towards us and the enemy. Ruhl and Hansen charged on ahead to the trench joining two concrete blockhouses. I turned around from watching our struggling platoon behind us just in time to see Ruhl and Hansen drop to their hands and knees and look over the edge of the trench.

They must have almost bumped heads with the Japanese, because they jerked back fast. Ruhl and Hansen had kneeled down side by side, now they lay that way. Immediately, over the side came an object much larger than the enemy's hand grenade. The large explosive charge landed between the two men.

Ruhl yelled at Hansen 'Look out, Hank!', then he flopped down on the object. We heard the muffled explosion. From the power and the shock, I saw Ruhl's body rise in the air then flop back. Hansen grabbed Ruhl by the pants leg and began dragging him back towards me, but I yelled and waved him to quit. One of Ruhl's shoulders fell back. It looked disconnected from his body, and I could see a great cavity that was once his chest.

There soon followed a fierce battle between the platoon and the Japanese in the trench. With rifle fire and grenades, the Marines held the line until the 'I' Company machine gunner set up his weapon and cleared that section. However, the

Japanese on the right flank launched an attack, and the machine gunner and his ammunition-bearer were both killed.

Wells and his men now turned their attention to a concrete bunker on their right, from which the enemy were showering them with hand grenades. Desperately needed supplies of fresh ammunition and charges were on their way in a supply tank, but a direct hit sent the tank and its crew skyward in a ball of fire.

As he climbed out of a crater, a Japanese mortar shell exploded almost at Lt. Wells's feet:

> The shock and blast of sound numbed my senses. It took me a few seconds to clear my mind. There was a sharp burning sensation in my neck, and no feeling from the waist down. With my hands, I felt behind me to see if I still had my legs. My hand came back wet with blood and water. A large piece of metal had hit my canteen as it exploded, another piece hit a stainless steel spoon in my hind pocket, turning the spoon inside out. Many small pieces of shrapnel buried themselves in my right cheek. A large piece of flesh was blown from my left leg just above the knee. Worst of all, a large piece of metal entered my left leg about a foot above my left knee, I found out later that a piece lodged in my neck. My clothes below the waist were almost gone. I lay on my stomach, and that saved my front.

The feeling gradually came back to his legs, and Corpsman Bradley dressed his wounds.

By now, two flamethrowers had arrived – Chuck Lindberg and Robert Goode – and they soon had the enemy blockhouse in flames. Exploding ammunition flew in all directions as the interior was reduced to a cinder. The Sherman tanks had also finally made it to the front line, and a second blockhouse, from which another fusillade of hand grenades now fell, was blasted by one of them. Within minutes, nineteen shells had pierced a hole in the wall, and Lindberg put his flamethrower nozzle through and let off a blast of flame. Seconds later, the back door of the blockhouse flew open and three Japanese figures ran out, straight into the path of Goode, who gave them another blast, which instantly incinerated them.

Wells now moved past the blockhouses to escape sniper fire, and found himself among a row of tripwires in a minefield. Dancing among them, he came face to face with a Japanese machine gun. The gunner blasted away at Wells: 'His bullets were hitting close to my privates, which was the only place where I still had some clothes. I quickly raised that leg and dived behind a small mound of dirt. The machine gunner continued trying to get me.'

Corpsman Bradley again bound up the unfortunate lieutenant's wounds and told him to go back for more treatment: 'I could feel myself running out of energy. My wounds were beginning to take their toll. I had not eaten, drunk water, urinated or defecated in two-and-a-half days.'

The events of the third day were still not over. As the afternoon light began to fade, a combined force of fifty Japanese fighters and bombers headed towards Iwo Jima from the north-west. They were *kamikazes* from the 2nd Milate Special Attack Unit based at Katori Airbase which had stopped over at Hachijo Jima, about 125 miles south of Tokyo, to refuel before continuing their one-way journey.

The aircraft carrier USS *Saratoga*, a veteran of many Pacific battles and invasions, picked up the aircraft on her radar when they were over a hundred miles out. The *Saratoga* was preparing to receive a squadron of Corsairs and Hellcats some thirty-five miles out from Iwo Jima. Six fighters were sent up to investigate, and twenty minutes later, an excited voice on the radio announced: 'Tally-ho! Splash two Zekes [Mitsubishi AGM Zero fighters].'

The invasion fleet, now on 'Condition Red', filled the sky with a blanket of anti-aircraft fire as six planes broke through the low-lying cloud and headed for the *Saratoga*. Two of the *kamikazes*, trailing black smoke and flames, slammed into the starboard side of the carrier near the waterline, smashing through the hull and turning the inside hangar into an inferno. Damage-control teams struggled to contain the blaze, and within an hour the fires were under control.

Within minutes of the first attack, a solitary flaming plane hit the flight deck and bounced into the sea, leaving a hole about a hundred feet from the bow. Despite the damage, the *Saratoga* was able to recover some of her aircraft by 8.15 p.m., while others were taken aboard the escort carriers USS *Wake Island* and USS *Natoma Bay*.

The *kamikazes* were not yet finished. A 'Betty' twin-engined bomber (Mitsubishi G4M) appeared as from nowhere and ploughed squarely into the hull of the escort carrier USS *Bismarck Sea*. The decks were crowded with aircraft, and the ensuing explosion sent the elevators plunging into the hangar below, causing more havoc. With fires out of control, 'Abandon Ship' was ordered at 7.00 p.m., and 800 men went over the side into the rough, cold sea. Within a few minutes, a tremendous explosion blew off the entire stern of the carrier, and she rolled over and sank. Escort vessels closed immediately, and began picking up survivors.

Three more ships were to fall victim to the Japanese attack. The escort carrier USS *Lunga Point* was showered with flaming debris when four aircraft were blasted out of the sky as they made a low-level pass. The minesweeper tender USS *Keokuk* was badly damaged when a 'Jill' dive-bomber (Nakajima B6N) tore into her top deck. LST 477, loaded with 3rd Division tanks, was struck a glancing blow, but was able to put her cargo ashore the next day before being towed to Saipan for repair. The *Saratoga*, still burning, left the invasion fleet with a destroyer escort and headed for Pearl Harbor – by the time the old veteran was repaired and seaworthy, the war was over.

The *kamikazes* had had a successful evening. The death toll stood at 123 for the *Saratoga*, 218 for the *Bismarck Sea* and 17 for the *Keokuk*. This attack, the only one at Iwo Jima, was an indication of the severe damage the *kamikaze* squadrons could cause: in the forthcoming invasion of Okinawa in April, the *kamikazes* wreaked havoc among the invasion fleet, and inflicted more casualties upon US Navy personnel than in any other Pacific engagement.

The US Navy practice of fitting wooden flight decks to aircraft carriers resulted in many carriers being withdrawn to Pearl Harbor or even the American west coast for lengthy repairs after *kamikaze* attacks. It is significant that the three carriers of Royal Navy Task Force 57 which participated in the Okinawa invasion were able to continue operations throughout the battle despite *kamikaze* attacks. Because they were all fitted with reinforced steel flight decks, the wrecked Japanese aircraft were simply bulldozed over the side into the sea. All postwar US carriers adopted the steel flight deck construction method as a result of the experience of Japanese *kamikaze* operations.

Seven

Corpsmen: 'Jewels of the Battlefield'

Those wonderful Corpsmen – what can you say about them?
(Pfc Clyde Washburn)

Throughout the Pacific campaign, from the jungle of the Solomons to the sands of Tarawa, among the Umurbrogol Mountains of Peleliu and the hillsides of Saipan, the cry 'Corpsman' could be heard above the roar of battle.

Corpsmen, the Navy medical aides who accompanied the Marines into battle and dealt with front-line casualties, were revered by the Marines, and justly regarded as their own. Though strictly Navy personnel, Corpsmen were allocated to the Marine Corps after their preliminary medical training, and thereafter were to all intents and purposes Marines.

The progression from Navy recruit to Marine Corpsman was a complex one that needs to be explained to clarify their unique status. After enlisting in the Navy, the recruit underwent the usual basic training – a process somewhat akin to Marine boot camp – and was passed out as an Apprentice Seaman (AS). It was at this stage that selection for medical training began.

For suitable candidates, a ten- to twelve-week period in the Hospital Corps School followed, which resulted in the classification of Hospital Apprentice 2nd Class (HA2/C). After further training, higher grades could be gained through examinations and suitability. There followed a period of general medical training in a multitude of subjects to give the recruit experience. It was from here that the final selection for

Marine Corpsmen took place. Those who were successful went to Field Medical Service School (FMSS) for an accelerated period of training, which included Marine Corps discipline, and classes to learn field medicine techniques and procedures. The course lasted eight weeks, during which time the Corpsman became a Marine in all but name. Marine Corps dress and regulations were mandatory, the only deference to their Navy status being their rank and serial number.

Corpsman Ernie Lang recalls:

After initial Navy boot camp training, we were given aptitude tests. From these tests, we were assigned to the duty stations and schooling where the Navy deemed we would be best suited. In my case, it was on a crash course in medical training for about six weeks. After our schooling, some went on to serve the medical needs of the ship crews at sea, others at Navy Hospitals in the states, some went to medical facilities on island outposts, and because the Marine Corps is a branch of the Navy, many of us Navy-trained Corpsmen were sent to serve in the various Marine units.

After several weeks of Marine field training, I was assigned to a rifle company, and after a year of medical field combat training with this company at tent camps in California and the mountains of Hawaii, we set sail for Iwo Jima.

After FMSS, the corpsman was allocated to a division – the USMC Division consists of 3 regiments of 3 battalions of 3 companies. In addition, there are the supporting units, tanks, transports, artillery, construction, communications, amphibious units and medical staff. Each battalion was assigned a Medical Section staffed by two doctors and forty or more Corpsmen. Of these seven Corpsmen were seconded to each company, and the remainder made up a unit known as the Battalion Aid Station

(BAS). The senior medical officer of the BAS – a Navy doctor – was in charge of the unit, and reported to the CO of the battalion.

The full range of Corpsmen ranks were: HA2/C, HA1/C, Pharmacist's Mate 3rd, 2nd and 1st class (PH3/C, PH2/C, PH1/C), and Chief Pharmacist's Mate (ChPhM). A ChPhM was responsible for the Navy personnel, and reported to the senior medical officer, while the Corpsmen in each company were usually led by a PH1/C.

While in training, Corpsmen accompanied their units wherever they went, and participated in all activities, including storming imaginary fortifications, boarding and leaving ships by nets, route marches – all the infantry training that was required of a Marine.

The Battalion Aid Station was a miniature hospital, usually staffed by two doctors and several Corpsmen, some of whom were specialists, such as surgery assistants, and there was a regular interchange between BAS staff and field Corpsmen, to enable them to learn each others' responsibilities.

Corpsman Stan Dabrowski experienced a typical training regime after enlisting from high school in July 1943:

After boot camp, I applied for and was accepted for training with the medical department, basic of which was a three-month accelerated course in the fundementals of medical science – i.e. anatomy and physiology, minor surgery, first aid, *materia medica* and therapeutics, hygiene and sanitation, VD, toxology and other related subjects.

Assignment to duty with the Fleet Marine Force resulted in courses in combat medicine, evacuating the wounded, along with a multitude of combat-related training in the Medical Field Service School, where Corpsmen were integrated for duty with Marine Corps units in combat training. During intensive training at Camp Pendleton in California and Camp Tawara in Hawaii, we not only honed our medical combat expertise, but also survival training with the infantry units.

In battle, the BAS became the first collection point for casualties, and was usually sited close to the action to provide the treatment the front-line Corpsmen were unable to give. This treatment was of necessity a stopgap in preparation for evacuation of the serious cases, although medical decisions made by the doctors at the BAS were very pertinent to the recovery of many casualties.

While a BAS served a battalion of around 2,000 men, a Field Hospital (FH) could serve a division, was fully equipped to handle the most serious cases, and was the next evacuation point after the BAS. Until enough territory had been captured to provide a relatively safe location for the FH, casualties were evacuated from the beachhead to hospital ships offshore, or to the troopships (APAs) that had transported the Marines to the battlefield.

The sickbay of the APAs contained a well-equipped operating room and beds for seriously wounded men. There were three hospital ships at Iwo Jima – *Samaritan* (AH-10), *Solace* (AH-5) and *Bountiful* (AH-9) – together with the auxiliary hospital ship *Pinkney* (named after a former Surgeon General). In addition, four LSTs – 929, 930, 931 and 1033 – were fitted out to handle near-shore casualties and to shuttle the wounded to the offshore hospital ships.

One LST was converted as a floating blood bank to process the whole blood flown in from the west coast of the USA, which was invaluable in combating severe shock. Iwo Jima saw the first use in the Pacific theatre of whole blood for transfusions. Blood donated in America, sometimes only days earlier, was rushed out by plane as soon as the first airfield became operational, and was a great innovation that saved countless lives.

Corpsmen in the front line worked under appalling conditions. It was always necessary for them to expose themselves to enemy fire to attend to casualties lying in open ground, and the casualty figures among their ranks were proportionately higher than any other Iwo Jima combatants. The front-line Corpsmen would try to assist the wounded to shelter if any was available, assess the severity of their wounds, stop bleeding, apply makeshift splints, dress wounds, try to prevent shock, alleviate pain, and send out calls for stretchers. Dabrowski recalls:

My first casualty was a sergeant with a sucking chest wound. He had taken a machine gun bullet right through the lungs. One of the paramount things we had trained for was sucking chest wounds. You had to do something immediately or the man would drown in his own blood. You had to close off the wound so that he could get air, then ram this big battle dressing into the wound and compress it as much as possible and tie it off, give him a shot of morphine, write out a tag, and mark him – you put a big 'M' on his forehead to indicate that he had already been given morphine, then someone would have to drag him off the beach. I could not do that. I had to advance with my unit.

As the Pacific war progressed, it seemed that the fighting became more and more violent. On Iwo Jima, where huge numbers of men were fighting within the limits of an island less than eight square miles in area, devastating wounds from shrapnel, mortars, artillery, landmines and the greatly underestimated Japanese sniper were common.

Although held in very high regard by the Marines, the Corpsmen were equally appreciative of the stretcher-bearers. Robert de Geus, a Corpsman with the 26th Regiment says:

The link between front-line Corpsman and the BAS and beyond were the stretcher-bearers, as they were the vital lifeline for many wounded Marines. The bravest warriors would not come close to matching the feats of many stretcher-bearers who risked everything to serve a seemingly endless number of calls from the front lines, and many became casualties as well. A four-man litter team would often be reduced to a one-man team, as trying to cross 'no man's land' was devastating.

After the initial bottlenecks on the invasion beaches had been cleared, it was often a surprisingly rapid trip from front line to hospital. One young Marine recalls that after being wounded when a mortar shell landed nearby, and being attended to almost immediately by a Corpsman, he was whisked away to the beach on the back of a Jeep on a makeshift stretcher, loaded onto an LVT and hoisted aboard a hospital ship, all within an hour. From the chaos, carnage and ear-shattering noise of the front line, here he was lying between crisp, white sheets with starched Navy nurses hovering over him and a Frank Sinatra record playing in the background: 'I finally made it to heaven,' he said. But such events were very much the exception. Ernest Lang, who described himself as a 'naive greenhorn kid of eighteen', was a Corpsman with the 28th Regiment:

By the fourth day, my clothes were stiff with dried blood from the men I gave first aid to. Often, I held their limbs, or whatever part of their body was torn open, on my lap or knee to treat them. The knees of my pants were ripped open from crawling too much. Then one of the wounded guys I was taking care of noticed this and offered me a pair from his backpack, as he was about to leave the island anyway.

Lang, who went through the whole battle physically unscathed, says that he will always appreciate the protective covering fire that the Marines of his company gave him when he was attending the wounded, many of whom, he recalls, were wounded two or even three times, and after partial healing, were sent back to the front to be wounded again or killed. One particular event will always remain with him: 'The Nips captured one of our men somehow, and after they severely tortured him, they left his body out in the open for all of us to see. His remains were such a gruesome sight that I shall not attempt to describe the details.'

The stress of battle and the appalling wounds that most Corpsmen were confronted with over weeks of front-line action would have been enough to unhinge many lesser beings, but few among their ranks succumbed. One Marine tells of how his friend had been shot in the head – a Corpsman said: 'I can't go on any more. I can't look at any more dead and wounded.' The Marine put his arm around his shoulder, but suddenly someone shouted 'Corpsman!', and he grabbed his bag and dashed away.

Dr Thomas Brown served on Iwo Jima, and remembers some of his experiences and those of his Corpsmen:

We were offshore in amphibious tractors for about thirty minutes before H-Hour. From the tractor that I was in we could see the battle scene ahead of us. There were several planes flying over the island – I saw one go down.

I could see destroyers and small craft cruising up and down parallel to the beach and firing at targets that had been spotted. I was in the third assault wave. The colonel in command said to me: 'Doc, I want you to go in on the third wave to take care of any of the wounded on the beaches that you see.'

All that I saw were dead on the beaches. We were told to set up a Battalion Aid Station as soon as we found something that looked like it might be a bit of a shelter. I went up the beach, and saw a blockhouse that had been pretty well beaten up by those 16 in naval guns, and I thought it might make a good aid station, but it turned out that it was full of Japs, and they started firing at me.

About this time, a Marine came by, and he saw what was going on and threw two hand grenades, and killed three Japanese. We then turned left and went along the east side of the air strip [Airfield No. 1]. When we got past the corner, another barrage of artillery came in, and we heard some cries for Corpsmen. With the two Corpsmen that were with me, we went over and found that one man was dying and another was badly wounded, so we started getting plasma into him, and told the Marines to take him back to the beach.

We went about another seventy-five yards across the island, and saw Lt. Hendricks of 'Easy' Company leaning against a small tree, and I asked him: 'Where is the front line?' He said: 'Doc, you dumb SOB, get out of here before you get your head shot off. We need you, so go back to the battalion CP.' I said: 'I'm not going back there.' So I took the two Corpsmen and went back about fifty to seventy-five yards and set up our first aid station. We were right in the open, behind piles of rocks or any security we could find – those 16 in shell holes were thirty or forty feet in diameter and six to eight feet deep, about as good an aid station as anything, as long as the Japs didn't spot us.

We set up two or three empty stretchers so that we could put wounded in them as they brought them in, and we could give them plasma, apply tourniquets or give them morphine surettes. Of course, they were tagged if they had been treated out front by one of our Platoon Corpsmen, and whatever we did with some of the more horribly wounded, after we finished, we put the tag on with the information of what we had administered and sent them on back by our Jeep ambulance, or about the second day, they began using amphibious tractors because they could haul four or five litters plus several ambulatory patients.

I remember one afternoon, the third or fourth day, we saw ninety-two casualties in two hours, and then maybe we wouldn't do much for a while. We were always under fire, we were right behind the lines. I remember seeing one fellow who came in with his eye all shot up. I told the Corpsman that surely his brain was destroyed by the bullet that went through his eye. I saw him ten years later at a Marine Reunion. I said: 'Don, you're not supposed to be here. You're dead.' He said: 'Well, I just came to spite you, Doc.'

It was Dr Brown who treated Medal of Honor winner Jack Lummus after he had been mortally wounded:

Jack Lummus, you may have heard about him, he was in our Battalion. He was a lieutenant, and played football for Baylor. He was put in command of what remained of the company and told to break through. He stepped on a landmine, and they brought him back on a stretcher. All that remained of his right leg was the femur, the bone in the thigh, and it was attached to the tibia by some fragments of ligaments, and there was a long artery, isolated, just hanging there.

His left foot was pretty well blown off, and the shrapnel had gone up into him and destroyed the genitalia. He just looked up at me and grinned rather weakly, and said: 'Well, Doc, the New York Giants lost a mighty good end today.' He died five hours later on the table in the surgery back in the Divisional Hospital.

As the battle dragged on and the casualties mounted, the problem of the disposal of the dead had to be dealt with. Drawing on experience from previous battles, the planners had already selected the sites for the cemeteries from aerial photographs before the first Marine set foot on Iwo Jima. The graves registration teams, responsible for cataloguing and burying the dead, were quickly on the scene, the first squad arriving on D-Day with their own bulldozers.

Little could be done for the first two days – most bodies had to be left where they fell, although some were reverently collected and laid in rows covered by ponchos. The areas designated as cemeteries had first to be cleared of mines and unexploded ammunition, and then levelled. Even during these operations, Japanese shells and mortars were frequently falling in the area.

The 3rd and 4th Division cemeteries were located side by side just off the north–south runway of Airfield No. 1. The 5th Division had their plot on the south side of the airfield under the shadow of Mt Suribachi. Touchingly, the 3rd and 4th Division cemeteries contained a special corner for war dogs killed in action.

The Marine Corps, as with all military organizations, had a strict procedure for the burial of the dead. The body was first fingerprinted and one dog tag removed – the other was buried with the body in a six-foot-deep trench dug by bulldozers. A distance of three feet was allowed between the centre of each body, with fifty bodies per row. Personal possessions such as letters, rings, watches and photographs were tagged and packaged to be returned to the next of kin, and the location of the body was marked on a master chart. When the situation on the invasion beaches had stabilized and the fighting shifted to the north of the island, the Seabees built fences around the plots, made from wood that had been salvaged from packing cases, and stone arches were erected at the entrances.

The Japanese dead were dealt with less ceremoniously. Where a number of bodies were found together, they were usually bulldozed over. The majority died in the labyrinth of caves they had so assiduously constructed before the battle, sealed in by Marine demolition charges. The Japanese were loath to leave the bodies of their dead in the open, and most were collected, usually at night, and dragged to the nearest cave.

Fifty years after the battle, parties of volunteers, known as 'bone diggers', were still arriving from Japan each year to look for the remains of missing soldiers, cremate the bones, and return the ashes to the mainland. As late as 1993, over nine thousand Japanese soldiers were still unaccounted for.

Ten years after the battle, all American bodies were exhumed and returned to American soil. For some, the final resting place would be the Punch Bowl, Hawaii's National Cemetery of the Pacific War, built into the huge cap of an extinct volcano. Others would be interred in Arlington Cemetery, across the Potomac River from Washington DC, close to the great bronze statue by Felix de Weldon depicting the Iwo Jima flag-raising, based on Joe Rosenthal's famous photograph. The remainder would go back to their home towns, to be interred in the local cemetery.

Stories of courage and devotion by Corpsmen are legion, an outstanding example which is typical of many is that of Albert Finkelstein. Since childhood, he had dreamed of becoming a physician, so when the time came for him to go into the forces, he enlisted in the US Navy so that he could choose the Hospital Corps. In 1944, he saw service in Normandy, and upon his return to the USA, was transferred to the Marine Corps and undertook further training at Camp Lejeune in North Carolina.

Landing on Iwo Jima with the 26th Regiment of the 5th Division on D-Day, he suffered a leg shrapnel wound, but refused to be evacuated. From 19 February, he was in the front line under appalling conditions until he was killed on 15 March (D+24). He was awarded the Silver Star, and his citation attests to his gallantry:

> Moving forward beyond the front line on repeated occasions, exposed continually to murderous enemy fire, he administered vital first aid and brought many wounded men back to safety and additional medical attention. Under murderous mortar and rifle concentration he heroically answered the cries of a helpless Marine, and, although he himself suffered a mortal wound, treated the casualty so skillfully that the man recovered.

In 1997, Albert's brother, Isidore, himself a Corpsman, received a letter from a stretcher-bearer who had known Albert on Iwo Jima: 'It was very dark that night. Someone started to throw hand grenades at three of us in a foxhole. Out we went. A machine gun cut us down, and I was hit. Your brother crawled over in the dark and gave me a shot of morphine and bandaged my arm. The fellow beside me got hit nine times. Your brother did a terrific job on him.' Isidore says: 'It is a wonderful irony that although Albert never realized his ambition, his nephew, my son, has become a physician.'

In all, 23 doctors and 827 Corpsmen were killed on Iwo Jima, and it is significant that of the twenty-seven Medals of Honor, America's highest decoration, that were awarded during the battle, four of the recipients were Corpsmen: PhM/1C Francis J. Pierce, PhM/2C George Whalen, PhM/3C Jack Williams and PhM/1C John H. Willis. Both Willis and Williams were given posthumous awards.

In reply to a request from Mrs Willis, the wife of Corpsman John H. Willis, for details of how her husband died, Herman J.

Dupont, a former 1st Sergeant in 'I' Company, 3rd Battalion of the 27th Regiment wrote:

> On February 28th 1945, both 'H' and 'I' Companies were engaged trying to defeat the enemy on Hill 362A on the west side of Iwo Jima. John was in the middle of the action helping wounded Marines when he was struck down by heavy mortar fire.
>
> John was ordered back to the Battalion Aid Station. Without waiting for official release from the doctor, he returned to the action. John went into a foxhole to aid a wounded Marine. The foxhole was at the base of a cliff of Hill 362A. A Japanese began dropping hand grenades into the hole John was in. John threw the first hand grenade out and continued to work. He also threw out the next seven hand grenades. When the next one landed in the hole, John grabbed it and it blew up in his hand. The explosion killed him instantly. John had remained with the wounded Marine trying to help him. Staying in the hole was beyond the call of duty. Mrs Willis, your husband died gallantly.

In his book, *This Here is 'G' Company*, author John Lane says:

> To return to the medical Corpsman, one hesitated to use the word 'love', but we loved them. Always called 'Doc', they had entered the Navy and been assigned to the Medical Corps, thinking of bright clean hospitals, spotless men of war, and of great brightly-lit hospital ships.
>
> Then somebody said, 'The Fleet Marine Force for you, lad,' and then it was sixty-pound packs, twenty-mile hikes, and the insanity and chaos of this war without mercy.

PhM/2C Stan Dabrowski sums up the Corpsman wonderfully:

Without sophisticated medical technology, without degrees in psychology and philosophy, the Corpsman was required to function with the versatility of no other enlisted man.

Wherever the troops engaged in combat, the ever-present Corpsman was physically exposed. Among the screaming, shouting and crying, surrounded by death, he tended to the injured and dying even as the plasma bottle shattered in his hand. When the battle had passed and the battlefield became graveyard quiet, the Corpsman, his clothes reeking of blood and sweat, mended gaping wounds and consoled his charges. Unlike a movie, the blood never left his boots, the stench never left his nose, the piercing screams never left his ears, and the taste of war never quite left his soul.

Eight

'The Flag Is Up!' (D+3–D+5)

You got so blasé that you could sit down next to a dead, mutilated Jap and eat your dinner – if you had any dinner. (Unknown Marine)

D+3

Thursday 22 February brought more rain. As daylight filtered through the heavy clouds, Mt Suribachi stood menacing the Marines of the 28th Regiment. Col. Atsuchi had around eight or nine hundred men left. His request for a grand final *banzai* charge had been ignored by Gen. Kuribayashi. The redoubtable leader was later to say: 'I had imagined that the first airfield would be overrun quickly, but what has happened to cause Mount Suribachi to fall in only three days?'

Col. Chandler Johnson ordered the regiment to consolidate their positions and bring up fresh supplies of ammunition and food prior to the assault, and at 8.00 a.m. the struggle was renewed. Men of the 3rd Battalion, drenched to the skin and bent by the wind, advanced against a maze of enemy strongpoints. There was little tank support in the deep mire, and the naval aircraft, even if they could have operated in the foul weather, were kept clear of the Suribachi area, as the Marine and Japanese lines were now indistinguishable. Maj. Yonomata's diary records:

We are surrounded by enemy craft of all sizes, shapes and descriptions. All night and thus far this morning, enemy shells have smashed at our above-ground installations and defences, their planes strafe and bomb our defending aircraft into absolute pyres of gutted nothingness, yet we remain strong and defiant. I have passed word to all defences in our fortification to withhold their fire. Not until I am certain that these enemies of Japan are sufficiently trapped shall I give the command to open fire and extinguish them. The Americans are leaving their stalled vehicles and are beginning to climb the first terrace towards the main plateau of our low land defences. Now they shall taste our steel and lead.

An ominous start to the day had been the death of the Regimental Surgeon, Lt.-Cdr. Daniel McCarthy, killed by a shell burst from the north of the island. Earlier, a bomb dropped by a 'friendly' aircraft had concussed a group of Marines.

The familiar assault with rifle, grenade, flamethrower and demolition charge continued throughout the day:

Because of extremely rugged terrain and limited room for manoeuvre, it was impossible to use supporting fire from tanks and artillery to maximum advantage. Demolitions and flamethrowers proved the only way to silence enemy fortifications. On the right flank the 3rd Battalion squeezed out 1/28 and a patrol from Company 'G' worked its way on down the west coast towards the southern tip. On the other side the 2nd Battalion continued mopping up and sent a group from Company 'E' along the east coast to meet the patrol from 3/28.

So ran the official report – what it fails to describe is the sheer misery and terror of fighting an almost invisible enemy in such appalling conditions. Each pillbox and foxhole saw a savage life-and-death struggle, mortar fire constantly rained down from the heights above, guns clogged in the mud and ash, and the cry 'Corpsman!' was all too familiar. One Marine fought a hand-to-hand battle with a sabre-wielding Japanese officer and won, but had to retire to the beach with deep lacerations to his hand because he had grabbed the blade. Another threw a grenade at a Japanese standing in the mouth of a cave, but forgot to pull the pin. The grinning enemy threw it back, with the pin still in place. John Lane describes the typical Marine in combat:

> Rifleman, BAR man, NCO, machine gunner, runners, officers, wire men – growing beards, hollow-eyed, filthy, their dungarees beginning to fray and become stiff with sweat, rain, spilled rations, oil from weapons, and sometimes blood. Hair matted with sweat, boots wearing out on the sharp rocks, skivvies beginning to stink and stick to the skin, loaded down with the bare bones of existence, mess gear, a change of socks (how many times could you change them without washing them?), a few toilet articles (if you wanted to use your water ration, you could shave in your helmet), some rations, water if you could get it, bandoleers of ammunition and a poncho. (The universal mark of the Marine infantryman was the dirty toothbrush sticking out of his breast pocket – it was used to clean his weapon, not his teeth.) A K-Bar combat knife and a first-aid kit hung from his web belt.

By afternoon, the patrols from Companies 'G' and 'E' met, and Mt Suribachi was surrounded. The struggle for the northern slopes had beaten the enemy down to a few hundred men – some were to infiltrate the American lines that night and join Kuribayashi's men in the north, others, using the labyrinth of tunnels, moved nearer the summit. For once, the night was relatively quiet with few infiltrators – the final assault would be left until tomorrow.

Howlin' Mad Smith, aboard the USS *Auburn*, was counting the cost. The 4th Division, fighting for Airfield No. 1 and The Quarry, had lost 2,517 men. The 5th Division, striking across the island and against Mt Suribachi, 2,057 men. Three days of fighting: 4,574 dead and wounded. The Marines were almost at the line that had been set as the first day's objective, and as they approached the hills, ravines, canyons, cliffs and gullies of the north, the worst was yet to come. The signs were ominous.

In the north of Iwo Jima, the 3rd Division reinforcements, the 21st Regiment, were now ready. Gen. Schmidt decided to place them in the centre of the line between the 4th and 5th Divisions. In this area, on and around Airfield No. 2, Col. Masuo Ikeda and his 145th Regiment held the strongest part of the Japanese defences. Literally hundreds of well-sited bunkers and artillery positions barred the American defence.

After four days of close-quarter fighting, the troops who had landed on D-Day were now reaching a low level of efficiency. Lack of sleep, heavy casualties, no hot food, and more recently, appalling weather had done little for morale. Genls Cates and Rockey, the 4th and 5th Division Commanders, knew this would be a good time to relieve some of the more hard-pressed units, but all did not go well during the changeover. The enemy kept up a fierce barrage, and the constant, driving rain added to a confused situation, during which Col. Trotti, CO of the 3rd Battalion of the 26th Regiment, and his Operations Officer, Maj. Day, were killed by an artillery burst.

The new 3rd Division men received a baptism of fire as they pressed forward towards the heavily defended high ground south of Airfield No. 2, with the day's gains amounting to no more than 250 yd, and with 'F' Company of the 2nd Battalion so badly mauled that they had to be withdrawn after only one day at the front. For the troops who have been 'relieved', the situation was only marginally improved. The enemy shells fell almost as thickly as at the front, and the procession of stretcher-bearers toiling back and forth only added to their depression. Hot coffee and doughnuts and a few hours of shallow sleep was the best they could hope for. Frank Gardner, a member of the Air Support Control Unit, was also in the rear:

We camped in an area between Mount Suribachi and Airfield No. 1 on a slope angling down toward the western beach. An AKA cargo ship loaded with ammunition approached fairly close to shore of the western beach.

Obviously, the captain was not aware that enemy artillery north of Airfield No. 2 was still within range to fire on it. It anchored just a couple of hundred yards below our camp. Before it could unload its explosive cargo, Japanese artillery spotted it and began firing. We watched from our camp with fascination as enemy artillery started splashing nearby the big ship. Others were watching with interest from 5th Amphibious Corps HQ, just up the slope next to our unit – they were General 'Howlin' Mad' Smith and Corps Commander Harry Schmidt.

One shell fell close enough to wound a sailor on the stern, the next salvo fell just ahead of the ship. Now the enemy gunners only needed to adjust their aim to hit the target, but fortunately for all of us, the ship picked up speed and departed.

On the eastern end of the line near The Quarry, Lt.-Col. Justin Chambers ('Jumpin' Joe' to the 3rd Battalion) had requested the support of rockets for his attack on the hills to his front. The rockets, mounted on racks on the rear of four-wheel-drive trucks, could unleash a storm of low-level fire, after which it was advisable to move rapidly to a new location before the Japanese artillery could home in. Two rocket launchers were available, and the ensuing fusillade caused the enemy to leave their hideouts and flee to the lower ground.

This was an opportunity the Marines had awaited for days. The machine gunners caught dozens of the enemy in the open, and cut them to ribbons. At 3.30 p.m., 'Jumpin' Joe' was struck by a burst of light machine gun fire. A bullet entered near the collar bone and punctured a lung. A Corpsman stuffed his wound with gauze, and a stretcher team carried him to the beach for evacuation.

From late afternoon until 6.00 p.m., the enemy launched a series of uncoordinated assaults on the left and centre of the American front, which were repulsed by heavy artillery and infantry fire. The weather was now becoming as formidable an enemy as the Japanese. The icy rain continued to fall in torrents, and low mists hampered visibility for patrolling naval vessels and troops alike. Flying had already been abandoned earlier in the day.

On the beaches, the casualties had mounted, but evacuation was proving impossible. The wounded were compelled to huddle under their ponchos in the bitter cold and rain, and wait. One LST, No. 807, remained on the beach under constant enemy fire, to act as an emergency aid station. Doctors worked throughout the night, with crew members performing the duties of nurses as best they could. Over two hundred wounded were treated that night, and remarkably, only two died.

It was during this night that Task Force 58 departed from Iwo Jima for a second strike against the Japanese mainland, significantly reducing the number of aircraft available to support the land forces. Admiral Spruance accompanied the fleet aboard his flagship, the USS *Indianapolis*.

The responsibility for providing air cover for the Marines now fell to the smaller escort carriers (CVEs) of Adm. Durgin's support force. This group was already heavily committed to anti-submarine patrols, combat air patrols, survivor searches and strikes against Chichi Jima. With the loss of the fleet carriers, each with eighty or more aircraft, Durgin would be hard pressed to provide the full coverage for ground attacks the Marines needed. It is difficult to understand why another foray to the already devastated Japanese mainland was considered more important than supporting three Marine Divisions in a battle that was still only a few days old and was proving to be much more difficult and protracted than the planners had envisaged.

Behind the lines, the 4th Division cemetery was inaugurated. Up till now, the dead had been left lying in rows under their ponchos, 'stacked like cordwood', as one Marine described it. Burials began on D+4, the bulldozers scooping out long trenches, and the War Graves team tagging and cataloguing the locations.

The same day, the Seabees set up their HQ. With the battle slowly moving north, it was time to bring ashore the masses of vehicles and heavy equipment that would enable them to start on the monumental task of turning Iwo Jima into one huge airfield complex – the main reason for the invasion. Sgt. Harold Best praises the work of the Seabee bulldozer drivers:

Each Engineer Platoon was assigned a TD14 Caterpillar dozer that was covered with three-eighth steel plate with narrow slits cut in so that the operator could see. These armoured dozers were used to cut crude roads as close to the front as possible so that wounded and dead could be taken back and supplies and troops moved forward.

Another major function was to seal cave openings. These caves sheltered enemy troops, and were lethal to us.

Two riflemen were assigned to each dozer to ward off attacking enemy troops. The Japs had magnetic mines which could be primed by hand and tossed to stick to the sides of the tanks and dozers to disable them. Three-inch by ten-inch wooden planks were secured onto the sides of the Tanks to ward off this threat: this protection was not on the dozer. However, our riflemen did a good job anyway.

One dozer operator was ordered by a tank officer to take his dozer forward to see if he drew fire. The operator replied: 'Hell no, I won't. You have four-inch armour plate, and I have three-eighth. You go damn it!' The officer walked away, hoping no one had heard the conversation – the tanks did their own testing after that. The operators of these dozers deserve much praise, as it was a nasty and dangerous job.

D+4

On 23 February, the 28th Regiment secured Mt Suribachi. This was a very significant event, both for the Japanese and the Americans. Gen. Kuribayashi had certainly not expected such an early capitulation, and when the survivors of Col. Atsuchi's command, who had infiltrated the Marine lines during the previous night, presented themselves at Kuribayashi's HQ, they were severely admonished.

For the Americans, the capture of Suribachi had two benefits: the troops fighting in the north and the supply and landing craft using the beaches no longer had to worry about artillery and mortar fire from this direction, and the 28th Regiment could now be diverted to join in the all-out push to the north. An added bonus was the psychological boost the Marines throughout the island and on ships off the coast would gain from seeing the Stars and Stripes flying from the highest point on Iwo Jima.

Even the weather favoured the Marines. The deluge of the

previous day had subsided, and a watery sun greeted the dawn – it was not to remain, as clouds formed a thin overcast, but at least the rain had gone for the time being.

The cliff-like southern slopes of the volcano were completely unsuitable for a mass assault, and on the gentler northern face there appeared to be room only for a limited force to ascend it. Lt.-Col. Chandler Johnson gave the order 'Secure and occupy the summit', and Marines from the 3rd Platoon, Lt. Keith Wells's outfit, started out at 8.00 a.m.

It was on this day that Maj. Yonomata made the final entry in his diary:

The enemy has now smashed our base and lower levels, and is working his way upwards towards the summit and us. Those of us that are left fully realize that our hopes of repelling the Americans or living to return to our homeland and loved ones are out of the question. We are doomed. But we will fight to the last man.

And later in the day:

It is late, and there are Americans all around us. I have had no contact with any of our forces for hours. I hope the enemy will presume our garrison has been wiped out and withdrawn from the mountain. We are tired, very hungry, thirstier than we have ever been through any other battles. Where our supplies vanished to is a mystery.

The time is uncertain, for we can do little but remain concealed, to wait for the proper moment to make our final attack. I imagine that the Ameri . . .

Two Marines, Cpl. Jack Hastings and Pfc John Castillo, blasted their way into a small, cubicle-shaped observation post and riddled its occupants. Cpl. Hastings found a Japanese major with a diary in his hand.

A forty-man patrol, led by Lt. Hal Schrier, who carried an American flag given to him by Col. Johnson, moved out towards the mountain, laden with weapons and ammunition. The going became increasingly difficult as the men laboured under their heavy loads, occasionally having to scramble on their hands and knees. To their amazement, there was as yet no resistance from the enemy.

Some time shortly before 10.00 a.m., they reached the rim of the crater. A quick survey revealed three shattered gun positions and a number of cave entrances, but no Japanese. Marines formed a cover as a few men descended into the crater to look for something on which to fly the flag. At last, the few remaining Japanese on Mt Suribachi made an appearance. One soldier rose from a cave entrance, only to be despatched by Cpl. Keller, and from another cave a flurry of hand grenades greeted the Marines.

While the exchange of grenades continued, two Marines had found a length of pipe, possibly from a water catchment system, and dragged it to the summit. One Marine fired shots through the pipe, and the flag was secured. At 10.20 a.m., the Stars and Stripes fluttered in the wind, and photographer Lou Lowery of *Leatherneck* magazine recorded the moment for posterity.

Throughout the island and on dozens of ships offshore, the shout was: 'The flag is up!' The Japanese on the summit were not pleased, to put it mildly. One solider jumped out of his shelter and fired at Lowery and another Marine. As he was shot down, a Japanese officer appeared brandishing a sword with only half a blade. Sgt. Snyder drew his .45 and fired, but nothing happened. Making a swift dive for cover, the sergeant saw the officer fall under a volley of rifle fire. The Marines now surrounded the cave entrance from which the hand grenades had been thrown, and enlisted the help of a flamethrower, who aimed a blast of fire into the entrance. Eventually, the cave was sealed with demolition charges, entombing the occupants for ever.

Just around noon, a larger flag, obtained from LST 779, was raised to replace the smaller one, and the event, photographed by Associated Press cameraman Joe Rosenthal, became the most famous photograph of the Second World War. (For a detailed account of the flag-raisings on Mt Suribachi, see Appendix 2.)

Halfway between the USS *Eldorado* and the beach, a landing craft carrying Gen. 'Howlin' Mad' Smith and Secretary of the Navy James Forrestal was ploughing through the heavy swell. When they both saw the flag fluttering on the top of Suribachi, Forrestal turned to Smith and said: 'Holland, the raising of that flag means a Marine Corps for the next five hundred years.'

As the hooters, sirens and whistles sounded around the fleet at the raising of the flag, Keith Wells, nursing his wounds aboard the USS *Eldorado*, was determined to be back on the island and among 'Easy' Company on top of the volcano:

The doctor loaded my BAR belt with twenty tubes of morphine and some sulphur drugs. The Corpsman and a doctor guided me to a passageway. They kept me there until a press boat was loaded and about to be lowered over the side of the ship. I strode across the deck and stepped into the back of the boat – nobody said a thing, and nothing was said on the way to the shore. I was going back to Iwo Jima.

When he reached the beach, Wells came across a pile of equipment collected from the dead and wounded. Poking among the heap, he was amazed to come across his own gear, and promptly kitted himself out. Arriving at Company HQ, he was dismayed to hear that Capt. Severence did not want him to go up the mountain, but having met Cpl. Lindberg and Pte. Goode, with whom he had been in action when he received his wounds, he accepted their offer to accompany him to the summit: 'With the two of them almost carrying me at times, we reached the top. After greeting everyone, I found a spot to set up my command post only a few feet away from the flag pole.'

Still on Suribachi when night came, Wells recalls that the Japanese who were still on the top started shooting flares, and the enemy on the northern end of the island soon joined in. He thought they were signalling to each other. This was soon followed by explosions overhead and shrapnel whistling to the ground. Col. Johnson rang up and wanted to know what was going on, but Wells was unable to enlighten him. The next morning, it was confirmed that the enemy had been firing at them with anti-aircraft shells.

For a number of nights, the Japanese would come out of their caves and forage for food and water. One Marine woke one night to find a Japanese stealing water from his canteen. He yelled at him, and he ran away. For Wells there was a more bizarre event, however: 'One night I slept soundly. When I awoke the next morning, I found a Japanese calling card lying in front of my face – that was all, just a card with a name on it. At first I thought the wind may have blown it there, but then I knew better. It became clear to me that the Jap let me know he was there. I still have that card.'

Contrary to popular mythology, the raising of the flag on Mt Suribachi was not the culmination of the battle. Although the highest point on Iwo Jima had been taken and the Marine front line was almost halfway up the island, the worst was yet to come.

The generals were now leaving their ships and setting up their headquarters ashore. Gen. Schmidt landed that day, as did Gen. Cates. Gen. Rockey was already set up in his HQ, and the three had a meeting to discuss the situation. After a long talk, a strategy was decided upon: the 3rd Division would take up the centre of the line, opening up the right and left flanks; the 5th Division would attack in the west, and the 4th Division in the east. The Navy would continue to give full support. Tanks from all three divisions would come under a single command, that of Lt.-Col. William Collins of the 5th Division, to support the main thrust.

War correspondent Robert Sherrod of *Time-Life*, a veteran of Tarawa and Saipan, met Gen. Schmidt that day and asked him how much longer he thought the battle would last: 'Five more days after today. I said last week it would take ten days, and I haven't changed my mind.' Unrealistic expectations still persisted.

Warrant Officer George Green was an artillery forward observer:

Got the word we are going to move up and attack tomorrow. Packed up, and we took off in single file as Japs were still hitting the beach. We moved along Airfield No. 1 to a spot where it is the shortest distance across the runway. On up to the hill, and deployed and dug in, as we will spend the night here. Still drizzly and damp. We have a nice view of Mount Suribachi from here – pretty good-size hill. We attack tomorrow. Got all the dope from Capt. Heinze. We will try to get Airfield No. 2 – seems as if all their attacks have been unable to get through.

After getting into position, we were watching a rather large bunker burn. It was quite long and had two entrances, one on each end, and two vents at the top. Smoke was coming out each of these, and every once in a while there was an explosion. I don't believe there were any Marines within a hundred yards of it. All of a sudden we saw a Jap poke his head out of one of the entrances. He had on a gas mask, and slowly looked the situation over, and then decided to come all the way out and make a run for it. Guess he must have taken three or four steps, and some Marine got him and down he went.

D+5

On 24 February, Gen. Schmidt decided that the stalemate on the northern front had to be broken, and Airfield No. 2 became the object of the American thrust. From the west coast, the battleship USS *Idaho* blasted the area just north of the airfield with her main 14 in guns, while from the east, the cruiser USS *Pensacola*, repaired after her D-Day battering, added her support.

Howitzers behind the American lines joined in, followed by planes from Adm. Durgan's escort carriers with bombs and rockets. The Air Support Control Unit played a vital part in the co-ordination of these air strikes, as Frank Gardner explains:

We maintained radio communications, not only with fliers, but with artillery and naval gunfire forward observers on the ground. This way we could choose the enemy targets that would need to be hit from the air. We had experienced pilots with us on the ground. They kept in radio contact with an airborne pilot who was our co-ordinator – he knew the terrain features and target locations. After an assignment of two or three hours on station, one carrier-based co-ordinator would pass on his duties to another.

When a new squadron reported on station for air strikes, the air co-ordinator would briefly explain the mission to all fliers and lead them on a 'dummy run' over the target area. When they all acknowledged that they had seen their targets, he would send them on a live run. Very often our planes were able to hit targets which were largely inaccessible to the limited trajectory of artillery and naval gunfire because the enemy positions were concealed in canyons or on the reverse sides of ridges or cliffs.

The 21st Regiment were to form the spearhead of the attack. On the left was the 2nd Battalion, and on the right the 3rd under Col. Wendell Duplantis, which had just replaced the shattered 1st Battalion. Two taxiways led from the northern extremity of Airfield No. 1 to the southern end of the main runway of Airfield No. 2: the plan was for massed tanks to precede the infantry along this route onto the plateau housing the airfield. However, Col. Ikeda had already anticipated such a move, and both taxiways were not only heavily mined, but were covered by anti-tank guns. As the first tank clattered along the western lane, there was a loud explosion and it ground to a halt. A second tank, attempting to manoeuvre around the disabled one, hit a buried aerial torpedo and was blown up, all the crew being killed. Anti-tank guns brought the remainder to a halt, and the tank commander called a temporary halt to the operation. Keith Wells, on the top of Mt Suribachi, watched the battle unfold around Airfield No. 1 through his binoculars:

The most spectacular thing I saw while watching was an American tank helping the Marines across the airfield. The Marines had tried to cross the airfield, and the Japanese mowed them down like a mower cuts grass. Some of the wounded would try to work their way back, while the others moved very little or not at all.

I watched the tank firing its big gun, and it looked as if it were circling or flanking the target. A monstrous explosion seemed to lift the tank completely off the ground. Smoke came out from under the tank, and the treads went slack. The turret, with the large gun attacked, left the tank. It rose another eight or ten feet into the air. A man sailed out of the tank with the turret. The man was very much alive – God knows how he survived that blast. When he hit the ground, he gathered his senses and tried to get out of the way of the turret that was coming down on him – he did not make it, the turret crushed him. To my surprise, at least two men crawled from the bottom of the tank, and they appeared to make their escape. I could not imagine the size of weapon capable of doing this kind of damage to a tank. Later, I had the opportunity of seeing this kind of weapon – an enemy anti-tank mine almost as large as a 55 gallon barrel was placed at the right spot to get the tank.

It was now up to the infantry. Col. Duplantis's 3rd Battalion had over 800 yd to cover before they could reach the first runway – a difficult task, even with tank support. Without it, the situation looked next to impossible, but the Marines moved on a 400 yd front. Under a hail of rifle fire, mortars, machine guns and shells, the advance took on the appearance of something from the worst days of the Western Front in the First World War. Bunkers and pillboxes were assaulted with satchel charges and flamethrowers. Shrieking, flaming figures fled their strongpoints and were gunned down in seconds. Corpsmen and stretcher-bearers moved among the wounded and dying, many becoming the targets of the Japanese riflemen. WO George Green witnessed some of the attack:

It was still dark, but dawn was beginning to break when we crawled into the Jap pillbox that Lt.-Col. Duplantis was using as his Battalion command post. The only specific thing I remember him saying was 'We have got to get the airfield today.'

We started the attack this morning with about 220 men, and before we got back in reserve, 'K' Company had about 90 left. We are to pass through the lines of the 1st Battalion, continue the attack, and get Airfield No. 2. We move into position, and get off behind a rolling barrage. The first thing I notice is a bunch of Japs in a low trench. Someone got them with a flamethrower, and they are still burning. Next, on this bright morning, I see a wounded Marine walking calmly back to the rear. The white bandages and the crimson red of his blood stand out over his dirty dungarees.

After seeing only dead Japs, I finally spot a live one. He is off to my right front in a shell hole, beyond reach of my carbine. He is a typical 'poster' Jap, wearing thick horned-rim glasses. He keeps putting his head up and down. I try to interest an infantryman to fire on him, but he says: 'He's in "I" Company sector, let them get him.'

It's funny how word travels in combat. Here we are, fighting away, when we get the news that Capt. Rockmore has been killed – shot through the neck.

WO Green set up a fire mission on the high ground where the runways crossed, and fired one round of smoke. Just as it hit, Capt. Heinze yelled that the men were going across the runway. He called off his fire mission after only one round:

Capt. Heinze is sitting on the edge of the runway, about ten feet from where I am, and he asks for my compass, as he has lost his. As I get ready to toss it up to him, he yells for me to look out. As I turn around, there is a Nip grenade spluttering about three feet in front of me. I am sitting in a small shell hole about two feet deep, and while I am looking at the grenade, it goes off. Instinctively, I duck my head, and then look back up, and start to aim my carbine. As I do, I see another one coming flying towards me from some bushes – it lands just about the same place as the other one did. This time, I get to duck my head before it goes off. I feel my face, expecting a handful of blood. I only got a little bit.

Capt. Heinze comes sliding down the slope with his pistol out and holding his leg. He got a good-size piece of one of those grenades in his right thigh on the inside. We help him back to a deep shell hole. I try to get my BAR man to spray the bushes, but he walks over to them then topples over. The Nip shoots him in the stomach.

I now see the Nip in a foxhole, with a top that he moves up and down like a spidertrap. We get a fire team directed at him, and they drop a few grenades in the hole. The next time I look at him when we are moving up again, he's plastered to one side of the hole – quite a mess.

By 11.40 a.m., Marines had crossed the intersection of the two runways and were attacking the enemy, who were entrenched on high ground. A few minutes later, another group struggled across the runway a few yards away, and they combined in a bayonet charge on the Japanese stronghold. Three times the position was cleared, only for the Marines to fall back under murderous artillery fire.

The previous day's bad weather caused many rifles to jam, clogged with a coating of wet volcanic ash, so many of their attacks were made with a variety of hand-held weapons: rifle butts, spades, picks and K-Bars (knives). The 2nd Battalion also had a tough time moving forward to their targets. Tank support was now becoming available, and units were gradually inching along the runway, until Japanese anti-tank guns halted them.

Shortly before 1.30 p.m., the naval guns resumed their pounding of the enemy lines, and aircraft swooped in low with bombs and rockets. As the planes wheeled away, the Navy guns fell silent, and a combined tank and infantry assault got under way. Company 'K' of the 21st Regiment, now down to less than two hundred men, charged the high ground beyond the airfield, only to meet Col. Ikeda's troops, bayonets fixed, and with the officers wielding their swords, charging down from the summit

In the ensuing mêlée, the Americans and the Japanese clubbed, stabbed, bayonetted and kicked at each other in a frenzy of violence. Pistols fired, grenades flew, K-Bar knives and swords slashed, and bodies fell, arms and legs were broken and blood spurted from gaping wounds. Within a few minutes, the grunting, cries of pain and cursing ceased, and over fifty of the enemy lay dead or dying at the foot of the hill.

Tanks were now operating on the runways at the western end of the airfield. Blasting pillboxes with their 75 mm guns and detonating horned mines with their machine guns, they provided excellent support to the hard-pressed infantry. The American Sherman tanks with their 75 mm guns were a constant thorn in the side of the Japanese. Maj. Horie states:

When American M4 Tanks appeared, General Kuribayashi was very anxious to know how to dispose of this tank. Even our 47 mm anti-tank guns could not destroy it, and at last came to the conclusion that bodily attacks with explosives were the only way to destroy it. He made special badges for the men who were in charge of bodily attacks against tanks and men in charge of cutting-in attacks.

A badly needed breakthrough had been achieved at the intersection of the two runways of Airfield No. 2, and the Marines were determined to exploit the gap. 'Hold at all costs!' ordered Col. Withers, the 21st Regiment CO, but the Marines were low on ammunition, and had sustained heavy casualties. With only four hours of daylight left, a desperate attempt was made to get supplies up to the troops on the airfield from the beaches two miles to the rear. At the same time, a convoy of Jeeps was pressed into service to shuttle the wounded and dead to the beachhead.

The redoubtable Seabees loaded trailers with supplies and ammunition, and brought them to the limits of Airfield No. 1, only 200 yd from the battlefront, and as darkness fell, the entrenched Marines stared in wonder as a tractor trundled towards them towing a trailer with ammunition, water and containers of hot food, preceded by two men on foot carrying flashlights to show the way. George Green remembers this incident well: 'How they did it, I don't know. After dark we hear a tractor coming, and sure enough there's a guy driving that thing in pitch black night pulling a trailer with food, water and ammo. To this day I don't know how he knew where he was going – to me, this guy had guts.'

On the right flank, the 4th Division's 24th Regiment fought a bitter day-long battle for 'Charlie Dog' ridge – an escarpment just south of the main east–west runway of Airfield No. 2, where the Japanese had over a hundred bunkers and strongpoints. Shortly before 11.30 a.m., the enemy on the ridge opened up with machine guns, mortars, artillery and rifle fire against the 2nd and 3rd Battalions immediately to their front. The Marines called for naval and air support, but because of the close proximity of the two front lines, this was rejected. With only their own howitzers and mortars to back them up, the troops advanced, and sustained heavy casualties as they blasted and burned their way to the crest of the ridge. Cpl. Earl Dunlap was having his own problems too:

On D+5, I moved up to a cave early in the morning to make sure it was still empty. Just as I approached the entrance, three hand grenades flew out and landed at my feet – I dropped to the ground and curled up like a ball before they exploded, and dropped my pistol in the process. I then had one of my men bring me an M1, and emptied two clips into the cave, killing the three occupants.

I was then evacuated to the beach for treatment, and while I was waiting to go to a hospital ship, I was approached by a Navy man who said that he had to take my pistol, as I couldn't take it aboard ship. I withdrew it from my holster, cocked it, and said, 'Come and get it!' – end of conversation.

At 4.08 p.m., the 3rd Battalion observation post was hit, and three men were killed. The Battalion Commander, Lt.-Col. Alexander Vandergrift Jr, the son of the Commandant of the Marine Corps, was wounded and had to be evacuated. Casualties had been so heavy during the assault that phosphorus flares had to be fired to screen the rescue parties, who bundled the wounded and dead onto ponchos and carried them to the rear. One Corspman recalls:

We soon ran out of stretcher-bearer teams. The white smoke was beginning to blow away – all that we could do was roll the casualties onto their ponchos and drag or carry them back to our lines. Because the ponchos were waterproofed, we found that many of the casualties were lying in a large pool of blood that sloshed around underneath them.

At 5.00 p.m., Col. Walter Jordan, CO of the 24th Regiment, ordered the men to dig in for the night. D+5 had seen significant gains after the stalemate of the previous day. Another regiment of the 3rd Division, the 9th, had come ashore to join the 21st (the last regiment, the 3rd, would not be landed on Iwo Jima), and with Mt Suribachi in American hands, the threat from the rear had been eliminated. The Marines now had a foothold along the southern perimeter of Airfield No. 2, with units holding the high ground north of the runway intersection. On the western side of the island, the 26th Regiment had advanced another 500 yd, and in the east, 'Charlie Dog' ridge had been stormed.

Behind the lines, the south of Iwo Jima became a hive of activity. Supplies were flowing freely onto the beaches on both sides of the island, tents and corrugated huts were springing up, telegraph posts sprouted everywhere, roads appeared overnight, and the temporary medical facilities gave way to field hospitals.

Ominously, the casualty figures were also multiplying. Between D+1 and D+5, 773 men had been killed, 261 had died of wounds, 3,741 were wounded, 5 were missing and 558 had suffered combat fatigue. Dale Worley's diary records: 'Had to go through the 5th Division cemetery. Plenty of dead lying about. They sure smell awful.'

Nine

'The Meatgrinder' (D+6–D+8)

In the last and final analysis, it is the guy with the rifle and machine gun who wins and pays the penalty to preserve our liberty. (James V. Forrestal, Secretary of the Navy)

D+6

Sunday 25 February was not a day of rest for the Marines on Iwo Jima. Having secured a foothold on Airfield No. 3, Gen. Schmidt and his staff now sought to press the advantage by thrusting across the relatively level central plateau towards the unfinished Airfield No. 3 and on to the northern coast. On either side of the plateau, the land descended into a chaotic, rocky jungle of hills, valleys, canyons, cave-ridden outcrops and ridges – if a military strategist had been given the task of selecting a perfect defensive position, he would have found it near impossible to pick one better than this.

Even in the centre of the island, the terrain north of Airfield No. 3 soon deteriorated into volcanic sandstone valleys and cliffs, among which the Japanese had spent many months constructing a maze of defences. By driving down the centre, the Marines hoped to be able to infiltrate into the valleys and rocks on both flanks, and join up with troops pressing forward on the east and west.

Other factors also influenced the commander's choice. The unpredictable wind conditions had made unloading on the invasion beaches a precarious business. On a number of occasions, unloading had had to be suspended as pounding surf battered smaller landing and supply craft. It was becoming imperative that the western beaches also became available, not only as an alternative, but to speed up the unloading of the huge mass of supplies and equipment the Marines and the Seabees required, so that the armada of supply ships could be released for the upcoming invasion of Okinawa. As the situation stood, the Japanese still commanded the heights west of Airfield No. 2, from which they could bombard the western shore with impunity.

At 9.30 a.m., the 3rd Division began its drive in the centre. The aim was to clear the remainder of Airfield No. 2, advance towards the village of Motoyama, then on to the unfinished Airfield No. 3. On the left flank, the 5th Division consolidated its position – they were already about 400 yd ahead of the 3rd Division lines, and could afford to wait until they caught up. On the right, the 4th Division faced a complex of four formidable defence positions that became known as 'The Meatgrinder'.

About 150 yd east of the end of the east–west runway of Airfield No. 2 stood Hill 382, named from its elevation above sea level. Its slopes were peppered with innumerable caves and pillboxes. Some 400 yd to the south lay a shallow, rocky depression known as 'The Amphitheater', and immediately to the east was 'Turkey Knob', a hill surmounted by a huge blockhouse. The fourth obstacle was the ruins of the village of Minami. All four positions were within a boundary of 600 yd and collectively formed a potential killing ground.

The Meatgrinder was defenced by Maj.-Gen. Senda's 2nd Mixed Brigade, which included a selection of Baron Nishi's 26th Tank Regiment – now devoid of their tanks. Further to the right, Marines of the 1st Battalion of the 24th Regiment were still fighting for the cliffs overlooking the invasion beaches. So far, the advance had been limited to about a quarter of a mile, and losses had been very heavy.

The south of the island was now becoming one gigantic construction site. The Seabees, over 2,000 of them, began the daunting task of turning Airfield No. 1 into a major airstrip capable of handling the giant B29 Superfortress bombers, Mustang P51 fighters and P61 Black Widow night-fighters.

Just off the shore of Mt Suribachi, a flying boat base had been established for the Catalina and Coronado PBYs engaged in the rescue of downed B29 crews between the Marianas and Japan. On the top of Suribachi, a radio and radar station was erected, with a road winding up to the rim of the crater – this despite the fact that the 28th Regiment were still mopping up some of the remaining troops of Col. Atsuchi's infantry, who were determined to remain on the mountain till the end.

The Seabees, along with the Marines' 2nd Engineers, combed the runways for undetected mines and shards of shrapnel. Shell holes were filled in, and runways extended, despite the occasional Japanese artillery salvo which rained down from the high ground in the north. The narrow isthmus at the base of the volcano was jammed with Nissen huts, tents, makeshift workshops and earth-moving equipment, with supply and transport vessels making almost unhindered trips to and from the armada of vessels that stretched to the horizon – a startling contrast to the drama that was unfolding in the centre of Iwo Jima.

In the centre, the 3rd Division's 21st Regiment went to the rear for rest and to re-equip. The 9th Regiment replaced them, and the drive up the centre of the island began. A battleship and two cruisers laid on a twenty-minute bombardment as carrier planes unloaded 500 lb bombs immediately to the front of the Marines, 1,200 rounds of artillery fire blasted the enemy lines around Airfield No. 2, and twenty-six Shermans lumbered forward to spearhead the assault.

The main thrust of the 3rd Division attack was against the western end of the airfield, the high ground to the north of the main runway, and the southern edge of the east–west runway where the 4th Division lines began. The Shermans moved out, and immediately ran into a blast of 5 in guns, anti-tank guns, mortars and small arms fire, as well as an assortment of mines. Two of the three leading tanks burst into flames and were abandoned, and the third, although operable, was of little use.

As the 9th Regiment moved towards the airfield, they soon realized that the stories they had been told about the ferocity of the Japanese defence were not exaggerated. The strongest point in the enemy line was a 360 ft high rocky prominence called 'Hill Peter' towards the northern end of the main runway. The 1st Battalion repeatedly stormed the hill, which was studded with caves and pillboxes, but casualties were so heavy that by 2.30 p.m. they had gained barely 200 yd. WO George Green, the Artillery Observer, recalls:

This was the best day we had in spotting live Japs. They could be seen running from hole to hole and manning trenches and machine gun positions. Off to our right, there was a sharp, conical hill that had a lot of holes in it like cave entrances, and you could see Japs running in and out – again, too far away to shoot at. We finally found a trench to our left front, and we watched them for a while to determine what they were doing. Every time someone opened up, they ducked back into the covered position.

Sergeant Chest hadn't fired a mission yet, so I told him to fire this one, and we could fire for effect or call with air bursts. He adjusted by using air burst, and darn it, the first or second shell was right on. We got Battalion set, and waited until the Japs filtered out of the concealed cover before giving the word to fire. I have never seen such a perfect shot – the first shell was aimed just above each of the trench positions, and those Japs were caught out in the open, then the rest were about 50–50, half air and half ground bursts. After the firing, we could not see any more live Japs.

The 2nd and 3rd Battalions had slightly better luck. By evening, their lines were north of the airfield, apart from Hill Peter and the area to its rear. Nine of the Shermans had been knocked out, and Marine casualties stood at nearly four hundred dead and wounded. On the 4th Division front, the 23rd and 24th Regiments, some 3,800 men prepared to take on The Meatgrinder, little knowing that this collection of defensive positions constituted the most impregnable fortress on Iwo Jima, and that it would take another week of slaughter to silence it.

Hill 382, honeycombed with tunnels and bristling with enfilading artillery and mortar positions, was surmounted by the wreckage of a radar station, long reduced to a heap of rubble by naval gunfire, and surrounded by machine guns and half-buried tanks.

Turkey Knob, the second-highest elevation on the island after Mt Suribachi, and only 600 yd from Hill 382, was an outcrop of rock the Japanese had turned into an observation post, which had commanding views of the whole of the south of Iwo Jima.

The Amphitheater, a natural, bowl-shaped depression, had been reinforced on its south-facing slopes by three tiers of concrete emplacements, all connected by a complex of tunnels from which all of the southern approaches to Turkey Knob could be covered.

Minami Village had long been reduced to rubble in the pre-invasion bombardment, but in the midst of the shattered brick and concrete, the Japanese had placed machine guns, mortar pits and concealed sniper positions that were designed to hamper the progress of the Marines at every step.

At 8.00 a.m., the assault on Hill 382, the major strongpoint in The Meatgrinder, got under way with the now customary naval barrage and sorties by carrier-based bombers and fighters. A novel addition was the use of armoured amphibious craft assembled off the east coast – they fired a few dozen rounds, but the choppy sea soon forced them to call off the operation.

Sherman tanks were again to spearhead the attack, but the terrain proved to be so rough that they had to divert through the 3rd Division lines and progress from the left flank – an ominous sign of the growing limitations of tank support in the appalling conditions. Lumbering through the deep volcanic ash, they became victims of the enemy anti-tank guns and the fields of mines that had been sown all around Hill 382.

As with the previous day, it was up to the infantrymen to attempt to clear the way. One platoon battled their way to the summit, only to be surrounded when the Japanese made a massive counter-attack. All morning, the Marines fought vicious hand-to-hand battles with the enemy before they could withdraw to the base of the hill under cover of smoke. Ten of the wounded had to be left behind, to be evacuated under cover of darkness by gallant volunteers.

As the day passed, it was obvious the struggle had developed into an impasse, and the Marines were ordered to consolidate their small gains and prepare for an artillery and air strike against the enemy. With darkness rapidly approaching, the Marine howitzers commenced a thirty-minute rolling barrage, followed by Navy bombers and fighters with bombs and rockets. George Green and his men had now retired to their reserve positions for the night:

While we were sitting around, Sergeant George Chest was facing the front line while one or other members of our team were sitting opposite but a little to the side of him. George suddenly grabbed his chest and we saw a bullet fall into his lap – a Jap bullet very near the end of its flight had struck him smack in the middle of his chest, but was not going fast enough to penetrate his clothing or his skin.

The first day in The Meatgrinder had resulted in complete stalemate – roughly a hundred yards had been gained at the cost of nearly five hundred men.

D+7

Monday 26 February dawned bright but chilly. Most Marines found it hard to register that it was only a week since they had first hit the beaches of Iwo Jima. To the survivors, it seemed like months.

In the centre, the 3rd Division were still faced with the prospect of capturing Hill Peter. At 8.00 a.m., the 9th Regiment, supported by half the available Marine artillery, moved out. The 1st and 2nd Battalions were in the vanguard, with tanks supporting. A flamethrower tank succeeded in getting behind the hill and incinerating a number of the enemy who were trying to escape from a tunnel, but the day ended with insignificant gains and the loss of eleven tanks.

On the left, the 5th Division had set their sights on Hill 362A, about 600 yd south of the village of Nishi. At 8.00 a.m., the 26th Regiment moved out to confront a Japanese strongpoint built around a complex of pillboxes and caves, but by 10.00 a.m. the Marines had advanced only 50 yd. Reinforcements were brought forward with tank support from the 5th Tank Battalion, and the enemy position was finally overwhelmed.

To the right of the line, the Shermans, supporting the 3rd Battalion, smashed through the enemy to a depth of 100 yd, knocking out many gun emplacement sites in the ravines leading from the central plateau. The 27th Regiment, operating to the left of the 26th, advanced up the west coast for 400 yd with the early assistance of the guns of the Amphibious Battalion close offshore. As the day progressed and the Marine forward elements merged into the Japanese lines, the boats were ordered to cease fire to prevent them endangering friendly troops.

The Marine combat photographers were operating with the front-line troops at this time, George Green witnessed one of them at work:

Now I ended up in another rather large crater with Capt. Stephenson. We were lying to the right of his SCR 300 radio operator when we started to get bullets from our rear. The radio operator was shot in the ankle. He let out with a yell about being hit. We got him patched up and off to the rear.

Then a rather heavy-set Marine jumped into our hole. He was spattered with blood and pretty well shaken up. He was a combat photographer, and told me he was taking movies next to this Marine – and he pointed one out, lying next to a bluff to our rear – when all of a sudden this Marine got hit with something heavy that sprayed the blood all over the place, and when he saw there was nothing he could do, he took off for our hole. I told him I thought he was nuts, and asked why he was up here with us when he could be back in the rear taking pictures. He stayed with us for a while, then took off after taking some shots of Corpsmen and the rest of us. I never did see him again, nor did I see any of the film he took that day. I often wondered if he took my advice.

The end of the day's fighting saw the 5th Division lines bulging in the centre to within 800 yd of Hill 362A, while the left and right flanks fell 400 yd to the rear. During the night, many of the Japanese troops in and around Hill 362A were seen heading for a cistern near the coast. In the bright moonlight, the Marine artillery were provided with an excellent target, and put an abrupt end to the enemy's nocturnal activities.

Day two of the battle for Hill 382 in The Meatgrinder began with the replacement of the 24th Regiment by the 25th, causing the 8.00 a.m. jump-off to be delayed for about half an hour while the 24th extracted themselves from their precarious forward positions. Artillery pounded the Japanese lines just ahead of the Marine front for fifteen minutes, and continued with a rolling barrage, lifting the fire 100 yd every five minutes.

The initial attack looked promising. The 1st Battalion on the left and the 2nd on the right gained over 100 yd – a substantial gain in this area – until vicious machine-gun fire from the emplacements around The Amphitheater and Turkey Knob brought the advance to a grinding halt. Shermans rolled forward to assist the beleaguered Marines, but immediately became the target for all the Japanese mortars in the area, and were forced to abandon the attempt.

Two 'Grasshopper' OY-1 spotter planes which had recently established themselves on Airfield No. 1 were called in to locate some of the enemy mortar positions, but the Japanese pre-invasion preparations proved to be too much. The 'Grasshoppers' failed to find any of the skilfully hidden fortifications.

The 23rd Regiment on the left flank worked its way through a minefield lying alongside the perimeter track of Airfield No. 2, and turned towards a shattered radio station lying below Hill 382. The enemy immediately laid down a hail of mortar and machine gun fire from the hill and nearby Turkey Knob. In less than thirty minutes, seventeen men lay dead and another twenty-six were wounded. Under cover of smoke grenades, stretcher-bearers evacuated them to the rear as the remnants of the attackers pressed forward to the base of Hill 382.

Much of the credit for this successful advance must go to nineteen-year-old Pfc Douglas Jacobson. Snatching a bazooka from the body of a dead Marine, he silenced one enemy position after another until his ammunition was expended. In less than thirty minutes, sixteen strongpoints had been destroyed and seventy-five of the enemy lay dead. The most remarkable thing about his feat is that it usually takes two men to operate a bazooka – Jacobson had managed single-handedly. The intrepid private was to become another of Iwo Jima's twenty-seven Medal of Honor winners.

A number of the Marines reached the top of the first ridge on Hill 382 and came under fire from mortars, machine guns and rifles from three different directions – even from Turkey Knob, which lay over 500 yd to their right. Pinned down and without any hope of retreating, they could only wait for reinforcements or darkness, whichever came first.

The casualties mounted by the hour, but Corpsmen and stretcher-bearers were unable to make any movement. Eventually, a smokescreen was laid over the area, and the men slithered back to the base of the ridge, dragging or carrying as many of the wounded as they could. The remainder of the wounded spent the night on the hill, surrounded by the enemy – not a pleasant prospect. One fortunate private was successful in feigning death when a party of four Japanese soldiers found him during the night. He was rescued the next day by a 2nd lieutenant, who was wounded in the process.

The weather had deteriorated during the course of the day. Early blue skies gave way to heavy rain by mid-afternoon, and at 4.30 p.m. Gen. Cates called it a day. The lines were consolidated, and in the mud and rain, parties worked throughout the night to replenish the stocks of ammunition that had been so lavishly expended during the day.

It was obvious to the General Staff that the Marines were up against the backbone of the Japanese defence line, and that the enemy had no intention of retreating any further. Capt. Awatsu's 309th Independent Infantry Battalion, which had previously held the line before Airfield No. 1 on D-Day, and had slowly been retreating towards The Meatgrinder ever since, was now virtually non-existent. In a message to Tokyo, Gen. Kuribayashi said: 'I am not afraid of the fighting powers of only three American Marine Divisions if there are no bombardments from aircraft and warship. This is the only reason we have to see such miserable conditions.'

In the light of the nightly parachute flares, Marines could see the enemy darting about on Turkey Knob and around the slopes of Hill 382, preparing for the inevitable attack of the following day.

'Took off my shoes for the first time. It felt wonderful,' wrote Dale Worley in his diary. 'My feet were beginning to get numb – they didn't feel like feet. North end of island is hell – thousands of pillboxes, I never saw so many caves and pillboxes in my life. We have five Nip prisoners now. Nips are jumping off the cliffs at north end. Our casualties are frightful. If it doesn't end soon, the 5th Division will be past history.'

Iwo Jima was becoming a sideline in the national newspapers in America. The war in Europe was entering its final stages, and the media was focusing its attention on the imminent downfall of Hitler's empire. Gen. Patton's lightning dash across France to the banks of the Rhine, the Canadian and British thrust through Belgium and Holland, and the spectacular Russian advance to the gates of Berlin were grabbing the headlines. In the minor columns, the words 'meanwhile, on Iwo Jima' were becoming a regular sight.

The hordes of news correspondents and photographers who

had accompanied Harry Hill's invasion fleet had dwindled to less than twenty, and Secretary of the Navy James Forrestal had left for Guam, together with Adm. Spruance, to prepare for the imminent invasion of Okinawa.

Off the coast of Japan, Task Force 58, whose heavy guns and hundreds of bombers and fighters could have made a significant contribution to the Marines' battle for the backbone of Iwo Jima, were frustrated by fog and torrential rain, and compelled to abandon their planned raids on industrial targets in the Nagoya area. The force split up, some returning to the harbour at Ulithi, the remainder sailing west to raid Okinawa.

The ever-mounting casualty figures were not reported to the media, and it was only the dreaded sight of the telegraph boy at the door that brought home to the ordinary American the harsh price the Marines were having to pay for that barren cinder in the north Pacific.

But at last the island was beginning to assume the role that had been the reason for the invasion – advanced elements of the Army Air Corps were setting up on the now-transformed Airfield No. 1. The 47th and 48th Squadrons of P51 Mustang fighters, scheduled to escort the B29 Superfortresses on the second leg of their flights to Japan, were in place, together with the first of the P61 Black Widow twin-engined, radar-equipped night-fighters that would patrol the skies around the island.

D+8

Tuesday 27 February finally saw the Marines in control of Airfield No. 2. Two Battalions of the 9th Regiment – Lt.-Col. Randall's 1st and Lt.-Col. Cushman's 2nd – launched their attack at 8.00 a.m. against the formidable Hill Peter and Hill Oboe complex.

1. Superfortresses return to North Field on Guam after a fire-raising attack on the Japanese mainland. (*National Archives*)

2. The *Enola Gay* and its pilot, Paul Tibbets. (*Paul Tibbets*)

3. Major-General Harry Schmidt, Commander 5th Amphibious Corps. (*National Archives*)

4. Major-General Clifton B. Cates, Commander 4th Marine Division. (*National Archives*)

5. Major-General Keller E. Rockey, Commander 5th Marine Division. (*National Archives*)

6. Lieutenant-General Holland 'Howlin' Mad' Smith, in two-tone helmet, and Secretary of the Navy, James Forrestal, with binoculars, pose on the beach with a group of Marines. (*National Archives*)

7. Formal portrait of General Kuribayashi, Japanese Commander on Iwo Jima. (*Taro Kuribayashi*)

8. General Kuribayashi organizing the defences of Iwo Jima shortly before the battle. (*Taro Kuribayashi*)

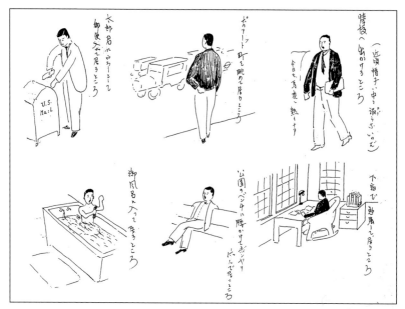

9. Letter from General Kuribayashi to his son, Taro, c. 1928–30. These letters tell of his travels in Canada and the United States. (*Taro Kuribayashi*)

10. The General commented in a letter to his wife about a large Canadian landlady with tattoos. This letter seems to illustrate her. (*Taro Kuribayashi*)

11. Rows of landing-craft head for the beaches, while two destroyers stand offshore. (*US Navy*)

12. Marines disembark into the black volcanic ash on the invasion beaches. (*National Archives*)

13. Marines prepare to move off the terraces on the beaches. (*National Archives*)

14. Near to Mount Suribachi, Marines wait for a lull in the Japanese barrage before moving out. (*US Navy*)

15. A bogged down tank and wrecked LVTs on the beaches. From the relaxed stance of the Marines, this appears to be after D-Day. (*National Archives*)

16. Chaos on the beaches. Landing operations were suspended for a while because there was nowhere to land the troops. (*National Archives*)

17. A communications team move rapidly across open ground with their wire. (*National Archives*)

18. A Japanese position at the base of Mount Suribachi is eliminated by a high explosive charge, detonated by the 5th Division Marines. (*USMC*)

19. A Marine howizer in action. (*National Archives*)

20. Amid a mound of spent ammunition, machine-gunners hammer enemy positions at the foot of Mount Suribachi with their .30 Browning.
(*National Archives*)

21. Stretcher bearers evacuating the wounded. Note the zealous wartime censor has scraped out the numbers on the landing craft. (*National Archives*)

22. 4th Division Navy doctors work on the wounded in an abandoned enemy installation. Note the doctor with scissors in his breast pocket and wearing knee pads. (*National Archives*)

23. Dale Worley, author of the 'unofficial diary', with knocked-out tank, between Airfields 1 & 2. (*Dale Worley*)

24. The Sherman tank 'Cairo' grinds to a halt after shedding a track. Note the wooden boards bolted to the sides as protection against magnetic mines. (*National Archives*)

25. Flamethrowers Pte Richard Klatt (*left*), and Pfc Wildred Voegeli (*right*), burn out an enemy strongpoint. (*National Archives*)

26. A row of rocket launchers blasts away with their 4.5 in missiles. (*National Archives*)

27. Unceremonial disposal of Japanese dead somewhere in the north of the island. (*USMC*)

28. A group of curious Marines watch as one of the few Japanese prisoners is captured somewhere on the east coast. (*National Archives*)

29. The inauguration of the 5th Division cemetery. (*USMC*)

30. Mr Taro Kuribayashi, the General's son, at the Japanese memorial at the summit of Mount Suribachi. (*Taro Kuribayashi*)

31. Robert R. Campbell's photograph of the first flag being lowered and the second one raised. (*USMC*)

With the help of flamethrower tanks and the now obligatory artillery barrage from the Marine howitzers, the troops inched forward against a murderous hail of machine gun and mortar fire. Suffering heavy casualties, the leading elements of the 1st Platoon reached the top of Hill Peter, but were pinned down by fire from the reverse slopes and from by-passed enemy positions to their rear. WO Green was now with a Navy gunfire team within the 9th Regiment lines:

Never in my life will I forget how those infantrymen just got up and took off into nothing. We saw no Japs, we just ran on a compass reading, and didn't stop until we were out of breath. This attack will live with me forever, and give me respect for the infantryman. As we approached a cliff, we stopped running due to being out of breath, and to determine where we were. Right in the middle of us pop up six Japs from out of the ground. They carried no arms, just wearing uniforms and helmets. Where they thought they were going, I don't know, but I am sure they were as surprised to see us as we were to see them. I raised my carbine to my shoulder and pulled the trigger, aiming at the first one. I heard a bang, and pulled the trigger again. No luck, it still didn't go off. By this time, all the Nips were on the deck, so I checked my carbine to see what was wrong. It dawned on me that I never unlocked the safety catch. The first bang I heard was the Marine next to me. I took the safety catch off, and never put it on again until we returned to our gun position.

The breakthrough came shortly before 1.00 p.m. Under cover of a short artillery barrage, both battalions launched a co-ordinated assault, and the 1st overran Hill Peter, relieving the beleaguered troops already pinned down on the summit, and storming forward to the crest of Hill Oboe. On the left, the 2nd Battalion advanced for 1,500 yd to straighten the line.

The first man on Hill Oboe was 23-year-old Pte. Wilson Watson. Silencing two Japanese pillboxes with grenades and rifle fire, he reached the top, to find that only one other Marine had succeeded in accompanying him – the remainder of the Platoon were pinned on the slopes under a hail of enemy fire.

Watson secured the position, killing sixty of the enemy in the process, until the remainder of his platoon could claw their way to the summit to relieve him. His day's work earned him the Medal of Honor.

Three days of bitter fighting and heavy casualties had finally gained the Marines the second airfield and the relatively level terrain to the north. Many isolated and by-passed enemy positions remained to be mopped up, but the 3rd Division were now in a good strategic position to continue their push northward towards Motoyama Village, the unfinished Airfield No. 3, and eventually to the northern coast.

Meanwhile, the 4th Division were still bogged down before the apparently impregnable Meatgrinder. Gen. Cates committed five battalions to the attack, with two battalions of the 23rd Regiment spearheading the assault on Hill 382, and three battalions of the 25th Regiment taking on Turkey Knob. A convoy of rocket-launching trucks was brought as far forward as the terrain allowed, and blasted off nearly five hundred rockets into Hill 382 before racing away under a torrent of Japanese mortar fire.

The battle see-sawed up and down the slopes of the hill all morning. One small group actually reached the top, where they repulsed constant enemy counter-attacks for two hours until shortage of ammunition forced them to fall back. At the foot of the hill, other Marines attempted an encircling manoeuvre – in bitter hand-to-hand fighting that lasted all morning, they overpowered one position after another, and by mid-afternoon the hill was surrounded by a very vulnerable ring of troops who were desperately trying to hold onto their precarious positions.

All during the day, the Marine Engineers had been busy attempting to clear a way through the rocks to allow the Shermans to operate within range of Hill 382 and Turkey Knob. A tankdozer cleared a path through the boulders and rubble, and by afternoon the tanks of Company 'B' were in position to support the infantry. The 25th Regiment called them in to lead the assault on Turkey Knob, but the Japanese were not prepared to give an inch. Constant anti-tank fire stalled any attempt by the Shermans to get within close range, and despite initial gains of around 100 yd in the morning, the 2nd Battalion were obliged to pull back in the afternoon to their original positions. WO Green recalls:

There is a Navy TBF Bomber [Grumman Avenger] flying overhead, whom I assume is an observer. As he makes several passes over our positions, I see an artillery shell hit the plane just behind the lower turret, knocking a big hole in the lower part of the fuselage, causing the plane to go into a steep dive to his left. I could see the pilot's reactions – as the plane makes an attempt to straighten up to level flight, the whole tail assembly falls off and he starts spinning down to our left rear and crashes. I wondered if any of those fellows got out of that crash alive.

Later on, I heard that several of them were thrown clear of the plane, but no one got to them because of the heat of the battle. I am sure that this fellow was unaware that when artillery was firing he was to stay above a specified altitude, and was probably being pressed by someone for the positions of our front lines, and came down low to see if we were Marines or Nips.

Yet another day in The Meatgrinder had resulted in insignificant gains, paid for with heavy casualties. The only grim consolation was that the Marine losses could be replaced. For the Japanese, it was an unsustainable haemorrhage.

That night, Japanese aircraft attempted to drop supplies to the beleaguered garrison. Three aircraft were shot down by carrier-based night-fighters, but the remainder succeeded in getting through, and a small number of parachutes containing medical supplies and some ammunition fell within the Japanese lines. Gen. Kuribayashi commented:

> I pay many respects to those brave aviators who supplied weapons to Iwo Jima by aircraft. They made arrangements with the Iwo Jima commander, started Isamamatsu [Japan] Airfield, and supplied hand grenades and flame projectiles. It is indeed difficult to express how the hearts of the fighting youth of Iwo Jima who stood before their death felt when they saw these brave flyers.

This was the one and only attempt to supply or support the garrison during the battle. The Japanese High Command had neither the will nor the ability to attempt a seaborne reinforcement or evacuation. For Kuribayashi and his defenders, there would indeed be no plans for their return.

Ten

'Oh God, Not Another Ridge'
(D+9–D+11)

Among the Marines who fought on Iwo Jima, uncommon valor was a common virtue. (Fleet Adm. Chester Nimitz)

D+9

Iwo Jima had become an island of dramatic contrasts. In the barren canyons and gullies of the north, the Marines were fighting a grim battle of attrition against an almost invisible enemy. 'Grasshopper' spotter planes, swooping over the valleys and rocky outcrops, observed hundreds of Marines in artillery emplacements, lining trenches, squatting in shell holes and behind hillocks. But beyond the American front line – nothing.

The Marines were fighting their battle wholly above ground; the Japanese were beneath it. Every cave, blockhouse, pillbox and observation post was connected by tunnel to another strongpoint, sometimes hundreds of yards away. The sight of a Japanese soldier – during the hours of daylight, at least – was a rare event.

In the southern half of Iwo Jima, the contrast was even more bizarre. Despite the occasional shell burst from the enemy, the Seabees pressed on with the transformation of Airfield No. 1, extending its runways. All around, a shanty town of tents, Quonset huts, supply compounds, transport depots and cookhouses had sprung up. A post office was even operating in a timber-covered hole in the 4th Division zone. Hospitals were springing up on the borders of the airfield. One was a Navy evacuation hospital, where whole blood was processed after being flown in from the American mainland. To the west, the 4th Division had established its own facility, and an Army hospital was in the process of moving in.

In the shadow of Mt Suribachi, three seaplane tenders were anchored to maintain the Catalina and Coronado PBY flying boats, so vital to the rescue of B29 bomber crews. The dream of a half-way haven between the Marianas and Japan was now becoming reality for the 20th Air Force. One of the greatest fears of the Superfortress crews was the prospect of ditching in the vast expanse of the Pacific during one of the daily trips to the enemy mainland. In the first two months of the bombing war, over 50 per cent of casualties were 'lost at sea'. The existing network of submarines, destroyers and flying boats had a near-impossible task in covering the tens of thousands of miles of sea around the 1,500-mile route from the Marianas to Japan. Many of the aircraft, crippled by anti-aircraft fire or from fighter attacks, came down close to the enemy coast, where their only hope of rescue was from US Navy submarines. The hazards of rough sea, rain squalls, poor visibility and even sharks was a constant worry. Ditching was a hair-raising business – putting down a 65-ton bomber into a rough sea usually resulted in the aircraft breaking up and sinking within minutes. The survivors, if any, were faced with the prospect of bobbing in an open dinghy in the hope that their distress signal had been picked up.

The 7th Fighter Command, equipped with P51 Mustang fighters, arrived on Iwo Jima in March. Their task was to escort the B29 Superfortresses to the Japanese mainland, and to fly cover during their bombing missions – a role for which they were superbly suited.

The story of the development of the Mustang, an aircraft that played a vital role in the Iwo Jima-based operations, is quite remarkable. As Britain realized in the late 1930s that war with Germany was almost inevitable, the chronic shortage of fighters compelled the Air Ministry to turn to the American market to supplement its meagre stocks of Spitfires and Hurricanes.

The British Purchasing Commission, which included Arthur Harris (later to become C.-in-C. RAF Bomber Command), toured the US aircraft industry in search of suitable aircraft. Fighters were top of the list of priorities, but although 200 Lockheed Hudsons were purchased for Coastal Command, as well as 200 North American NA16 trainers (called 'The Harvard' by the RAF), the choice of fighters was bleak. Only the Bell P39 Airacobra and the Curtiss P40 Tomahawk began to approach the desired specification, and production of both was heavily committed to the US Army Air Corps.

A delay in delivery was unacceptable, and a solution to the problem was suggested by having one of the major aircraft manufacturers which had spare production capacity build the P40 under licence. North American Aviation were approached with the idea, but rejected it out of hand – they were not prepared to build a rival company's plane. Instead, they came up with an idea that startled the Commission: they would design and build an entirely new aircraft in 120 days (in Britain, such an undertaking would have taken years). Still sceptical, the British signed a contract for 320 aircraft, and to their amazement, the prototype rolled off the production line just two days after the target date.

Named the Mustang by the British, the first model arrived at the Aircraft and Armament Experimental Establishment at Boscombe Down for evaluation in 1941, but the performance of the Allison engine was a bitter disappointment at altitudes of over 13,700 ft, the region where most aerial combat would take place.

The Battle of Britain was now over, and the demand for fighters had lost much of its urgency, so the Mustang was relegated to the role of Army Co-operation, flying photo-reconnaissance missions over Europe.

It was in 1942 that the great breakthrough in the Mustang story occurred. Rolls-Royce test pilot Ronnie Harker was invited to fly the Mark I model at Duxford airfield near Cambridge, and immediately realized that here was a superb aircraft suffering the constraints of an inferior engine. After discussion with Rolls-Royce, a Mustang was fitted with a Merlin 61 engine – and the rest, as they say, is history. With continued developments to the airframe – a redesigned tail unit, bubble canopy, four-bladed propellor, and more importantly, a Merlin engine built under licence by the Packard Automobile Company, the Mustang became one of the great aircraft of the Second World War. With long-range fuel tanks, it was able to escort the B17 Flying Fortress bombers of the 8th Air Force to Berlin and back, and soon swept the Luftwaffe from the skies of Europe.

Now, in the Pacific, its immense range and devastating firepower was to shock the pilots of the Japanese Air Force. Lined up behind the Superfortresses to navigate them to the mainland, the Mustangs could easily span the 750-mile trip with over an hour's flying time in enemy airspace. On their very first mission on 7 April, a hundred Mustangs escorted a hundred B29s to Tokyo, destroying twenty-one Japanese fighters for the loss of only two planes and three Superfortresses. Later, when Gen. LeMay switched to his preferred programme of night-bombing, the Mustangs, guided by a couple of B29s, devastated the airfields of Kyushu, blasted enemy shipping with rocket fire, and shot up railway engines and rolling stock in a highly successful series of independent sorties.

The last day of February, D+9, saw the Marines holding just under half of Iwo Jima. Ironically, this was the date given by Gen. Schmidt for the end of the battle. Today, Schmidt's orders for the 3rd Division were blunt – press forward in the centre of the island, and reach the north coast.

In the pre-dawn gloom, the 21st Regiment moved forward to relieve the battered 9th. By 9.00 a.m., the changeover had been made, and the now customary half-hour of naval gunfire and carrier plane attacks succeeded in temporarily stunning the enemy. Moving under a rolling barrage from the corps' 155 mm guns, the 1st Battalion advanced for 150 yd before they were halted by accurate fire from the high ground to their front. Company 'I' made good progress until they were confronted by the tanks of the 26th Regiment under the command of the flamboyant Baron Nishi.

Taken aback by this most unusual display of armour, the Marines soon rallied and made a counter-attack with flamethrowers and bazookas, destroying most of the flimsy Go-Ha Tanks. Marauding aircraft were called in by the ground control unit and disabled two more Go-Has with 20 mm cannon fire. The Baron was now left with only three serviceable tanks on the island.

Recovering from the naval and aerial pounding, the Japanese resistance stiffened during the morning, and by noon the general advance ground to a halt. Working on the principle that what had worked once could work again, another massive artillery barrage was laid down, and by 1.00 p.m., the Marines were once more on the move.

This time, the momentum was maintained. Storming their way through clusters of pillboxes and bunkers, the troops came upon the shambles of what once had been the village of Motoyama, the largest settlement on Iwo Jima. All that remained of the village that once had welcomed Gen.

Kuribayashi with flags and cheering children was a pile of rubble and the shattered evaporation vats of the one-time sulphur mine. Col. Duplantis's Battalion soon overcame the machine gunners and snipers who had set up their defences among the ruins, and swept on to establish themselves on the high ground overlooking the unfinished Airfield No. 3.

By Iwo Jima standards, this had been a very good day. An advance of over 600 yd was a major achievement in comparison with recent gains, and the Marines settled into a defensive position that had all the signs of being an excellent jumping-off point for the next attack. As Col. Duplantis's men spearheaded the 21st Regiment advance on Motoyama, the 1st and 2nd Battalions of Col. Randall and Col. Cushman on the flanks dealt with the mass of by-passed positions. In a bitter afternoon of fighting, the Marine flamethrowers and demolition teams slowly secured the flanks, and by evening all three battalions were again together.

During the evening, the C.-in-C. of the 21st Regiment, Col. Hartnoll Withers, spoke to Gen. Erskine on the field telephone to give his report of the day's progress. 'Shall I keep going?' he asked. 'Go ahead, we will send a Higgins Boat so you won't have to walk back,' he joked. Little did he know that the 3rd Division faced another six days of slaughter before they would cover the mile between them and the sea.

Lt. Keith Wells, to his disgust, had been forbidden to rejoin his platoon. Instead, he migrated to the aid station near the beach. The doctor allowed it because Wells acted as his helper when he needed him. Some of the wounded presented a grim sight:

A Marine was half-sitting and half-lying, his lower jaw was blown away, the socket bones appeared to be intact. As I watched, they clamped blood vessels off as fast as they could.

When they finished he must have had fifteen or more scissor-like clamps sticking out of what looked like his throat.

I know I could not see anything, but I watched them tie veins off and pack his mouth with cotton. Most of the skin that went over his jaw was still there, and they sewed his mouth shut. Later, I used a writing tablet to converse with this man in the hospital at Pearl Harbor.

On the 5th Division front, Hill 362A still barred the way. The top was dotted with anti-tank guns, mortars and assorted artillery pieces. On its barren slopes, machine guns poked out of every cave entrance, and at the base, every rocky outcrop and valley hid lines of pillboxes and bunkers.

Two battalions of the 27th Regiment, the 1st and the 3rd, moved out at 8.15 a.m., supported by six Shermans, and almost immediately ran into a wall of concentrated small arms fire. In a frenzy of activity, the combined infantry and tanks assaulted the Japanese positions with flamethrowers, demolition charges and 75 mm gunfire, until the leading Shermans retired because of lack of ammunition.

The result of an attack on an enemy position by flamethrower crews is described by Pte. James Justice:

This was where the flamethrower came in – they would saturate the entrance to a cave with fuel. The liquid and the flames would then travel back into the cave and ignite. The Japs would come running and screaming out of the cave, flaming like torches. This was the only way of getting them out without physically going in after them.

Hill 362A, which had earlier been blasted by heavy naval guns and aircraft, was now to be subjected to an assault by the 3rd Rocket Detachment. Blasting off two salvoes of 4.5 in rockets, the six trucks immediately left the area before the enemy could locate their position and destroy the vulnerable trucks with mortars.

By noon, the base of the hill had been reached, but the Marines were taking heavy fire from the caves above and from both flanks. Some of the men from 'I' Company reached the top, but were soon forced to abandon their gains. On the right flank, over a hundred Japanese made a vigorous counter-attack, but were beaten back by 'H' Company, while on the left, the 1st Battalion, pushing back strong opposition, skirted Hill 362A and gained 300 yd. Meanwhile, the 28th Regiment, still clearing up around Mt Suribachi, were alerted to move up towards the 5th Division front in preparation for the continued advance.

In The Meatgrinder, the 4th Division prepared for yet another attack on Hill 382 and Turkey Knob. The 25th Regiment moved out at 8.15 a.m. The 1st Battalion was to assault Turkey Knob from the north in an encircling movement, but the Japanese rained down grenades from the high ground, and the attempt was foiled. Hill 382 had also been encircled, and rocket trucks in convoys of six made repeated assaults with their 4.5 in rockets, and dashed away within five minutes.

The day's progress had been minuscule, and at 4.45 p.m., orders went out to close down for the day. Smoke shells had to be fired to enable some of the forward troops to get back to the relative safety of the very lines they had left that morning. Cpl. Roland Chiasson of the 2nd Platoon of B-1-26 remembers the gallantry of his buddy, John Reilly, that day – gallantry that went unrecorded and unrecognized:

The enemy resistance was delaying our advance, and Lieutenant Miller called for a bazooka team. A few days earlier, our bazooka Marine, Sheldon Calhoun, had been killed, so

John Reilly and I grabbed the weapon and the ammunition and volunteered. There were several machine gun nests about sixty-five yards ahead, so we made our way up an incline.

In a crater were some Japs, but they let us go by – they knew that we would be taken care of higher up, and presumably they didn't want to give away their position. When we reached the caves, I fired the bazooka and Reilly put in the ammunition, wired the projectiles and tapped my shoulder to indicate that he was out of the way of the blast. When we ran out of ammunition, we threw grenades. As I threw the last one, I shouted to John: 'Let's get out of here!'

At that moment, a Jap grenade tore into my arms. I turned around, and a second grenade tore into my buttocks, leg and thighs. In both instances, I protected Reilly, and for that reason he was able to get this bloody, wounded Marine back to the safety of our front line. How he did it, neither he nor I know. It was miraculous, and he saved my life.

In June 1945, at Balboa Naval Hospital, Roland Chiasson was presented with the Silver Star. He had not seen Reilly since that day on 28 February and it was not until he reached St Alban's Hospital in New York City that he heard that Reilly had not been given the Silver Star, nor even a recommendation. Chiasson was devastated, and for years during the Reagan and Bush administrations petitioned to get Reilly an award – but to no avail. Whenever Roland Chiasson shows his Silver Star citation, signed by Gen. 'Howlin' Mad' Smith, the reader will see an addition: 'When you read my name, please put in the name of Corporal John Reilly – what the citation says is what we both did.'

Nobody who fought on Iwo Jima will forget the night of 28 February/1 March. For some unknown reason, the Japanese stepped up their previously sporadic artillery fire against the south of the island, and a storm of shells began falling all around Airfield No. 1. It is surprising that they had not done this earlier, as the whole area was now a small town, crowded with supply dumps, vehicles, hospitals and thousands of sleeping Seabees and reserve Marines.

Shortly after 2.00 p.m., a shell found a large ammunition dump, and the whole of the southern end of Iwo Jima erupted in a pyrotechnic display of gigantic proportions. Shells shot hundreds of feet in the air, mortar and artillery rounds exploded with an ear-shattering violence that awoke everyone ashore and at sea, bullets popped and crackled, and huge clouds of smoke covered almost everything from the foot of Suribachi to the approaches to Airfield No. 2. To add to the chaos, the gas warning and the air raid warning sounded at around 2.30 a.m. at the height of the inferno – someone had mistaken the phosphorus artillery rounds for a gas attack. Seabees manned their bulldozers and braved the flames to pile mounds of earth onto the exploding ammunition, but the fires raged on until dawn.

Although the gas warning was the result of panic, the air raid warning was genuine. A single Japanese bomber, almost certainly from Chichi Jima, launched a torpedo attack on the destroyer USS *Terry*. The torpedo passed 50 ft astern as the plane made a rapid exit to the north. Spurred on by their success, the Japanese launched a rocket bombardment against Mt Suribachi. The huge, unwieldy missiles howled across the night sky, trailing sparks and flames in their erratic trajectory. Some sailed across the mountain and fizzled out in the sea, others exploded in a spectacular fireball on the hillside. The front-line Marines watched the Fourth of July display and wondered if the Japanese had a tunnel to the airfield.

It was a tragic night for the USS *Terry*. Having survived the torpedo attack, a salvo from a battery of 6 in coastal guns straddled the destroyer shortly after dawn, hitting her deck and engine room. Eleven of the crew were killed, and nineteen others wounded. The battleship USS *Nevada* and the cruiser USS *Pensacola* silenced the enemy guns, and the *Terry* limped away to Pearl Harbor on one engine. Miraculously, there were no casualties from the ammunition dump explosion, but the 5th Division had lost almost a quarter of its stocks.

D+10

By 1 March, casualties among the Marines of all three divisions had reached a critical stage. The combat-efficiency of many units had plummeted, and officers in particular were becoming an endangered species. It was not uncommon in some units for the command to have passed from captain to lieutenant and down to sergeant, and in some cases to private first class. Gen. Erskine in particular was concerned that a whole Regiment of his 3rd Division was being held in reserve in offshore troopships, while the 4th and 5th Divisions were at full strength. The fact that these reserves, the 3rd Regiment, were never landed on Iwo Jima remained a contentious issue for years, and soured relations between Erskine and 'Howlin' Mad' Smith forever.

Smith's reasoning is unclear. Some thought that he wanted the regiment as a standby in case of some unforeseen reversal – an unlikely scenario. Others said that there was not enough room on Iwo Jima for another nine thousand men. Yet another view was that Smith had wanted the Regiment kept intact for Okinawa.

A meeting aboard the *Auburn*, Smith's command ship, on the morning of 1 March ended acrimoniously, with Erskine being told: 'Fight the battle with the troops you have.' Even more contentious around this time was the use of 'battle replacements', as opposed to 'organic replacements'. John Lane of the 25th Regiment, 4th Division explains:

The great majority of the battle replacements were recruits who had gone through Parris Island in the summer of 1944, where they had fired for qualification once.

In early September, they were formed into an Infantry Training Unit at Camp Lejeune, where they went through 'musketry range' once. They threw one live hand grenade, fired one rifle grenade, and went through one live fire exercise, crawling under machine-gun fire.

The unit was designated as the 30th Replacement Draft in late October, travelling by rail to Camp Pendleton, and almost immediately embarked for Maui. Throughout November and December of 1944 the draft was employed on working parties and mess duties. No additional training, even as shore party troops, was provided. The day after Christmas Day, the draft was sent to Kahalui Docks to begin boarding for Iwo Jima. Those replacements who survived Iwo went back to Maui with their new outfits and began receiving the training that might have helped them before the operation.

Gen. Erskine was scathing in his criticism of the quality of the replacements: 'They get killed the day they go into battle,' he said, and Lt.-Col. Cushman, an experienced veteran of Bougainville and Guam (and a future Commandant of the Marine Corps) said: 'Almost all of the infantry were replacements. They lacked the will to close with the enemy.'

Gen. Erskine's comments are echoed in an incident Pfc Otis Thomas witnessed: 'A new replacement kept crawling around piling up rocks and saying, "I'll be careful." All the others lay tight. He straightened up a little too high once, and a Jap from the other cliff rim shot him through the head. He left a wife and one-year-old twins back in New Jersey. He had shown us all pictures of them.'

The 3rd Division spent the night on the high ground just short of Airfield No. 3, and at 8.30 a.m. Gen. Erskine, still seething from his encounter with Gen. Smith, ordered the 2nd and 3rd Battalions of the 21st Regiment forward. For once, the now customary naval bombardment was dispensed with, and only a Marine artillery barrage paved the way as the battalions bore down on the unfinished runways.

Resistance was comparatively light, and by noon the forward troops had advanced 500 yd and were across the airfield. Meanwhile, the 1st Battalion on the left flank spent the day mopping up by-passed enemy pockets that were left over from the previous day. In the afternoon, tanks moved forward to stiffen the attack, and a rolling artillery barrage helped dampen enemy resistance. But as the day wore on, the Marines reached the vicinity of Hills 362B and 362C, two more strongpoints of the same elevation as 362A, which was proving to be such a trial for the 5th Division on the west coast.

Gen. Erskine ordered the troops to consolidate their lines at 4.00 p.m., and the commanders began counting the cost: 600 yd of ground had been secured – one of the Divisions' best days – but 200 more casualties were added to the mounting list. Dale Worley's diary records:

5th Division having hell with Hill 362. Nips don't seem to want to give it up – we have south side, they have north, and no one on top. It's been a hand grenade battle for three days now. The damn Army has hot chow and joe all the time. They are bitching because they were landed before the island was secured – the bastards.

The conquerors of Mt Suribachi, the 5th Division's 28th Regiment, were again in the front line. All three battalions were engaged, the 1st and 2nd directly against Hill 362A, and the 3rd along the coast, it was to be a costly day.

At 8.30 a.m., the assault on Hill 362A began with a 45-minute bombardment by the Divisional 155 mm howitzers, then a battleship and two cruisers – the USS *Nevada*, the USS *Pensacola* and Adm. Spruance's flagship, the USS *Indianapolis* – added 30 minutes' worth of heavy shelling. The 1st and 2nd Battalions stormed the slopes of the hill, and by noon had reached the top, but the Japanese had escaped through their labyrinth of tunnels, and had established themselves on Nishi Ridge, a ragged cliff line almost as high as Hill 362A, and 200 yd to the front.

The capture of Hill 362A was a significant achievement, and would provide the Marines with the means of breaking the stalemate on the west coast. Tanks moved in to support the attack, blasting the positions the troops had by-passed with their 75 mm guns, while the 'Zippo' flamethrowers incinerated the more accessible positions. The 3rd Battalion, despite fierce mortar fire, advanced for 350 yd, but had to call a halt as they were moving too far ahead of the 2nd Battalion. Once again, the casualties had been appalling, and the haemorrhage of officers continued – one captain, one lieutenant and four 2nd lieutenants among the 28th Regiment, and 'Easy' Company alone had thirty-eight dead and wounded.

Among the dead that day were Cpl. Tony Stein, who had earned the Medal of Honor on D-Day with his 'stinger', and three of the flag-raisers on Mt Suribachi – Sgt. Hansen, who had helped raise the first flag, and Sgt. Michael Strank and Cpl. Harlon Block, both of whom featured in Joe Rosenthal's famous photograph. Sadly, none of them would realize how famous they were to become.

In The Meatgrinder, Hill 382 was again the primary target for the 4th Division. The hill was the key to the impasse – until it was secured, the eastern side of Iwo Jima would remain firmly in Japanese hands.

In the pre-dawn darkness, the 24th Regiment moved silently forward to replace the 23rd. Once the transfer was complete, a 45-minute artillery and naval gunfire barrage rocked the enemy lines. The 1st and 2nd Battalions moved out abreast with the 2nd on the left, and immediately caught a fusillade of mortar fire which caused the advance to grind to halt. For the next three hours, the hill was pounded by Marine artillery and gunfire from offshore naval units, with carrier aircraft lending support with napalm canisters, many of which failed to ignite.

As the 1st Battalion resumed their attack, the Japanese returned from the depth of the tunnels where they had sheltered, and resumed their machine gun and small arms fire from the high ground. In a bitter yard-by-yard struggle, the men of 'G' Company of the 2nd Battalion, using bazookas, grenades and flamethrowers, grappled their way to the western crest of the two-ridge hill and immediately faced fierce opposition from the Japanese entrenched on the other ridge 100 yd to the east. All afternoon the battle raged, but by evening it was a stalemate.

Meanwhile, the 2nd Battalion were attempting to infiltrate to the south side of the hill and towards Turkey Knob, but met such fanatical resistance and suffered such severe casualties that they were compelled, under constant withering enemy fire, to return to their jumping-off positions. The day's losses were 374 killed and wounded. In all, the 4th Division had suffered 5,595 casualties of various kinds since D-Day, and fighting efficiency had plummeted to 55 per cent.

Although the extent of the enemy's losses was not known, it was becoming apparent that the use of ammunition was becoming more selective. No longer did the Seabees working around Airfield No. 1 have to worry about random Japanese artillery fire: mortars were only fired when the Americans offered a positive target, and small arms fire was more discriminating. Unknown to the Marines, Gen. Kuribayashi had moved his HQ from the centre of the island to a prepared location in the north-west.

D+11

The following day saw no let-up in the pressure on Hill 382 and Turkey Knob. In an unusual pre-dawn infiltration, the 1st Battalion of the 25th Regiment moved out of their night positions and eased their way towards Turkey Knob, but the Japanese were not fooled, and at 7.00 a.m. delivered a storm of mortar shells from the heights above. The Marines retaliated with mortars, and eight tanks moved forward in support.

The Shermans pounded the blockhouse on the top of Turkey Knob, while the 'Zippos' expended over 1,000 gallons of fuel on caves and pillboxes, but the enemy simply slid back into the depths of their tunnels and sat out the inferno.

Meanwhile, the 26th Regiment following up a 45-minute naval and air pounding, launched a three-pronged attack on Hill 382. After a period of some of the fiercest fighting for days, the 2nd Battalion finally reached the summit of the hill to secure a tenuous foothold alongside the men of 'E' Company, who had spent the night on the western ridge under constant harassing fire. The casualty toll had again been high: one unit alone had suffered the loss of five officers – two were fatally wounded, and another had his leg blown off below the knee.

Marine artillery could not be used in support at ranges of under 100 yd, so the bulk of the fighting had to be at close quarters, machine guns, grenades and flamethrowers reducing the Japanese strongpoints in a slow, grinding and bloody day of attrition. Official casualty figures for the day were 610, 207 of them killed. Combat-efficiency was not the only problem the Marines had to cope with: combat fatigue – the point at which a fighting man has reached the limit of his physical and mental endurance – was becoming increasingly obvious. Pfc Otis Thomas speaks of one incident:

Wolf had to leave. After twenty-eight days and nights, the tension had evolved into combat fatigue. His eyes were bloodshot, he would whirl and fire at any sound behind him. The Corpsman asked him to go back to the aid station for a few days. Wolf refused, saying: 'I am not leaving my boys.' 'Go back for three days, get some chow and rest, and then come back,' he said. He left, and they kept him.

Hopes of a rapid dash to the sea in the 3rd Division sector proved to be wildly optimistic. Although the north coast was only 1,500 yd from the front line, the Japanese had no intention of allowing the Marines an easy passage.

On the left flank stood Hill 362B, which was actually in the 5th Division zone, but which had been giving the 3rd Division a great deal of trouble. After a 30-minute artillery barrage, the division moved out in a two-pronged assault with over 4,000 men. One group thrust towards Hill 362B, and the remainder towards Airfield No. 3. The 3rd Battalion of the 9th Regiment under Col. Boehm moved out against Hill 362B, but the approach was a flat area overlooked by artillery and pillboxes, and the cover was virtually nil. Tanks were called forward, and under their cover, the 3rd Battalion advanced for 500 yd to the foot of the hill.

On their right, the 2nd Battalion moved against the airfield, but made only limited progress as they came across the lines held by Baron Nishi. The Baron, now without most of his tank command, was resigned to fighting to the death on this bare island hundreds of miles from home. Gone were the glory days when he had won an Olympic medal on his horse Uranus, a lock of whose mane he kept in his pocket, and had socialized with influential Los Angeles society and Hollywood stars.

The 2nd Battalion commander, Lt.-Col. English, received his second wound of the day at around 5.30 p.m., and was hauled away to a dressing station. His place was taken by his executive officer, Maj. George Percy – at forty-seven, over-age and over-weight, he was a most unlikely battlefront officer, but had wangled his way into the Marines and into the battle, where he proved to be a natural leader. Already twice wounded, he was to continue until the end of the battle.

Nishi Ridge lay 200 yd beyond Hill 362A on the 5th Division front. 'Oh God, not another Ridge,' complained one Marine, and it seemed that he was right. The troops were now encountering fewer blockhouses and pillboxes on the western side of Iwo Jima. The terrain was so rocky and filled with valleys, draws and canyons that the Japanese had all the defensive cover they needed without the need to build any more.

Col. Chandler Johnson's 28th Regiment advanced along the left side of Hill 362A, but drew heavy fire. A riddle of tunnels threaded through the hill with outlets on the far slopes, but the two battalions pushed forward. In the ravine between the hill and Nishi Ridge, tanks and bulldozers of the 5th Engineers edged forward. An anti-tank ditch ran north to the ridge, and the bulldozers were determined to fill it. Under constant mortar fire and with the support of the Shermans, the ditch was finally covered, and the Marines had a firm foothold between the hill and the ridge from which to blast both cliff faces.

Although the Americans held the top of Hill 362A, the Japanese still clung tenaciously to both sides, and when the attack began, the Marines were confronted with fire from ahead and behind. Both the 26th and 28th Regiments were called in, and by early afternoon they were at the foot of Nishi Ridge. 'E' Company, the first Marines to reach the top of Suribachi, dug in after repulsing a determined counter-attack.

Chandler Johnson, well known for being up front with his men, walked towards a shell crater expecting to see Marines sheltering inside. Instead, all he saw were dead Japanese. As he turned to leave, a shell exploded within feet of him, and he was blown to pieces. 'The biggest bit I found of him was his rib cage,' said an 'E' Company Marine. Another found a hand and wrist with a watch miraculously still ticking. The shell, almost certainly a misplaced American round, also killed and wounded a number of others. Dale Worley's diary records:

I can't relax enough at night to get any sleep – this thing is really getting on my nerves. Rhine was killed today. He was on the FO [forward observation], and a sniper shot him in the head, killing him instantly.

Eleven

Stalemate (D+12–D+15)

O living soul in this abyss, see what a sentence has been passed upon me and search Hell to find one to equal this. (Dante, *The Inferno*, Canto XXVIII)

D+12

By 3 March, the Americans were in control of approximately two-thirds of Iwo Jima. The battle was dragging on way beyond the most pessimistic forecasts of the Chiefs of Staff, however. The casualty figures were also assuming tragic proportions. So far, the US tally stood at over 16,000, of whom more than 3,000 were dead. For the Japanese, the toll was staggering – of the 21,000 troops in Gen. Kuribayashi's command on 19 February, only 7,000 remained, of which barely half were effective fighting troops.

The Marines were also having serious problems with combat-efficiency. Officers in particular were being lost at an alarming rate. Many units found the chain of command passing to very junior ranks, and a senior medical officer had recently remarked on the 'zombie-like attitude' of the troops. Many Marines were seen with a fixed, blank, uncomprehending stare – 'the thousand-yard stare' to the Marines, who were familiar with this type of fatigue from previous campaigns.

The divisional commanders were also worried about the fighting capabilities of some of the replacements, among whom the casualty rates were shocking. No one doubted their courage or enthusiasm, but there were serious questions about their training.

On the other hand, the Japanese, desperately short of food and almost devoid of water, were reduced to an animal-like existence. Living a largely subterranean life, they would emerge at night and prowl the American lines, as much concerned with stealing food and water as killing the enemy. At the back of the minds of the Marines was the knowledge that eventually they would win the battle. The Japanese were equally certain that they would soon be dead.

D+12 was a day of incredible heroism. Five Medals of Honor were awarded for valour in the field – a record for the Marine Corps. Two Marines, Cpl. Charles Berry and Pfc William Caddy, died saving the lives of their companions by throwing themselves onto spluttering hand grenades, and two Corpsmen, George Wahlen and Jack Williams, further enhanced the reputation of the Navy medics by their acts.

Pharmacist's Mate 2nd Class Wahlen, who had already been wounded twice, was back in the line near Hill 362B amid a vicious hand-to-hand battle with the enemy. Dashing from one wounded Marine to another, Wahlen was exhausted and almost out of medical supplies when he was wounded for a third time, but still continued to attempt to minister to the wounded until he passed out from loss of blood and was evacuated.

Pharmacist's Mate 3rd Class Jack Williams, a twenty-year-old from Harrison, Arkansas, was with troops near Nishi Ridge. Attending to his fifteenth casualty that day, Williams was hit three times in the abdomen by fire from a Japanese sniper, but continued attending to his patient before attempting to stem the flow of blood from his own wounds. Knowing that the only way he could get help for himself and his wounded Marine was to get to the rear of the lines, he dashed across an open stretch of land, and was immediately shot in the chest and killed.

For Sgt. William Harrell, the night of 3 March would be branded on his mind for the rest of his days. Sharing a foxhole with Pfc Andrew Carter in the Marine front line near Nishi Ridge, Carter wakened the dozing sergeant around midnight to tell him that the Japanese were infiltrating their lines from a nearby ravine. After killing three of the enemy, Carter's gun jammed, and he left to find another one. Moments later, a grenade landed in the foxhole, wounded Harrell in the leg and left arm as he was attempting to reload his carbine. Carter returned just in time to see two of the enemy approaching the foxhole. One, swinging a vicious-looking sabre, lunged at Carter as he was about to fire, but again his gun misfired, and in desperation, he grabbed a Japanese rifle he had acquired on D-Day as a souvenir and bayonetted the attacker. His reactions had been just that fraction too slow, for the dying Japanese sliced his left hand almost in two. The second intruder was shot dead by Harrell with his Colt .45 revolver.

A desperate battle was now raging all along the front line, and Harrell, unable to move, told Carter to go back for medical aid. Carter left, promising to return with help as soon as possible. Lying helpless in the foxhole, bleeding from a multitude of wounds and with his left hand hanging by its tendons, Harrell's ordeal was just beginning.

Within minutes, two more Japanese arrived. One jumped into the foxhole with Harrell and activated a hand grenade, which he dropped at the sergeant's feet. As he sprang from the hole, Harrell shot him with his Colt, grabbed the grenade, and attempted to throw it out. The ensuing explosion killed the other enemy soldier and blew off Harrell's right hand.

The enemy attack petered out, and as daylight broke, Carter returned with stretcher-bearers to evacuate the semi-conscious sergeant. After prolonged hospital treatment, Harrell, fitted with mechanical hands, returned to civilian life, gaining a degree at Texas A&M College, and becoming a successful cattle rancher.

Meanwhile, the battle was becoming an inexorable slog from ridge to ridge, shell hole to shell hole, the Japanese only retreating when their position was blasted away or incinerated by flamethrower teams. The Marines doggedly advanced through the lunar landscape of the north of Iwo Jima, giving no quarter, and inflicting and sustaining fearful casualties in a seemingly endless struggle of attrition.

Gen. Schmidt, still determined to split the enemy through the middle of the island, had ordered Gen. Rockey to realign his sector to include Hill 362B, thus relieving the pressure on Erskine's left flank and allowing him to press forward to the north-east coast. The 3rd Division was now free to direct all its attention to Hill 357 – some 500 yd to the east, and according to intelligent reports, the only obstacle between them and the sea.

The 1st and 2nd Battalions of the 9th Regiment advanced against an in-depth defence line of pillboxes, trenches, dug-in tanks and caves, from which the enemy rained down a hail of rifle, machine gun and mortar fire that slowed the Marines to a crawl. Shermans were brought forward, a slow and ponderous procession grinding its way among the boulders and rocks until they finally reached the front. Because of the conditions, they were only able to operate in small groups or individually, but succeeded in damping down the opposition sufficiently for the Marines to storm Hill 357 with flamethrowers and grenades. By 11.00 a.m., elements of both battalions were on the summit, and spent the rest of the day consolidating their gains and mopping up by-passed enemy pockets.

In the northern half of the 3rd Division zone, all the high ground north-east of Airfield No. 3 had been seized, and there appeared to be nothing between the Marines and the sea.

After midnight, the Japanese launched a major counter-attack in the direction of the airfield, and vicious close-quarter fighting erupted along the front line, the 2nd Battalion taking the brunt of the assault by an estimated two hundred Japanese troops. After a brutal battle, the enemy were beaten back with heavy casualties, and the gains of the day were secure.

Back at Airfield No. 1, the first American aircraft to land on Iwo Jima were circling. Two transports from the Marianas packed with medical supplies edged around Mt Suribachi and lined up on the newly resurfaced thousand-yard main runway. The arrivals did not escape the attention of the Japanese in the north, who immediately laid on a mortar barrage.

Seabees and Marines who dashed to the aircraft as they taxied to the northern limit of the airfield were amazed to see a woman step out of one of the planes. She was Barbara Finch, a Reuters war correspondent. As the mortar shells crumped around the end of the runway, Mrs Finch was unceremoniously bundled under a nearby Jeep, and within thirty minutes was on her way back to Saipan in the first unloaded aircraft. Questions were later asked by Gen. Schmidt about why she had been allowed to hitch a lift in the transport, and public relations men on Guam who had authorized the trip received a severe reprimand from the usually placid Adm. Nimitz.

Other planes arriving during that day also bore the brunt of the Japanese artillerymen's wrath, and it was decided that for the time being it would be safer for deliveries to be made by parachute.

The 5th Division resumed their offensive along the northern coast at 7.45 a.m., the 26th Regiment attacking Hill 362B, previously in the 3rd Division zone, and the 28th once more pitting themselves against Nishi Ridge. In a bloody day's fighting in which they suffered appalling casualties, the 26th burned and blasted their way to the summit of Hill 362B, but not before one entire company had had to be withdrawn after only ninety minutes in the field, with devastating losses. The greatest achievement of the day was the conquest of Nishi Ridge by the 28th Regiment. The final removal of this obstacle was a great boost to the division.

At the end of the day, the Marines held an irregular line from the top of Hill 362B across the northern edge of the Motoyama plain and along the west coast to about 200 yd north of Nishi Ridge. Once more, the Japanese attempted to regain some of the lost ground by mounting a night-time counter-attack, but as usual, it was a failure. Of about a hundred infiltrators who attempted to breach the 26th Regiment perimeter, ninety-seven dead were counted the following morning.

One of the greatest problems facing the Americans in their attempts to advance to the north in this sector was the terrain. In his report, the 5th Division Intelligence Officer gives a graphic account of the problems facing the troops:

In the final defensive area north of Nishi the increased natural strength of the ground and its subterranean defense features compensate for the reduced amounts of concrete and steel used by the Japanese.

Volcanic eruptions have littered the whole north end of the island with outcrops of sandstone and loose rock. The sandstone outcrops make cave-digging easy for the Japanese. Our troops obtain cover only by defilade or by piling loose rocks on the surface to form rock-reverted positions. A series of irregularly eroded criss-crossed gorges with precipitous sides resulted in a series of compartments of various shapes.

These were usually small, but some extended for several hundred yards. The compartments were lined with a labyrinth of natural and artificial caves which covered the approaches from all directions. Fields of fire were usually limited to 25 yards, and a unique or at least unusual characteristic of the Japanese defensive positions in this area was that the reverse slopes were as strongly fortified as were the forward slopes.

In an attempt to confuse the Japanese, the 3rd Division renewed their attack against The Meatgrinder without the benefit of artillery or air support. Moving off at dawn, Col. Jordan's 24th Regiment renewed the battle of Hill 382, and Col. Wensinger and his 23rd tackled the complex of Turkey Knob, The Amphitheater and Minami Village.

Shermans of 'C' Company, 4th Tank Battalion had been assigned to both units, but soon ground to a halt before an impenetrable wall of boulders. In the few clear areas, the enemy had sown a field of mines. Engineers braved heavy machine gun and rifle fire throughout the day to clear a path for the tanks, but with only limited success. The 24th drove beyond Hill 382 to assault strong defensive positions to the north-east while the 23rd swung south-east above The Amphitheater in an attempt to reduce Turkey Knob. Initially, the move looked as though it might succeed, but as the Marines approached Turkey Knob, fire from the huge blockhouse on the summit brought the attack to a grinding halt, and that marked the limit of the day's advance.

The 24th Regiment had moved out early, at 6.30 a.m., again without any preparatory artillery fire, and were immediately confronted with a cluster of concrete pillboxes set among mounds, corridors and hillocks. Once again, the tanks were stymied by the terrain, and the few that were able to reach the front could only operate with limited fields of fire.

It was once again left to the individual Marine with his grenade, bazooka and flamethrower to move the line forward – inevitably, with heavy casualties. As the Marines prepared to dig in for the night, the 24th had advanced 350 yd, but Turkey Knob, The Amphitheater and Minami Village were still firmly in enemy hands, although Hill 382 had been surrounded, and was now of little strategic value.

D+13

For a few days, the Marines had enjoyed reasonable weather – dry days and cool nights – but on Sunday, even the elements appeared to be against them. Grey, lowering clouds hung over the whole of the island, and a cold drizzle greeted the dawn.

The planned carrier strikes were suspended, and the customary naval bombardment of the northern half of the island was cancelled because of poor visibility. Again, The Meatgrinder was the focal point of the 4th Division, but the axis of the attack was shifted to the east, so that the Marines could attempt to clear the Japanese from the multitude of valleys and draws that led to the sea.

Wherever they could operate, the tanks and rocket launchers blasted the enemy, particularly around the encircled Amphitheater. The dog-tired Marines again pitted themselves against the deeply entrenched enemy, who defended stubbornly and inflicted heavy casualties. A general weariness had permeated the entire front. The 5th Division in the north relied on flamethrower tanks to clear the more exposed Japanese positions, while the troops slogged on with grenades and flamethrowers. In a now fixed pattern of attack, the frustrated Marines battled against an invisible enemy for every yard of ground. Sgt. Harold Best recalls the following incident around this time:

Nearly halfway into the battle, our platoon was digging in for the night. I had just given the shovel to my foxhole buddy, Jack Phillips, and sat down at one end, as it was his turn to dig. Suddenly, there was a terrific blast. I knew exactly what had happened – a shell had burst in our midst.

I looked at Jack just as he said, 'I'm hit.' I noticed the blood above his right eye. I saw that others had been hit too. I know that Morrison was filling his canteen at a jerry can, and now a glance showed that a long, red slash had opened down his back. Others also were down. The man crouching in a hole to my right was dead with his brains lying back on his helmet.

Scott, wounded himself, had picked up Marenna, whose right arm was dangling by a thread of flesh, and started off to the nearest aid station. There, Marenna's arm was released from his body. There was also someone injured who I can't recall. Jack's wound was worse than I thought. A piece of shrapnel had embedded within his forehead – the wound was troublesome to Jack for many years to come.

The 3rd Division in the centre had taken nine days of bitter fighting to advance the 3,000 yd from the edge of Airfield No. 2 to their present position, and today, Gen. Erskine delayed the attack until 11.40 a.m. until fresh troops were brought forward, but the gains were negligible, and the day ended with the lines much as they were at dawn.

The highlight of the day was the arrival of the first B29 Superfortress to land on Iwo Jima. 'Dinah Might' was returning to Saipan from a bombing mission south-west of Tokyo with her bomb bays jammed in the open position and a malfunction in the reserve fuel tank transfer valve. Without fuel for the 1,400-mile trip back to base, the pilot, Lt. Raymond Malo, had two options: ditch at sea and hope that they would be picked up by one of the rescue services, or attempt a landing on Iwo Jima. The latter choice looked the best.

The plane's distress signals were picked up by USS *Auburn*, Gen. Smith's floating HQ, and the giant bomber was directed towards the island, while the Seabees were ordered to clear the runway, and a Catalina flying boat was scrambled in case the plane was forced to ditch in the sea.

After circling the island twice, Lt. Malo brought the B29 down onto the runway, and it ground to a halt in a cloud of dust at the northern extremity. The landing had not escaped the attention of the Japanese, and a steady hail of shellfire began landing in the area. 'Dinah Might' was quickly swung around, and taxied away to the Suribachi end of the airfield, where she attracted a large gathering of interested viewers while repairs were carried out. Within thirty minutes, the bomber was thundering back along the runway, and lifted off into a weak barrage of anti-aircraft fire.

'Dinah Might' seemed to have opened the floodgates, for within a week the airfield was taking up to twenty-five flights of various kinds each day. The large-scale air evacuation of the seriously wounded began around this time – one artillery observer was recovering in hospital in Guam, 700 miles south of Iwo Jima, only five hours after being wounded near Motoyama Village in the centre of the island – and between D+12 and D+35, over 124 casualties a day were airlifted from the island. During the battle, a total of 2,449 wounded were flown to the hospitals of the Marianas.

Gen. Kuribayashi had now realized that the battle had swung irrevocably in favour of the Americans, and radioed to Tokyo:

Our strongpoints may be able to fight delaying actions for several more days. Even when the strongpoints fall, we hope the survivors will continue to fight to the end. I comfort myself a little in seeing my officers and men die without regret after struggling in this inch-by-inch battle against an overwhelming enemy with many tanks, and being exposed to indescribable bombardments. Although my own death is near, I calmly pray to God for a good future for my mother country.

Kuribayashi's estimation of the course of the battle was a little pessimistic. The Japanese garrison would continue to hold out for another three weeks before it finally succumbed to the overwhelming power of the American forces.

There will be no general attack tomorrow. Except for limited adjustments of positions, each Division will utilize the day for rest, refitting and reorganization in preparation for resumption of action on 6th March.

Thus ran the 5.00 p.m. communiqués from the Command Posts of Genls Rockey, Cates and Erskine. It was clear that the Marines were desperate for rest. Two weeks of the bloodiest fighting the Marine Corps had ever experienced had seen eleven Battalion Commanders killed or wounded, and an appalling depletion of junior officers and senior NCOs.

As with many other Pacific campaigns, the planners had misjudged both the determination of the enemy and the strength of their defences. At Tarawa, the Marines were told that the giant naval barrage would 'sink the island'. Instead, the huge 16 in shells, fired from close inshore from a low trajectory, bounced off the coral and into the sea. Now, on Iwo Jima, the abbreviated pre-invasion bombardment, reduced from the ten days requested by Genls Smith and Schmidt to the three days authorized by Adm. Spruance ('I know that your people will get away with it.'), left many of the Japanese defences intact.

D+14

On D+14, the Marine front ran along a line almost identical to that designated as the goal for D+1. Although the Japanese were drastically reduced in numbers and desperately short of ammunition, food, and particularly water, they were compensated by an ever-increasing advantage in their defence positions. The further north the battle progressed, the worse the terrain became, and the easier the ground was to hold.

The Motoyama Plateau, the relatively level area of central Iwo Jima on which the third airfield had been started, gave way to a moonscape of valleys, rocky outcrops, ravines, draws, caves and hills, in which tanks were almost unable to move without a vanguard of bulldozers. Every cave held an enemy machine gun or mortar, every movement was observed from the nearest hill, and when a Marine squad advanced, it would never know from which direction the next bullet would come. Progress of a few hundred yards was a major advance, and casualties were frightening.

At Airfield No. 1, Seabees continued to widen and lengthen runways and hardstands, now secure from enemy shellfire. All around, the land that had so recently been a bloody battlefield resembled a suburban shanty town of huts, shacks, tents, compounds and telegraph wires. The contrast was bizarre: here normality, less than a mile away carnage and slaughter on a scale resembling the worst excesses of Passchendaele and the Somme of the First World War.

Although 5 March was a day of rest, the generals had forgotten to tell the Japanese, and shells and mortars fell all day on the weary Marines as they regrouped, straightened the lines and brought forward replacements, supplies and ammunition. Tank crews used the time to service their machines, containers of fresh water were brought to the front from the newly-installed distillation plants, and coffee and doughnuts were supplied by the bakery near Airfield No. 1.

As the new replacements filtered through, the veterans eyed them up and did what they could to prepare them for the next onslaught. Many – too many – were fresh out of Hawaii, and unprepared for the bloody battles of attrition that had become the norm on Iwo Jima. One replacement, upon being assigned to a machine gun unit, was asked if he had any questions. 'Only one,' he replied, 'How do you operate this thing?'

With two-thirds of the island occupied, the rundown of Navy support continued. Adm. Spruance in the *Indianapolis* had departed for Guam along with Navy Secretary Forrestal. More controversial was the sailing of the 3rd Regiment of the 3rd Division – troops that Gen. Schmidt and his Divisional Commanders would have dearly liked to have seen as replacements instead of the green kids arriving from Hawaii. Instead, they sailed back to the Marianas having never set foot on Iwo Jima.

There were new arrivals. The Army, who were to garrison the island once the battle was over, sent their preliminary units, and the 28 Mustangs and 12 Black Widow aircraft under the command of Brig.-Gen. Ernest C. Moore now had their hardstands on the airfield. As the day of 'rest' ended, the casualty figures for the last twenty-four hours were totted up – 400 dead and wounded.

D+15

As if to underline that the day of rest was over, the Marines and Navy put up one of the heaviest bombardments of the battle on Tuesday morning, when 132 artillery pieces fired a total of 22,500 rounds within 67 minutes, blasting the western region first, and then shifting to the east. From offshore, a battleship, a cruiser and three destroyers added 450 rounds of

14 in and 8 in shells and salvoes of smaller-calibre ordnance, while the carrier-based Corsairs and Dauntlesses strafed and dropped napalm and bombs.

The attack was staggered – in the west, the 5th Division moved out at 8.00 a.m., and in the east the 4th waited until 9.00 a.m., but on both fronts the enemy resistance was as fierce as ever. The huge barrage seems to have had little effect. The 21st and 27th Regiments were the first to move out in the western sector, but fierce machine gun and mortar fire halted the attack almost before it got started, and even though flamethrower tanks were brought up to incinerate the more troublesome enemy positions, the gains for the day could only be measured in yards. Dale Worley's diary states:

Days are long and lonely on the front. You don't go to sleep if you want to wake up. Not much activity today, mainly blowing up caves that had Nips in them. They have almost blown Hill 362 off the map, there are bodies everywhere, the ground is spotted with blood, the smell is sickening. Planes have been bombing and strafing with rockets all day. We are on a ridge by a sulphur bank. Steam comes out of the ground, and the holes are warm. Last night, one Nip came out and stole a box of 'K' rations. We watched him eat for a while, then a Marine shot him. He crawled off into the rocks, wounded. This morning, a Marine went out and killed him.

In the centre, the 3rd Division made only marginal progress. An element of the 21st Regiment under the command of Lt. William Mulvey blasted and burned their way to the summit of yet another of the seemingly endless series of ridges, and gazed upon the prize that had for so long eluded Gen. Schmidt – the sea.

Mulvey estimated that it was no more than a quarter of a mile to his front, but almost sensing the elation felt by the

American vanguard, the Japanese piled on a storm of deadly accurate mortar and small arms fire that had the group completely pinned down. Mulvey sent back for reinforcements, and a dozen flamethrower and demolition men rushed out. Before they could get to the ridge, six were killed and two wounded, and the Marines had to sit where they were and ride out the storm. It was not until late afternoon that Mulvey and his survivors could work their way back to their lines north of Motoyama Village.

The day had seen advances of less than 200 yd at an equal cost in dead and wounded. Col. Wensinger's 23rd and Col. Jordan's 24th Regiments were the spearhead of the 4th Division assault in the east, but the best of the day's advance was a mere 350 yd by the 3rd Battalion of the 24th, aided by four flamethrower Sherman tanks.

For a number of days, the 5th Division had been receiving intermittent gunfire from enemy installations sited on Kangoku and Kama Rocks – two groups of small islands 1½ and ½ mile respectively off the north-west coast. Three batteries of the Army's 506th Anti-aircraft Artillery Gun Battalion were given the task of silencing them. Originally, it had been intended to let the Navy do the job, but the Army requested the privilege, and blasted the rocks all afternoon. The results were not impressive, and the Navy complained that they were still receiving light volleys whenever they approached the islands. The Army were given clearance to resume fire whenever the Japanese showed any sign of activity.

Dale Worley's diary for the day records: 'There is a quiet, deadly stillness in the air, the tension is strong, everyone is waiting. Some will die – how many, no one knows. God knows, enough have died already.'

Twelve

On To the Sea (D+16–D+19)

Victory was never in doubt. What was in doubt in all of our minds was whether there would be any of us left to dedicate our cemetery at the end, or whether the last Marine would be knocking out the last Japanese gun and gunner. (Maj.-Gen. Graves B. Erskine)

Gen. Schmidt was a worried man. The battle was not progressing as he and most of the planners had anticipated. Only 'Howlin' Mad' Smith had made a realistic prediction.

On 6 March, D+15, the Marine casualties stood at 2,777 dead and 8,051 wounded, and a further 1,102 men were out of action with battle fatigue. With the departure of the 3rd Division's 3rd Regiment for Guam, the commanders were scouring the rear echelons for front-line replacements. Almost anyone – cooks, mechanics, clerks, musicians, drivers and storemen – found themselves donning combat gear and moving to the front line.

Gen. Erskine, a veteran of the First World War, had long nurtured a plan for a night attack – a tactic that had seldom been used by the Marines in the Pacific, but which Erskine had seen succeed on the Western Front in 1918. At a meeting with Schmidt, he argued his case, and won approval from the Commander-in-Chief, who was desperate to see an end to the stalemate.

The attack was scheduled for the early hours of D+16, and the objective was relatively straightforward – infiltrate for 250 yd into the Japanese lines and capture Hill 362C, the last major stronghold in the 3rd Division zone between the Americans and the sea. The attack would be spearheaded by the 3rd Battalion of the 9th Regiment under the command of Lt.-Col. Harold Boehm. This battalion was presently in reserve, and had to move through the 21st Regiment to take up position.

Boehm had misgivings about the plan: night attacks were not the Marines' style, and in the rugged terrain north of Airfield No. 2, one hill looked much like another. He was told to bring his company commanders up to the front, and in the flickering light of a Navy star shell, Hill 362C was pointed out. An azimuth sighting was taken – if the attack was to be made in total darkness, at least he would have a compass bearing to follow.

D+16

In the early hours of 7 March, it started to rain, and as the Marines moved forward, total radio silence was ordered all along the line. On the right flank of Boehm's men, the 1st Battalion under Maj. William Glass and the 2nd Battalion under Lt.-Col. Cushman were to make a diversionary attack, and had already taken up their positions. As the Marines readied themselves, a star shell from an offshore destroyer burst directly to their front and lazily floated down under its parachute. There was momentary panic, and everyone froze – had they been seen? Cursing officers phoned the gunnery control to order the Navy to stop the firing of star shells, and as the spluttering flare finally hit the ground, a barrage of smoke shells whooshed overhead to screen the assault.

Shortly after 5.00 a.m., the Marines eased their way forward into the Japanese lines. Surprise was complete as they by-passed enemy pillboxes and fortifications without detection. For thirty minutes, the enemy remained silent, until an observant machine gunner opened up at the left of the battalion. He was swiftly incinerated by one of the flamethrowers, but the enemy were now aroused, and began offering mounting resistance.

At 6.00 a.m., Boehm broke radio silence with the news that his men were on top of Hill 362C. Erskine was delighted: 'We caught the bastards asleep, just as we thought we would,' he told his intelligence officer, and further news was that many enemy positions had been eliminated, and that casualties were light.

But the euphoria was short-lived. At 6.30 a.m., Boehm made a startling discovery. Checking his maps and aerial photographs, he realized that he was on Hill 331, not 362C as he had thought – 362C was another 250 yd further forward. In the pitch darkness and driving rain, distinguishing one of Iwo Jima's plethora of hills from another had proved to be an almost impossible task. Boehm decided he would press forward now that he knew exactly where he was, and asked for an artillery barrage on Hill 362C and the surrounding area.

Japanese resistance was now fierce, not only from the front, but from the many by-passed positions in the rear, but the Marines slowly blasted and burned their way forward, and by 2.00 p.m., elements of Company 'K' finally reached their objective, and Hill 362C was permanently in American hands. On the right, the 1st and 2nd Battalions had also achieved initial surprise, but at 7.30 a.m., the Japanese, attacking from the front and from by-passed positions on both flanks, showered down a hail of mortar and small arms fire that not only brought the Marines to a halt, but rapidly cut them off. Maj. Glass and Lt.-Col. Cushman had inadvertently stumbled across the remains of Baron Nishi's 26th Tank Regiment, one of Gen. Kuribayashi's toughest outfits, and fighting as bitter as any in the whole battle would continue in this area – soon to be known as 'Cushman's Pocket' – for another six days.

Tanks were brought up in an attempt to extricate the two Battalions, but they were repeatedly foiled by the ground conditions, and at dusk Maj. Glass sent word to 'B' Company, the unit isolated at the front of the platoon, to attempt to withdraw. Despite withering enemy fire, the survivors staggered back under a protective screen of mortar fire, many Marines carrying wounded comrades on their back. Of the original company, twenty-three were dead and another twenty wounded.

The Company Commander, Lt. John Leims, showed conspicuous courage in extricating his men. Crawling for 400 yd, he brought them back in the gathering darkness. Upon finding that there were still wounded men left behind, he made repeated trips into enemy territory to rescue them. For his actions, he was awarded the Medal of Honor.

Two of Col. Cushman's companies were still surrounded in the Pocket, and had to remain there overnight until they could be evacuated the following day. Lt. O'Bannon had only nineteen men left from his original forty-one, and Capt. Schmidt had only nine survivors. Lt. O'Bannon vividly recalls the event:

After we had advanced about seventy-five yards, I observed a dark, jagged rock formation directly to our front. All hell broke loose after we had advanced another twenty yards or so. Intense machine gun fire and grenades seemed to be the order of the day.

Knowing that we had by-passed enemy defence positions, it was plain that we were behind their lines and completely surrounded . . . we dashed to our rear and found a large shell crater which was already housing three or four men, including a Sergeant 'Ski'. From immediately to my left and only fifteen yards or so distant, we were receiving heavy and devastating machine gun fire. One toss of a grenade from my supply silenced them. Then the radio man excitedly tossed off his radio pack and exclaimed: 'I see them! I see them!' As he lifted his carbine to his shoulder to fire, he pitched over to his left, almost falling on me, with a sound as if he had been struck in the stomach by a tank. He had been hit at belt level. The bullet had split his stomach from just above his navel to his right hip bone, an eight-inch gash. By this time it was breaking day, and I thought that I should let Col. Cushman know our situation. He wasn't very pleased with my report, but was sympathetic to our predicament. He asked if supporting mortar and artillery fire would be effective.

In about five minutes we started receiving punishing artillery fire – damaging our own personnel as well as the enemy. I called the Colonel and asked if the fire could be lifted, and it was. It was getting pretty bright now, and I got busy with my canteen cup in an effort to improve the hole we were in. As half the hole was deepened I moved the wounded men into it. About this time, I heard the sound of running footsteps, and a voice rang out: 'Lieutenant! Lieutenant!' I scrambled to my knees, thus my head was above ground level. A shot rang out, and I ducked for cover and heard the man's body slam into the ground.

It was fully daylight now, and to my surprise we weren't attacked and completely annihilated at this point. I contacted Col. Cushman again, and informed him of our situation – number of men, casualties and supply of ammunition. Later, he informed me that he was sending 'G' Company with tanks to get us out. They would start early afternoon. We heard the roar of tanks a little later, together with machine gun fire and large-calibre weapons. We learned an hour later that 'G' Company had suffered considerable casualties, and one tank had been lost. They would try again later. Later was about 4.00 p.m. the next day.

At noon the next day, three tanks started in our direction – only thing was, they did not know exactly where we were. A jumble of craters, rocks, crevices, mounds and depressions look all the same. It was suggested that a tank fire two smoke rounds at different angles, and I could take a compass bearing, then relay the reading to BH [Battalion Headquarters], who could compute the readings with those of the tank that fired the rounds. Soon, we heard the tanks in the distance. As the tanks arrived, the Japs fired smoke shells in an attempt to blind the drivers, but the determination of the crews prevailed.

As we were loading the wounded, a bullet struck Sergeant 'Ski' between the eyes. He pitched forward in my lap, his blood seeping onto my canvas leggings. We got back to Colonel Cushman, and a Corpsman started removing my leggings, thinking that I had been hit. I assured him that I was OK. Before sundown, I had some warm 'C' Rations and an extra blanket. I slept till noon the next day.

Lt. O'Bannon was awarded the Navy Cross.

Despite the heavy losses, the attack had been a success. Hill 362C was secure, and although Cushman's Pocket would remain a threat to the flank of the 3rd Division for some considerable time, the prize that had for so long eluded Gen. Erskine – the north coast – was only 800 yd beyond his front line, and there was an excellent prospect of splitting the enemy down the middle.

It was to be a memorable day on the 5th Division front. Driving forward towards Kitano Point, the most northerly area of Iwo Jima, the 26th Regiment had moved out without the benefit of the customary artillery barrage – not as a new tactic to foil the Japanese, but simply because the artillery were short of ammunition.

Approaching a ridge just north of the ruins of what had been Nishi Village, the vanguard of the regiment were more than a little surprised at the lack of any serious opposition. A few rifle shots rang out, and an occasional hand grenade explosion was heard, but on the ridge itself there was an eerie silence.

The Marines proceeded with caution to the summit, expecting to receive a fusillade of fire from the far side, as had happened so often in the past. Instead, the whole ridge vanished in a huge explosion that could be heard clearly as far away as Mt Suribachi. Flames and rubble shot into the air, leaving a smoking crater and the charred and shattered bodies of forty-three Marines. The Japanese had blown up their local command post – a tactic they were to repeat as the perimeters of their territory grew smaller.

Along the coast, the 28th Regiment under Col. Harry Liversedge made steady progress among the gorges and valleys that riddled this part of the island. Helped by gunfire from offshore destoyers, they advanced for 500 yd before sundown closed the day's operations. A false gas alarm late in the evening caused some disruption before it was revealed that a combination of sulphur vapours and a smouldering enemy ammunition dump had triggered the alert.

For the first time in the battle, the 4th Division found an opportunity to manoeuvre. The 23rd and 24th Regiments deployed to the east and then swung to the south, edging the enemy towards the 25th Regiment, which had formed a defensive line.

Trapped between the three regiments were the troops of Gen. Senda and Navy Capt. Inouye, with about 1,500 men between them. Seeing the hopelessness of the situation, the two officers planned a *banzai* attack, a manoeuvre strictly forbidden by Gen. Kuribayashi. Fantastic plans were discussed for a breakthrough to the south, destroying American aircraft en route, and ending with the recapture of Mt Suribachi and the replacement of the Stars and Stripes with the Rising Sun.

Leaving their sick and wounded behind to fend for themselves, a column of men moved south at around midnight armed with sacks of grenades, bamboo spears, with some rigged as human bombs carrying demolition charges wrapped around their bodies. In the front were the officers carrying their traditional swords.

As the nightly star shells descended, the Americans saw large numbers of the enemy crawling towards them, and sounded a general alarm. A massive barrage of artillery, machine gun fire and small arms shredded the Japanese, and they died in their hundreds. The few that did reach the Marine lines set about the Marines, and many a sabre-wielding officer was despatched with a .45 pistol. Grenades flew thick and fast, and hand-to-hand fighting continued into the early hours.

D+17

The dawn revealed a scene of carnage, with scores of Japanese bodies and parts of bodies littering the front. Among the dead lay Capt. Inouye, sword in hand, killed leading a futile charge. This was the type of attack Gen. Kuribayashi had tried so hard to avoid, and which he had forbidden in his pre-invasion battle strategy. His tactic of sickening the Americans by his policy of attrition had so far been highly successful.

As dawn broke, one of the giant Japanese rockets that frequently roared across the sky trailing flames and sparks like an oversized firework made a lucky hit on the command post of the 23rd Regiment's 2nd Battalion, killing the communications officer and wounding six of the other staff.

Thursday 9 March saw steady if unspectacular progress. The 3rd Division still had Cushman's Pocket to deal with, and the

4th Division had yet to silence the remaining Japanese, who were grimly hanging on to Turkey Knob.

The 2nd Battalion of the 27th Regiment attacked at 7.50 a.m., but had to await the arrival of the Shermans at 9.00 a.m. before they could make any impression on the cave-infested and heavily mined enemy fortifications. With the aid of a 75 mm howitzer which had been manhandled through the rocks, an advance of 150 yd was achieved by noon, and on the right, Company 'E' made a breakthrough of 300 yd that brought them to the cliffs overlooking the sea.

The day is best remembered for the outstanding heroism of two of Iwo Jima's Medal of Honor winners. Pfc James LaBelle, a nineteen-year-old from Minnesota, had led a charmed life since D-Day. In the dash across the narrows below Mt Suribachi, he had seen three men shot down beside him. A few days later, while sharing a shell hole with four other Marines, a mortar shell had exploded within feet of the rim, miraculously leaving LaBelle the only unwounded man in the group, and on D+10 his best friend had died at his side as they advanced on Nishi Ridge.

Now, in the 5th Division zone, his luck was finally to run out. Pinned down among a group of boulders near the mouth of a cave, LaBelle and two others waited for the hail of enemy fire to slacken before attempting to move out. Looking to the cave entrance, he saw a Japanese soldier throw a hand grenade in their direction. It landed a few feet from the group, and LaBelle threw himself on top of it and died, saving the lives of his comrades.

In the same area, 'E' Company of the 2nd Battalion of the 27th Regiment were engaged in the push towards Kitano Point. Lt. Jack Lummus, a 29-year-old former professional football player who had abandoned a promising career with the New York Giants to join the Marines, ran out in front of his platoon, but was floored by the blast of a grenade. Jumping up, he ran to an enemy gun emplacement and silenced it. Another grenade exploded nearby, wounding him in the shoulder. Again, he got to his feet, and attacked a second emplacement killing all of its occupants.

He turned and shouted to his men to move forward, and as they did, they saw Lummus disappear in a cloud of dust and debris. He had stepped on a mine, and both his legs had been blown off. To his men, he looked as if he were in a hole, but to their amazement, they saw that he was standing on his bloody stumps, urging them forward.

Lummus, from Ennis in north Texas, survived until late afternoon, but died from shock and loss of blood in the 5th Division Hospital in the shadow of Mt Suribachi. Before leaving Camp Pendleton in California for Hawaii, Jack Lummus had been dating a Nebraska girl, Mary Hartman, who had moved to Hollywood to work. They planned to marry on his return. In 1987, she returned to Jack's home town:

I follow a rock road through Ennis Myrtle Cemetery. I spotted a small replica of the Medal of Honor next to a flat tombstone. On the granite was engraved Jack's name and the dates October 22nd 1912–March 8th 1945. Once a year now I visit the grave. A gnarled old elm tree shades me as I sit remembering. When I leave, I place a single rose on the grave marker. I have found Jack at last.

D+18

On Friday, the final breakthrough was achieved when a 28-man patrol led by Lt. Paul Connally reached the north coast in the 3rd Division sector. The men stood staring down at the sea, hardly believing that they had finally split the Japanese forces in two. They gingerly scrambled down to shore, and as some swilled their grimy faces in the cold water, others took of their boots and socks and soothed their swollen feet. All was quiet for ten minutes, but then mortar rounds began to fall among them, and there was a mad rush back to the protection of the cliffs.

Connally, perhaps sensing the significance of the occasion, had filled his water bottle with sea water, and when the patrol returned, he gave it to Col. Withers, his CO. He in turn forwarded it to Gen. Erskine with the message: 'For inspection – not consumption.' Erskine was delighted, but the cost had been appalling. Of the original 3rd Division troops who had landed on 19 February, 3,563 had so far been killed, wounded or were missing.

That night, as the Marines bedded down as best they could among the shell holes and rocks of northern Iwo Jima, the B29 crews in the Marines were preparing for a raid on Tokyo that was destined to alter the nature of the American bombing campaign.

The concept of daylight precision bombing which had been developed in Europe was to be abandoned. After tonight, 'area bombing', which the RAF had practised against Germany since 1941, would be adopted against all the major Japanese cities. Earlier in the day, at the operational briefing, the crews had been stunned to learn the details of the raid – flying at 5,000–8,000 ft with an all-incendiary bomb load, minus all guns and with a minimum fuel load, they were sceptical about the success of the mission.

At 7.05 p.m., the giant Superfortresses rolled from their hardstands and were soon thundering down the multiple runways of their airfields on Saipan, Guam and Tinian, and by 8.10 p.m., 325 aircraft of the 21st Bomber Command were heading for Japan. With Tokyo over five hours' flying time away, the crews settled down to a long, straight course, interrupted only by a slight detour around Iwo Jima, which they were ordered to avoid because it was not yet officially under American control. As they approached the Japanese mainland, the crews were surprised to hear American popular songs being transmitted by Radio Tokyo. Ironically, one of the numbers was 'I don't want to set the world on fire'.

Gen. LeMay was confident about the outcome: 'If this raid works the way I think it will, we can shorten the war. We've figured out a punch he's not expecting this time. I don't think that he can keep his cities from being burned down – wiped right off the map.' At exactly 00.07 a.m., the lead aircraft released 122 gasoline gel bombs on central Tokyo, and as other bomb loads showered into the city – which contained a large proportion of timber-built dwellings – large areas became roaring infernos. One B29 of the 498th Bomb Group, which was over a hundred miles away on its approach to the city, saw a glow on the horizon and took it for a jettisoned bomb load. Only when the glow grew brighter as they approached landfall did they realize that this was Tokyo burning.

From midnight to dawn, the inferno raged, as thousands of citizens abandoned their homes and fled the all-engulfing flames. The all-clear sounded at 3.20 a.m., but the fires continued until after 6.00 a.m., when the worst of the conflagration began to subside, although isolated areas continued to burn for days. The last of the Superfortresses landed shortly after noon on the following day, and Gen. Powers, LeMay's second in command, who had overflown the raid at 20,000 ft, reported a devastating raid. The final results, which were obtained from the Tokyo Metropolitan Bureau after the war, disclosed that 267,171 dwellings had been destroyed (about 25 per cent of all the buildings in Tokyo). 1,008,000 people were left homeless, 83,793 people were killed and 40,918 suffered injuries.

In retrospect, it is difficult to understand why the Japanese

Government did not seek a negotiated peace at this stage. Every major city on the mainland was now vulnerable to similar attacks, the Americans were about to occupy Iwo Jima, and the Imperial Navy had been routed at the battles of the Philippines Sea and Leyte Gulf. Instead, the Mayor of Tokyo told his citizens to be 'unafraid of the air raids', and issued a bizarre announcement that for the next four days they could ride free of charge on the municipal buses and transport.

D+19

By Saturday 10 March, it was clear that the battle was reaching its final stages. Though still resisting fiercely, the Japanese troops were fragmented, and had no overall command. Bitter and bloody fighting continued in Cushman's Pocket east of Airfield No. 3, but the survivors of The Meatgrinder and Turkey Knob were nearing the end of their tether.

Only in the north-west, where Gen. Kuribayashi had chosen to make his last stand, was there a problem. This was to be the last section of the island to fall to the Marines, and already it had earned itself the title of 'The Gorge' or 'Death Valley'. Situated about 500 yd south of Kitano Point, the northern tip of Iwo Jima, it was a mass of ravines, rocks, caves and gullies that harboured about 1,500 of the enemy. Deep underground, amid a labyrinth of tunnels, Kuribayashi's HQ was a model of defensive planning. Anticipating the course of the battle to perfection, Kuribayashi was holed up, and it was for the Marines to prise him out. He sent the following message to Tokyo:

The enemy's bombardments are very severe, especially the bombing and machine gun fire against Divisional Headquarters – so fierce that I cannot express or write it here. The troops are still fighting bravely and holding their positions thoroughly.

Thirteen

The Last Round (D+20–D+26)

We cannot hallow this ground – the brave men, living and dead, who struggled here have consecrated it far above our powers to add or detract. (Abraham Lincoln)

When the War Department released the casualty figures for Iwo Jima, it caused consternation in America. People were asking why so many young men were dying for a useless piece of real estate hundreds of miles from Japan. Their concerns were fuelled by the pro-MacArthur factions in the national press. The Hearst-controlled *San Francisco Examiner* ran a headline, 'General MacArthur is our best strategist . . . he saves the lives of his own men . . . why don't we use him more?', while Robert McCormick's formerly isolationist *Chicago Tribune* continued its vendetta against Holland Smith.

As a gesture to placate public opinion, Iwo Jima was declared 'secure' on 14 March. In a ceremony most Marines still consider to have been cynically premature, an honour guard of twenty-four Marines, eight from each division, oversaw a flag-raising ceremony 200 yd north of Mt Suribachi.

As explosions rumbled in the north of the island and columns of smoke rose in the sky, Gen. Schmidt's personnel officer read from a prepared statement:

I, Chester William Nimitz, Fleet Admiral United States Navy, Commander-in-Chief of the United States Pacific Fleet and

Pacific Ocean area, do hereby proclaim as follows: United States forces under my command have occupied this and other of the Volcano Islands and . . .

His words were lost as an artillery barrage blasted Japanese strongpoints in Cushman's Pocket. The irony of the situation was apparent to all. 'Howlin' Mad' Smith was there for one of the last engagements of his wartime career: 'This was the worst yet, Bobbie,' he said to Gen. Erskine, with tears streaming down his face.

With the Japanese now confined to three distinct areas – Cushman's Pocket, the east coast and The Gorge – the bulk of the remaining fighting was up to the infantrymen. Flamethrowers, demolition squads and riflemen were left to slug it out with a now desperate enemy. Tanks could only be used in areas where the bulldozers could clear a path for them, artillery was reduced dramatically for fear of hitting the Marine forward positions, and many gunners found themselves donning combat gear.

The heavy naval vessels left for Guam, leaving a few destroyers to provide illumination for the hours of darkness. The P51 Mustangs operating from Airfield No. 1 took over from the carrier-based aircraft and provided excellent ground support with their bombs, napalm and rockets.

On the very day the island was declared 'secure', two more Medals of Honor were won. Pte. George Phillips an eighteen-year-old who had only been at the front for two days, threw himself onto an enemy grenade and died saving the lives of his three companions. Pte. Franklin Sigler, taking over his leaderless squad, destroyed an enemy emplacement, and although badly wounded, carried three comrades to safety and continued the battle until ordered to the rear for medical treatment.

Dale Worley's diary states: 'The fight is still raging. It has developed into hand-to-hand fighting with bayonets and grenades. There isn't much infantry left – 'E' Company, 27th has 41 left out of 250. No officers – a buck sergeant in charge.'

Airfield No. 1 was a hive of activity. The daily shuttle of transport and hospital planes gave precedence to damaged B29s returning from raids on Japan. Interspersed with this traffic, the P51 Mustangs constantly roared off the runway to batter the remaining enemy positions a few hundred yards to the north, and at dusk, the twin-boomed Black Widows left to patrol Iwo Jima's skies.

Around this time, a wild rumour swept the island that the war in Europe was over. How it originated is unclear, but the result was spectacular: offshore destroyers and transports fired hundreds of rounds, and dozens of star shells into the air, the news was blared over loudspeaker systems, and men cheered and yelled in wild excitement. It was over an hour before Gen. Schmidt issued a red alert to cease firing, and much longer before the rumour was revealed as a hoax.

As the 5th Division Marines recouped and prepared themselves for the final onslaught on Gen. Kuribayashi's headquarters in The Gorge, the 3rd Division were fighting a bloody battle in Cushman's Pocket, slowly and painfully reducing the enemy in fierce fighting. Baron Nishi, believed to have been partially blinded during the fighting, had held out for longer than most of his compatriots. Using dug-in tanks and fighting from caves, Nishi and his men put up a cruel resistance against the weary Marines until 16 March, when Cushman's Pocket fell silent. Baron Nishi's fate is unclear – one view is that he remained underground and killed himself on 22 March. His body was never identified, and none of his staff lived to verify the story.

Gen. Senda and his remaining men still held a small area near the east coast, between the village of Higashi and the sea. A captured prisoner estimated his strength at around three hundred men, and the 4th Division were still under fire from mortars and rockets from this sector. In an attempt to lessen the carnage, Gen. Erskine arranged for loudspeakers to broadcast in Japanese to the defenders, explaining the futility of resistance and imploring them to lay down their arms. Unfortunately, the generators for the loudspeakers failed to work, and the messages were never transmitted. The grim struggle raged on for four more days before the Japanese in this area were annihilated. The body of Gen. Senda was never found.

On 17 March, D+26, Adm. Nimitz issued a bulletin – Iwo Jima has been officially secured at 6.00 p.m., and Japanese resistance was at an end. One incredulous Marine was heard to say: 'If this damn place has been secured, where the hell is all this gunfire coming from?' Nimitz's communiqué ended with the now famous phrase: 'Among the Americans who served on Iwo Jima, uncommon valor was a common virtue.'

Dale Worley was less than happy with the impression given that the fighting on the island was at an end: 'This morning the island was officially secured. They ran the flag up at the base of Hot Rocks. We are still fighting, but it's called "mopping up operations".'

In a battle that will always be remembered for its ferocity, the final phase reached heights of savagery that shocked even battle-hardened campaigners. Another ten days of carnage and 1,724 casualties lay ahead of the battered Marines before the fighting would be over. The Gorge was about 700 yd long and 300–500 yd wide, and had a series of small canyons leading off it on both sides. Into this area, Gen. Kuribayashi had concentrated the remains of his garrison, estimated by the

Marines at around five hundred men. Deep underground among this labyrinth, Kuribayashi planned his last stand.

The 28th Regiment under Col. Liversedge moved up the west coast and took up positions on the cliffs overlooking The Gorge, while the remainder of the Division attacked from the centre and the east. A 5th Division report states:

In attacking these positions no Japanese were to be seen, all being in caves or crevices in the rocks and so disposed as to give an all-round, interlocking, ghost-like defense to each small compartment. Attacking troops were subjected to fire from flanks and rear more often than from the front. It was always difficult and often impossible to locate where the defensive fire originated. The field of fire of the individual Japanese defender in his cave position was often limited to an arc of 10 degrees or less. Conversely, he was protected from fire, except that coming back on this arc. The Japanese smokeless, flashless powder for small arms, always advantageous, was of particular usefulness here. When the position was overrun or threatened, the enemy retreated further into his cave, where he usually was safe from gunfire, only to pop out again as soon as the occasion warranted, unless the cave was immediately blown.

In a week of frantic fighting, the Marines gradually squeezed the enemy further and further back into this ever-shrinking pocket. Col. Wornham's 27th Regiment at the eastern end cleared a passage for the flamethrowing Sherman tanks (the 'Ronsons') which expended up to 10,000 gallons of flame oil per day to burn the enemy out of their caves and crevices, but even so, the losses were appalling. The 2nd Battalion had to be withdrawn. So badly mauled that it ceased to exist as a fighting force, the 1st Battalion was down to its third commander in nine days – the first had been decapitated, the second maimed by a landmine, and now the third had his left arm shattered by a burst of machine gun fire.

As the Marines pressed relentlessly down The Gorge, enemy resistance concentrated for a while on a large blockhouse near the eastern end. Tanks battered it with their 75 mm guns, and demolition teams attempted to blast it into submission. It took a massive 8,500 lb explosive charge to demolish the building. By 24 March, D+33, the Japanese had been edged into an area measuring only 50 yd square, and the last hours of resistance were approaching. Maj. Hori reports:

> General Kuribayashi commanded his battle under candle light without having a single rest or sleep, day after day. Radio broadcasts, newspapers and magazines from Japan encouraged him thoroughly, especially when the old and young men, boys and girls of his native place prayed to God for his victory.

Gen. Erskine again tried to persuade the Japanese to give up the hopeless struggle. *Nisei* (Japanese Americans) and POWs contacted a few of the defenders and told them to ask their leaders to surrender, but his efforts came to nothing. Kuribayashi reported to Chichi Jima:

> I have 400 men under my control. The enemy besieged us by firing and flame from their tanks. In particular, they are trying to approach the entrance of our cave with explosives. My men and officers are still fighting. The enemy's front line is 300 metres from us, and they are attacking by tank firing. They advised us to surrender by loudspeaker, but we only laughed at this childish trick, and did not set ourselves against them.

Maj. Horie on Chichi Jima anxiously monitored the broadcasts from Iwo Jima, and on 17 March transmitted a message informing Kuribayashi of his promotion to full General – the message was never acknowledged. Late in the evening of 23 March, a last transmission was received: 'All officers and men of Chichi Jima – goodbye from Iwo.' Horie says: 'I tried to communicate with them for three days after that, but in the end I received no answer.'

In his section of Iwo Jima, things had quietened down sufficiently for Sgt. Harold Best to go looking for a Seabee friend:

Glen was a Seabee, that great and mighty arm of the Navy who accomplish amazing construction feats under difficult and dangerous conditions. I started out on foot and walked towards Suribachi. Along came a Seabee truck and gave me a ride right to their camp. The road passed the 5th Division cemetery and I saw burial crews still working. It was about 5.00 p.m. Then I saw what few Americans saw during the war, because news photographers were under orders not to take pictures of great numbers of American dead together. Piled up on the roadside was a row of dead bodies, four feet high and about a hundred and fifty feet long. Each Marine was wrapped in his poncho with his exposed shoe towards the road. I've seen many piles of roadside wood in my profession, and each one brings this scene to mind. They must have been part of that day's dead because I didn't smell the odour of death. I suppose even then their telegrams were being prepared: 'The President of the United States regrets to inform you that your son . . .'

In the pre-dawn darkness of 26 March, D+35, the final act of the tragedy was being prepared. Between 200 and 300 Japanese troops from The Gorge and other positions along the west coast silently infiltrated through the rocks and ravines of the 5th Division sector and headed for a tented bivouac between Airfield No. 2 and the west coast. Led by sword-wielding officers and armed with grenades, machine guns and an assortment of Japanese and American rifles, this was a well-organized and co-ordinated assault, not a mad, last-ditch *banzai* attack. The target held a mixture of Marine shore parties, Air Force crewmen, AA gunners and Seabees – most of them sleeping, confident in the knowledge that Iwo Jima was now secure.

In a three-pronged attack, the Japanese slashed tents, stabbed sleeping men and lobbed hand grenades. One of the first to react was Lt. Harry Martin of the 5th Pioneers, who hurriedly organized a defence line, and then dashed into the mêlée to rescue injured men. As the assault continued, the noise brought nearby Marines from the Pioneer Battalions, who were due to leave the island that day, and men from an all-Negro shore party unit that had never before seen combat.

Meanwhile, Lt. Martin had single-handedly killed a group of four enemy machine gunners, and rallied the scattered troops to make a charge which momentarily repelled the attackers. Regrouping, the Japanese came back more determined than ever, and in the ensuing onrush, Martin was killed.

As the confused and macabre battle continued, Americans from an assortment of units grabbed whatever weapon came to hand and joined in the fray. Men struggled and cursed, knives and bayonets slashed, fists and boots flew, grenades exploded and pistols cracked as the fighting reached a furious climax.

With daylight gradually illuminating the grotesque scene, a detachment of the Army's 147th Infantry, complete with tanks, arrived on the scene, but by then the worst was over. Sgt. Best was witness to part of the scene:

We were eating our breakfast on a bench high on the north side of the island. The battle was over and we were about to board ship. Suddenly, we heard explosions on the beach below. We saw men in white skivvies running from their tents, being chased by Japs – the men in white skivvies were American airmen. The Japs had come from caves in a co-ordinated attack upon the near-helpless airmen. A number were killed and wounded.

A nearby Marine Company was ordered to sweep the area and finish off the Japs. Later, as we were going down the slope to board our ship, several truckloads of dead Jap bodies passed us on the way for burial. On the rough road, the freshly killed bodies bounced like Jello.

Dawn was to reveal the full extent of the carnage – among the blood-stained tents, 44 airmen lay dead, and another 88 had been wounded; 9 Marines were also killed, and 31 wounded. Of the Japanese attackers, 262 were dead, and 18 captured. It was rumoured that Gen. Kuribayashi led the attack, but there was nothing to prove this assumption, and his body was not found among the dead.

To Lt. Martin, killed so late in the battle, would go Iwo Jima's final Medal of Honor, bringing the total to an incredible twenty-seven – an indication of the 'uncommon valor' Adm. Nimitz had praised so highly. Dale Worley's diary records:

We left Iwo at 1800 hrs. I stood on the rail of the ship as it pulled out. As we left I thought of my friends that had fallen and were buried there. I felt like we were leaving them back there alone, that we were deserting them. We are Marines, fighting men, that are supposed to be hard, with no feelings, but we have them. We talk of our fallen buddies as though they were transferred – we sound indifferent, but when we are alone we would cry. A buddy is something precious, and to lose that buddy is a hard blow.

I have found the meaning of 'killed in action'. It is the body of a man that is torn with bullets and shrapnel, bloated from lying in the sun, the face black, with the skin falling off parts of the body, and with dried blood on the ground – that is 'killed in action'. There is no glory or honor in it. People talk of this glory and honor, but they don't see the facts. There is no death compared to the death of a man killed on the battlefield.

At last, the island began to pay back its debt of human lives. The Seabees swarmed over Airfield No. 2 and began the task of converting it into the biggest airfield in the north Pacific. The Motoyama Plateau was levelled, and landmarks such as Hill 382 and Charlie Dog Ridge disappeared for ever. Tank farms, breakwaters and twenty miles of road appeared as from nowhere, and Motoyama No. 2, with a 10,000 ft long runway, became (and still is) Iwo Jima's principal airfield.

The P51 Mustang fighters rose to accompany the B29s from the Marianas on the last leg of their fire-bombing missions to Japan, and by the end of the war, 2,400 Superfortresses, with crews totalling over 70,000, had set down on the island for one reason or other.

The Marines began to leave on the morning of the Japanese raid on the west coast bivouac, and control was passed to Gen. Clancey and the US Army's 147th Regiment, which had been shipped in from New Caledonia. During April, they were credited with killing 1,600 and capturing 867 survivors of the battle who had been hiding in underground tunnels and caves.

Lt. Musashino, CO of the Pioneer Company of the Japanese 2nd Mixed Brigade, survived the battle along with some hundreds of other Japanese troops, and lived to relate his adventures while attempting to evade the occupying Army troops. He continued to live in caves on the east coast with Lt. Taki. Many times he had wanted to kill himself with a hand grenade, but each time Taki dissuaded him. By mid-May, he estimated that there were around 1,500 Japanese still on the island. They were spending their entire time hunting for food and water. Every night, they would go to the places where they were most likely to find food, but always met other Japanese at the same place. During the day, they would hide from the Americans, but at night 'we became thieves and burglars'.

On 8 or 9 June, Musashino and Taki trudged to their old Brigade HQ, but found it full of bodies and thousands of flies. Nevertheless, they stayed for three nights. Later, while climbing under some barbed wire, a machine gun opened up on them and Taki was hit in the head. Musashino stayed with him until he died, then continued on to the east coast.

Musashino finally decided he had had enough, and would starve himself to death. He hid under a large rock and awaited the end. By 16 June he was delirious and terribly emaciated. His next recollection was of a dog scratching and many soldiers pointing guns. Contrary to his expectations, he was well treated by the Americans, spending a while in hospital, and being given plenty of food. He soon recovered, and spent the remaining months of the war in a POW camp.

The dirty, weary and emaciated Marines trudged down from the north onto the eastern beaches, and were shipped out to the waiting transports. Many were too weak to pull themselves up the netting which had been lowered over the sides of the ships, so sailors clambered down and hauled them aboard. As the ships got under way, they were given clean clothes, good food and had showers. The food was initially difficult to eat for many, as weeks of 'K' rations had shrunk their stomachs, but they soon returned to normal – physically at least. Twenty-five days after their departure from Iwo Jima, and as if to signify that the long struggle was finally almost over, the war in Europe came to an end.

Fourteen

Epilogue (D+27–D+36)

When you go home, tell them of us and say: 'For their tomorrows, we gave our todays.' (John Maxwell Edmonds)

On 1 June 1945, the 509th Composite Group of B29 Superfortresses arrived at North Field on Tinian. Gen. LeMay had been informed about the Manhattan Project, and knew exactly what the 509th were expected to accomplish. He also knew that training in the southern states of the USA was a different ball game to flying from the Marianas to Japan, and that like any other Bomb Group, they would have to prepare accordingly. Starting with practice runs to adjacent islands, the 509th progressed to making regular bombing runs to Truk and Marcus Island, both still held by the Japanese.

As the plans were being drawn up for the first atom bomb raid, a disagreement arose between LeMay and Gen. Leslie Groves, the overseer of the Manhattan Project. Groves, an Army man, had little experience of flying, and insisted that every available B29 of the 21st Bomber Command should fly the mission as escort for the aircraft carrying the bomb. It took a while for LeMay to convince him that individual planes had been overflying Japan for weeks on meteorological flights without coming to harm. LeMay insisted that only three aircraft were required: the A-bomber and two observation planes.

The larger components of the bomb, code-named 'Fat Man', had been shipped directly to Tinian on the deck of Adm. Spruance's old flagship, the USS *Indianapolis*, in May.

The fissionable material was to come a little later, after the first test firing at the proving ground at Alamogordo in New Mexico.

The subsequent fate of the *Indianapolis* has been the subject of a number of films and books. Sailing without escort from Guam to Leyte in the Philippines, she was torpedoed on the night of 30 July by a Japanese submarine, and sank within minutes without giving a distress signal. Because of anomalies in the Navy's procedures for reporting overdue ships at that time, she was not listed as missing for four days. Of the 850 men who went into the water, only 316 survived. The remainder died from injuries, thirst and shark attacks before a chance sighting by an American patrol aircraft alerted the rescue services.

Gen. Carl Spaatz had allowed LeMay to choose the day for the attack, and all looked clear for 5 August. At 9.15 a.m., the 'Enola Gay' (named after the mother of the pilot, Col. Paul Tibbets) released its bomb at 31,600 ft over the centre of Hiroshima. The crew felt two shock waves that buffeted the plane even though it was speeding away from the city, and a huge, mushroom-shaped cloud rose to a height of 50,000 ft. In the ensuing inferno, 71,379 people died instantly, and 68,023 were injured, mostly from burns and the later effects of radiation.

Many post-war revisionists have condemned the bombing of Hiroshima and Nagasaki, along with LeMay's fire-bombing campaign, as mere acts of terrorism against helpless civilians – it is perhaps pertinent to consider the alternatives.

Had the war not ended with the dropping of the A-bombs, or even as a result of the bombing campaign by the 20th Air Force, then the Marines and the US Army would have had to undertake the invasion of the Japanese mainland. The invasion had already been planned as OPERATION DOWNFALL, and the prospect filled the Government, the Army and the USMC alike with foreboding.

From experience gleaned in Saipan, Iwo Jima and Okinawa, it was obvious to them that every beach, town, village and field would be defended to the death, not only by the armed forces (and Japan still had six armies on the mainland) but also by the remnants of the Navy, *kamikazes*, and by millions of civilians. Here were the ingredients for a titanic battle that would make Tarawa, Peleliu, Saipan, Iwo Jima and Okinawa pale into insignificance. A leading Marine General estimated that 70 per cent of the landing force would become casualties, and the war was expected to continue into 1946, or even 1947. Plans were already laid for large contingents of allied troops from the European theatre to move to the Pacific, and some of these forces, Tiger Force, were already on their way when the A-bombs were dropped.

Speaking and corresponding with scores of Pacific veterans, the author has yet to find one who does not wholeheartedly agree with the bombing of Hiroshima and Nagasaki – indeed, most consider that they owe their lives to these events, and are certain that they would have died in the invasion of the Japanese mainland.

In what was probably the understatement of all time, Emperor Hirohito announced to the Japanese nation: 'The war is not necessarily proceeding to Japan's advantage.' At a formal ceremony aboard the battleship USS *Missouri* in Tokyo Bay on 2 September 1945, a glittering array of American and Allied service chiefs witnessed the signing of the surrender document by Gen. MacArthur and the Japanese delegation led by Foreign Secretary Shigemitsu and Gen. Umeza.

Conspicuous by his absence was 'Howlin' Mad' Smith. Adm. Hill had written to Adm. Nimitz urging him to invite Smith to the ceremony, but his request had been returned with the word 'No' written across it. It seems that his enemies had finally won – his sacking of two Army Generals for 'lack of aggression' had not been forgotten in high places. Smith was less worried about this personal slight than what he saw as an affront to his Marines, who had turned the tide in the Central Pacific and driven the enemy back from the approaches to Australia to the very shores of Japan.

As they so often did, the planners had underestimated both the timescale and the number of casualties for the operation to secure Iwo Jima. What had been envisaged as a short, sharp battle had developed into the grimmest and most costly battle in Marine Corps history. In all, 5,885 Marines died, and 17,272 were wounded. The US Navy lost 881 men, with a further 1,917 wounded.

Grim as these figures were, the Japanese losses were simply staggering. An exact figure is impossible – at the time of writing (1998), Japanese 'bone diggers' still make visits to the island to recover the remains of war dead from caves and underground tunnels. It is known that the garrison stood at 21,060 shortly before the battle, and that 216 Navy and 867 Army personnel were taken prisoner – few of them voluntarily – so the Japanese death toll can be assumed at 19,977. Gen. Kuribayashi's order that each of his men should die taking ten Marines with him was hyperbole: in reality, each Marine who died accounted for three of the enemy.

As some compensation for all the suffering and loss of life, Gen. Paul Tibbets cites the fact that thousands of B29 crews were able to use Iwo Jima: 'On 4 March 1945, when the first B29 in distress landed on Iwo Jima, until the end of the war, more than 2,200 aircraft made emergency landings on Iwo, many with wounded crewmen on board who would not have made the return trip to their home bases. Had it not been for the heroic valour of the Marines in securing the island and the Navy

Seabees who built the runways, more than 22,000 pilots and air crewmen would have perished in crash landings at sea.'

Prior to the return of the island to Japan in 1968, all the American dead were removed, and although the US Air Force maintained a base on Iwo Jima for twenty years after the war, only a thirty-man US Coast Guard contingent remained in 1968 to operate the LORAN (Long-Range Aid to Navigation) station on Kitano Point. This token presence vanished in 1993, when the facility was turned over to the Japanese Maritime Safety Agency, and forty-eight years after the battle, Iwo Jima once again came under Japanese jurisdiction.

Still a remote, forbidding and almost inaccessible dot in the north Pacific, Iwo Jima is regarded as a Japanese national war monument. Occasional parties of Marine Corps veterans are allowed to visit for one day – there are no hotels, and the old men scramble among the black volcanic ash, ascend Mt Suribachi in trucks, or simply stand and remember.

Appendix 1

Medal of Honor Winners

The Medal of Honor, sometimes mistakenly called the Congressional Medal of Honor, is the United States' highest military decoration, and was awarded to 27 combatants at Iwo Jima, of which 22 were Marines, 4 Navy corpsmen, and 1 a Navy officer – 13 were awarded posthumously.

Some indication of the ferocity of the battle can be gained from the fact that the medals awarded at Iwo Jima constitute a third of the total number awarded to members of the United States Marine Corps during the whole of the Second World War. The prefix 'For conspicuous gallantry and intrepidity at the risk of his life above and beyond the call of duty' echoes the famous words of Fleet Adm. Chester Nimitz: 'Among the Americans who served on Iwo Jima, uncommon valor was a common virtue.'

Cpl. CHARLES J. BERRY, 1st Battalion, 26th Regiment, 5th Division, 3 March 1945, Posthumous

Charles Berry was a 21-year-old from Lorain, Ohio. For thirteen days he had been slowly advancing with the 26th Regiment, and was finally dug in among the rocks and gorges west of Nishi Ridge. On the night of 3 March, he and two other riflemen were in a foxhole on the perimeter of their area. By the occasional light of Navy star shells, stooping figures of enemy troops could be made out scurrying among the rocks from one position to another.

Some time in the early hours, the Japanese made a frenzied attack with rifle fire and a fusillade of grenades. Berry and his companions immediately returned fire, until one of the grenades bounced over the edge of the foxhole and landed at the feet of the group. Charles Berry threw himself onto the grenade, and was killed instantly. The two other Marines were wounded in the explosion, but owe their lives to Berry's sacrifice.

Pfc WILLIAM R. CADDY, 3rd Battalion, 26th Regiment, 5th Division, 3 March 1945, Posthumous

Near Hill 362B, north of the unfinished Airfield No. 3, William Caddy, a nineteen-year-old from Quincy, Massachusetts, was sheltering in a shell hole with two other Marines among the rugged outcrop of gullies and rocks. The day had seen savage fighting in this area, and Caddy and his companions had been unable to move for nearly two hours.

Around 4.00 p.m., one of the Marines scrambled to the edge of the hole in an attempt to locate a particularly troublesome Japanese sniper. Spotting the Marine, the enemy threw a hand grenade into the shell hole. Without a thought for his personal safety, William Caddy threw himself onto the grenade and took the full blast of the explosion in his chest and stomach, dying immediately.

Lt.-Col. JUSTICE M. CHAMBERS, 3rd Battalion, 25th Regiment, 4th Division, 19–22 February 1945

Classed as one of the 'old men' of the battle, 38-year-old Chambers, from Huntington, West Virginia, was a career Marine. Affectionately known to his men as 'Jumpin' Joe' because of his ungainly, loping walk, he was a veteran of the Solomons and Tinian. He had been a Captain with a Raider Battalion in the early days of the war.

The 3rd Battalion were engaged in assaulting Charlie Dog Ridge on the approaches to Airfield No. 2. Evening was approaching, and Chambers was anxious to gain the high ground before nightfall so that he would have the advantage for the following day. Calling for a salvo of rockets from a nearby mobile launcher, he rushed to the head of his men and led the attack on the enemy positions. A burst of Japanese machine gun fire hit Chambers in the upper part of his chest, leaving a gaping hole. He was dragged back to his observation post, where the Regimental Surgeon, Lt.-Cdr Michael Kelleher, treated him.

Dr Kelleher recalls the event:

About 4.00 p.m., I got word that Colonel Joe Chambers had been wounded. He was in the forward battalion observation post. He had been shot through the chest and back. He was perhaps only one hundred yards from our aid station, over as rough, rocky, hilly ground as anywhere on the plateau of Iwo Jima. I took two Corpsmen and a stretcher and went forward – crawling forward is a better description, because we dare not raise up for fear of being shot ourselves. Joe's wounds were very serious. One bullet had hit him in the left lung, he was bleeding and going into shock.

Joe was a big man, about 6 ft 3 in tall and over two hundred pounds. He was fully awake and alert. We got him on the stretcher, and by lifting him as far off the ground as we dared, carried him – and I'm afraid bounced him at times when we drew enemy fire – and somehow got him back to the aid station, where at least we had some protection from gunfire. I could then examine his wound better, dressed them with some pressure dressings to help control the bleeding, got three units of plasma into his veins rapidly, and got ready to evacuate him to the beach about a thousand yards away.

I had no ambulance or any other means of transportation at the time – they were all busy elsewhere. An amphibious truck – called a 'duck' – driven by a young black Marine lumbered along outside our station. I commandeered him and his truck, and got ready to put the Colonel aboard. The driver said he wasn't going back to the beach. 'They're shooting people down there,' he said, really very frightened. I took out my .45 handgun and said: 'There's some people up here that are going to get shot if that duck doesn't take my patient down to the beach – right now.'

It was now rapidly getting dark – about 5.00 p.m. At dark, the beach 'closed down'. The beachmaster would be stopping all traffic to and from the ships until daylight next morning. If the Colonel didn't get to an operating room soon, he wouldn't live. He certainly would not survive until morning without emergency surgery. So we loaded him and several other casualties aboard the truck, and our Marine driver drove down to the beach, where they were promptly loaded on the last boat to leave that evening, and were taken to a hospital ship. The Colonel survived.

Chambers's citation reads: 'Exposing himself repeatedly to enemy fire, he inspired his men by fearless example and aggressive leadership during the first bloody days, until seriously wounded, he was evacuated.' He later received his Medal of Honor from President Harry Truman at the White House in Washington.

Sgt. DARRELL S. COLE, 1st Battalion, 23rd Regiment, 4th Division, 19 February 1945, Posthumous

When his platoon came under very heavy fire on Yellow Beaches 1 and 2 on D-Day, Cole, a 22-year-old from Flat River, Missouri, decided to mount a one-man attack. Armed with a few hand grenades and a .45 pistol, he stormed the half-dozen pillboxes that were pinning down his men, lobbing grenades through the firing slits. Darrell Cole returned to his lines twice for more grenades until most of the enemy positions fell silent, but on his third foray, a Japanese grenade landed at his feet, killing him instantly.

Capt. ROBERT H. DUNLAP, 1st Battalion, 26th Regiment, 5th Division, 20–21 February 1945

Dunlap, from Abingdon, Illinois, was serving with 'A' Company. Pinned down at a steep cliff, they were unable to advance as the Japanese poured a rain of mortar and rifle fire onto the approaches to Airfield No. 1. Calling for covering fire from his men, Dunlap dashed forward to locate the source of the enemy fire and called up artillery support from the rear. Returning to his own lines, he obtained a field telephone and moved to an isolated position only fifty yards from the enemy, and for the next forty-eight hours directed devastating fire onto the Japanese positions from various directions.

Robert Dunlap's actions played a significant role in clearing the western section of the island. Five days later, he was severely wounded in the hip and evacuated to Saipan.

Sgt. ROSS F. GRAY, 1st Battalion, 25th Regiment, 4th Division, 21 February 1945

Gray was a 24-year-old from Marvel Valley, Alabama. Engaged in the bloody fighting around Airfield No. 2, his platoon was pinned down among a nest of enemy pillboxes. Grabbing a satchel charge, he zig-zagged his way under heavy fire to the nearest emplacement and lobbed the charge through the firing aperture, killing all inside. In short order, he repeated the process until six of the Japanese positions fell silent.

Now able to advance, the platoon approached a minefield, but Gray cleared a path, enabling his men to move on. Known as 'The Preacher' because of his strong religious convictions, Ross Gray's God was certainly with him on this day.

Sgt. WILLIAM G. HARRELL, 1st Battalion, 28th Regiment, 5th Division, 3 March 1945

Only yards from Nishi Ridge, Harrell, a 22-year-old Texan from Rio Grande City, and Pfc Andrew Carter were dug in for the night in their foxhole. Soon after midnight, Carter opened fire on a group of enemy infiltrators he had seen by the light of a flare. Within minutes, the Japanese were on the edge of the foxhole, and Harrell and Carter had accounted for four of them before Carter's gun jammed. Dashing off for a replacement, he yelled: 'Be right back!'

Moments later, the enemy attacked with hand grenades, and one of them exploded within feet of Harrell, almost severing his left hand, and injuring his thigh. Within minutes, Carter had returned with another carbine, just in time for the next attack. Two Japanese charged into the foxhole, one of them swinging a sabre. Carter's second weapon failed to work, and he struggled with the sword-wielding enemy, finally killing him, but not before he severely injured his hand. Harrell, now only able to handle his Colt .45 pistol, shot the second intruder, and ordered Carter back to the command post to summon help and have his wounds attended to.

In extreme pain and bleeding profusely, Harrell prayed that the enemy would not return, but it was wishful thinking, as yet another two Japanese approached the foxhole. One jumped into the hole, placed a grenade alongside Harrell, and began clambering out. Harrell shot him with his pistol and lobbed the grenade with his good right hand at the second intruder.

The blast killed the Japanese at once, but it also blew off Harrell's right hand. As daylight broke, Carter returned with stretcher-bearers, and the half-dead Sergeant was evacuated.

After the war, the indomitable Harrell, with the aid of mechanical hands, became a successful rancher.

Lt. RUFUS G. HERRING, USNR, LCI (G) 449, 17 February 1945

Herring, a 25-year-old from Roseboro, North Carolina, was Captain of Gunboat No. 449. Two days before D-Day, flotillas of gunboats were laying down a carpet of rockets onto the invasion beaches and carrying frogmen to within 250 yd of the shore. The tiny craft were coming under very heavy fire from the Japanese shore batteries, which were under the impression that this was the main invasion. A near hit seriously wounded Herring, and a direct hit demolished the bridge and killed twelve of the crew.

Bleeding profusely, Herring struggled for thirty minutes to steer his vessel and his wounded crew away from the enemy barrage. Finally, he came alongside the destroyer USS *Terror*, and remained propped up by empty shell cases, refusing to be evacuated until the remainder of his crew were taken aboard.

Pfc DOUGLAS T. JACOBSON, 3rd Battalion, 23rd Regiment, 4th Division, 26 February 1945

As the 4th Division battled to take Hill 382, nineteen-year-old Jacobson from Rochester, New York, a veteran of Saipan, seized a bazooka from a dead Marine and began to wage his own war against the Japanese.

For thirty minutes he dashed from blockhouse to blockhouse blasting everything in sight, until he had expended all his ammunition, sixteen enemy positions were obliterated and seventy-five of the enemy lay dead. Using a bazooka is usually a two-man operation, but Jacobson managed alone, and opened up a gap in the Japanese lines, enabling his company to temporarily reach the summit of the hill.

Sgt. JOSEPH R. JULIAN, 1st Battalion, 27th Regiment,
5th Division, 9 March 1945, Posthumous

The battle was in its eighteenth day, and heavy fighting was going on around Kitano Point, one of the final pockets of Japanese resistance. Julian, a regular Marine from Sturbridge Village, Massachusetts, was determined to break the stalemate holding up his platoon.

Using hand grenades, he silenced a four-man enemy emplacement, then wiped out a machine gun nest with his carbine. Dashing back to his lines, Joseph Julian collected demolition charges and a bazooka, and once more charged the enemy positions. This time, he silenced four more strongpoints before he was hit in the chest by a burst of machine gun fire, which killed him instantly.

Pfc JAMES D. LaBELLE, 2nd Battalion, 27th Regiment,
5th Division, 8 March 1945, Posthumous

It seems that James LaBelle, a nineteen-year-old from Columbia Heights, Minnesota, was fated to die on Iwo Jima. He had missed death by inches on three previous occasions: during the dash across the island at the base of Mt Suribachi, three of his companions fell to machine-gun fire, three days later he was the only man to remain unhurt when a grenade landed in the shell hole he was sharing with four other Marines, and on the tenth day of the battle he had seen his best friend die at his side near Nishi Ridge.

Now LaBelle's Platoon were at the northern end of the 5th Division sector. Taking cover behind a pile of boulders with two companions, LaBelle saw a solitary Japanese soldier dash to the front of a nearby cave and lob a hand grenade in their direction. Shouting a warning, James LaBelle threw himself onto the grenade and was killed instantly in the explosion, saving the lives of his comrades.

2nd Lt. JOHN H. LEIMS, 1st Battalion, 9th Regiment, 3rd Division, 7 March 1945

After a night attack against Hill 362C, east of Cushman's Pocket, Leims, a 22-year-old from Chicago, and his company found themselves in a precariously advanced position with the enemy rapidly surrounding them. When it became apparent that they were cut off, he personally advanced and laid telephone lines across the isolated expanse of open, fire-swept terrain.

After being ordered to withdraw his men, he was informed that several casualties had been left in an abandoned position beyond the front line. He instantly went forward despite darkness, carried a wounded Marine to safety and returned again under heavy enemy fire to recover a second man. John Leims showed himself to be a dauntless leader, concerned at all times with the welfare of his men.

Pfc JACKLYN H. LUCAS, 1st Battalion, 26th Regiment, 5th Division, 20 February 1945

Lucas was hell bent on being a Marine. He lied about his age, and enlisted when he was fourteen. Now, aged seventeen, the young rebel from Plymouth, North Carolina, was wanted by the Military Police in Hawaii for being AWOL. He had stowed away on a troopship with his unit when they left for Iwo Jima, and his buddies fed and watered him on the long trip.

On the second day of the battle, near Airfield No. 1, he was one of three riflemen who were pinned down by a group of Japanese, and was fighting a fierce battle with hand grenades and rifles. When a grenade fell in the middle of the group, Jacklyn Lucas smothered it with his body, then grabbed a second grenade and pulled it underneath him.

Miraculously, he survived the blasts, and although severely wounded, recovered after seven months in hospital, with only a partially paralysed arm as a memento of Iwo Jima.

1st Lt. JACK LUMMUS, 2nd Battalion, 27th Regiment, 5th Division, 8 March 1945, Posthumous

Towards the end of the battle, around Kitano Point, the 2nd Battalion moved forward against a complex of enemy caves and bunkers, and became bogged down. Determined to move forward, Lummus, a 29-year-old ex-football star from Ennis, Texas, spearheaded an attack, charging forward and immediately coming under heavy enemy fire. He was knocked to the ground by a grenade blast, but jumped to his feet and attacked the position to his front, killing the occupants. Although wounded in the shoulder, he stormed another strongpoint and waved his men forward.

While leading his men on yet another charge, Lummus stepped on a landmine, and both his legs were blown off. As the dust and debris settled, the men of the 2nd Battalion were amazed and horrified to see their leader on his bloody stumps, still urging his men forward. Although fatally wounded, Jack Lummus lived for several hours before dying in a field hospital.

Capt. JOSEPH J. McCARTHY, 2nd Battalion, 24th Regiment, 4th Division, 21 February 1945

In the fighting around the approaches to Airfield No. 2, the 24th Regiment had come under very heavy fire from several enemy pillboxes, and their advance was grinding to a halt. Chicago-born 33-year-old McCarthy (another 'Jumpin' Joe' to his men) filled a bag with grenades, mustered a three-man flamethrower team and headed towards the Japanese positions yelling 'Let's get the bastards before they get us!'

Charging across open terrain, they plunged to the ground only yards from the nearest position. Joe McCarthy flung three grenades through the firing vents, shooting down three of the enemy when they bolted from the rear exit. Within the space of five minutes, three more pillboxes were silenced in the same fashion, allowing the company to advance.

1st Lt. HARRY L. MARTIN, 5th Pioneer Battalion, 26 March 1945, Posthumous

Shortly before dawn on 26 March, 200–300 Japanese troops launched a mass attack west of Airfield No. 2 against a rest area occupied by Marine shore parties, Seabees, aircrew, AA gunners and other mainly non-combat troops. Striking from three different directions, the enemy were everywhere, throwing grenades, firing guns and slashing sleeping men in their tents.

Martin, a 34-year-old from Bucyrus, Ohio, immediately formed a line manned mainly by black troops, and held the enemy in check. Seeing that a number of Marines were wounded, he dashed forward to help them, then attacked a machine gun position, killing four Japanese, before being seriously wounded by a grenade.

In the early light, the scene of carnage unfolded: 44 Airmen, and 9 Marines lay dead, with a further 31 men wounded.

The bodies of 262 of the enemy were strewn about the camp. Among the dead was Harry Martin, the last of Iwo Jima's twenty-seven Medal of Honor heroes.

Pte. GEORGE PHILLIPS, 2nd Battalion, 28th Regiment, 5th Division, 14 March 1945, Posthumous

On the very day Iwo Jima was declared 'secure', Pte. Phillips, an eighteen-year-old replacement from Rich Hill, Missouri, who had only been in action for two days, was taking cover with three other Marines near a cave when a hand grenade landed in their midst. George Phillips unhesitatingly threw himself on the missile and died instantly, saving the lives of his comrades.

Pharmacist's Mate 1st Class FRANCIS PIERCE Jr, 2nd Battalion, 24th Regiment, 4th Division, 15 March 1945

While evacuating wounded Marines, Corpsman Francis Pierce and a party of stretcher-bearers were ambushed. Pierce, a 21-year-old from Earlville, Iowa, immediately moved two seriously wounded men to safety and directed the withdrawal of the others, covering them with rifle fire until they were clear. He then carried one of the badly wounded Marines over his shoulder for 200 yd under intense enemy fire, and returned for the second man.

The following day, Pierce was badly wounded while aiding an injured Marine. Refusing aid for himself, he treated the casualty and maintained protective covering fire for his comrades. His actions were typical of the Corpsmen of Iwo Jima, and show why they were held in such high respect by the Marines.

Pfc DONALD J. RUHL, 2nd Battalion, 28th Regiment,
5th Division, 19–21 February 1945, Posthumous

After a group of Japanese had been driven from a blockhouse on D-Day, Ruhl, a 21-year-old from Columbus, Montana, attacked them, killing one of the enemy with his bayonet, and another with his rifle. The following morning, he moved towards the enemy lines under very heavy mortar and machine gun fire to rescue a wounded Marine lying in an exposed position.

On 20 February, he occupied an abandoned gun emplacement, and stayed overnight to prevent the enemy from re-occupying it. As dawn broke, Ruhl accompanied his Platoon Sergeant to a camouflaged bunker to bring fire to bear on the enemy on the far side. A hand grenade landed between the pair, and Donald Ruhl, without a thought for his own safety, threw himself onto it and took the full force of the explosion, dying immediately.

Pte. FRANKLIN E. SIGLER, 2nd Battalion, 26th Regiment,
5th Division, 14 March 1945

During the fighting in The Gorge, Pte. Sigler, a twenty-year-old from Glen Ridge, New Jersey, took command of his leaderless squad and led them in a fearless charge against a gun emplacement that had held up the advance of his company for several days. In the face of fierce enemy fire, he attacked the position with hand grenades, killing the entire crew.

Nearby Japanese troops opened fire on Sigler, severely wounding him, but he continued attacking, sealing several cave entrances before crawling back to his own lines. Refusing medical treatment, he carried three wounded squad members to safety, then continued to direct rocket and machine gun fire at the enemy until ordered to the rear to have his wounds attended to.

Cpl. TONY STEIN, 1st Battalion, 28th Regiment, 5th Division, 19 February 1945

As the 28th Regiment hit the beaches on D-Day, Stein, a 24-year-old from Dayton, Ohio, was the first man from his unit in position. Using his own improvised weapon, which he called his 'stinger' – an adapted .50 aircraft machine gun – he assaulted ten enemy positions, killing at least twenty of the enemy.

When his ammunition ran out, he shed his boots and helmet, and made repeated forays to the beach for more, helping or carrying a wounded Marine on each trip. On the ninth trip, he was wounded in the shoulder by shrapnel, but stayed in the fight. Towards the end of the day, Stein personally supervised the withdrawal of his platoon, despite having his 'stinger' twice shot from his hands.

Tony Stein was killed later in the battle, near Hill 362A, never knowing of his Medal of Honour citation.

Pharmacist's Mate 2nd Class GEORGE E. WAHLEN, 2nd Battalion, 26th Regiment, 5th Division, 3 March 1945

Wahlen, a 21-year-old from Ogden, Utah, epitomized the selfless courage of the Navy Corpsman at Iwo Jima. He had been wounded on 26 February, but continued to aid injured Marines on the battlefield despite a terrific concentration of enemy fire. Wounded again on 3 March, he gallantly refused evacuation, and continued to administer medical aid.

After sustaining a third wound and unable to walk, he disregarded the hail of bullets and mortar fire around him and crawled for fifty yards to administer to a fallen Marine. When finally evacuated, George Wahlen had been treating wounded Marines non-stop for five days and nights.

Gunnery Sgt. WILLIAM G. WALSH, 3rd Battalion,
27th Regiment, 5th Division, 27 February 1945, Posthumous

Moving against Hill 362A, Walsh, a 22-year-old from Roxbury, Massachusetts, led his platoon against a complex of enemy pillboxes and machine guns on a heavily defended ridge which guarded this key Japanese strongpoint. After very heavy fighting, the platoon reached the summit, but were forced to retreat when they came under devastating fire from three different directions.

Mounting a second assault, Walsh again reached the top of the ridge with six men from his platoon, and took cover in a trench. The enemy immediately staged a suicidal counter-attack with hand grenades from the reverse slopes. When a grenade fell in their midst, William Walsh threw himself onto it and died instantly.

Pte. WILSON D. WATSON, 2nd Battalion, 9th Regiment,
3rd Division, 26–27 February 1945

Two hills, code-named Peter and Oboe, were a formidable obstacle for the 9th Regiment as they attacked Airfield No. 2. Moving forward under a heavy artillery barrage, Watson, a 23-year-old from Tuscumbia, Alabama, was the first man on the top of Hill Oboe. On the way, he had silenced a Japanese bunker and a machine gun nest.

Finding that only one other Marine had made it to the top, he helped stave off repeated attacks for thirty minutes, until reinforcements arrived. Advancing again, he neutralized another strongpoint, and was attacking yet another when he was wounded by mortar fire and sent to the rear for medical treatment. Within forty-eight hours, he was back with his platoon. In two days, Wilson Watson had killed over ninety of the enemy, and played a significant role in the capture of these important positions.

Cpl. HERSHEL W. WILLIAMS, 1st Battalion, 21st Regiment, 3rd Division, 23 February 1945

On the fourth day of the battle, in the centre of the island, the 21st Regiment were confronted by a network of bunkers and anti-tank guns adjoining Airfield No. 2. Maj. Robert Houser called upon Williams, a 21-year-old from Quiet Dell, Virginia, the last of his flamethrowers.

With an escort of riflemen, he attacked the first pillbox ahead of the Marines, and incinerated the occupants and a group of Japanese troops who attempted to shoot him down. Moving from one position to another, he burned out bunkers and strongpoints until the way ahead was clear. In four hours, Hershel Williams had neutralized one of the most stubborn obstacles so far encountered by his regiment, and was the first 3rd Division Marine on Iwo Jima to win the Medal of Honor.

Pharmacist's Mate 3rd Class JACK WILLIAMS, 3rd Battalion, 28th Regiment, 5th Division, 20 March 1945, Posthumous

'I'm just a hillbilly who wants to get away from the hills and see the world,' said Jack Williams from Harrison, Arkansas, as he boarded the bus for Little Rock, but the 21-year-old from the Ozarks was to join the list of posthumous Corpsmen who were admired by the Marines on Iwo Jima.

His story is best told by his Medal of Honor citation:

Gallantly going forward on the front lines under intense enemy small arms fire to assist a Marine wounded in a fierce grenade battle, Williams dragged the man to a shallow depression and was kneeling, using his own body as a screen from the sustained enemy fire as he administered first aid, when he was struck in the abdomen and groin three times by hostile fire. Momentarily stunned, he quickly recovered and completed his administrations before applying battle dressings to his own multiple wounds. Unmindful of his own urgent need for medical attention, he remained in the perilous, fire-swept area to care for another Marine casualty. Heroically completing his task despite pain and profuse bleeding he endeavored to make his way to the rear and was struck down by a Japanese sniper bullet which caused his collapse. He gallantly gave his life for his country.

Pharmacist's Mate 1st Class JOHN H. WILLIS, 3rd Battalion, 27th Regiment, 5th Division, 28 February 1945, Posthumous

All day long Willis, a 24-year-old from Columbia, Tennessee, had been tending wounded Marines around Hill 362. Inevitably, he was himself wounded by shrapnel from an enemy mortar, and was ordered to the rear for medical attention. Within hours he had discharged himself and was back with the front line troops, attending to a casualty lying in a shell hole.

With his rifle stuck in the ground, Willis was administering plasma when a grenade rolled down beside him. Steadying the plasma with his left hand, he threw the grenade out of the shell hole with his right. Seven more grenades followed in rapid succession, and each was quickly thrown out. John Willis's luck finally ran out when the last grenade exploded in his hand, killing him instantly.

Appendix 2

The Flag-raising

Associated Press photographer Joe Rosenthal's picture of Marines raising the Stars and Stripes on the summit of Mt Suribachi on 23 February 1945 is the most famous photograph to come out of the Second World War (see cover). Because of its superb composition and the fact that it was the second flag to be raised that day, there have always been doubts about its authenticity, and speculation that it was posed. At the time, this was compounded by a statement that Rosenthal made a few days later, saying that he had indeed taken a posed picture on the summit that day. Over the years, in numerous books and articles on the battle, the story has been distorted and misquoted to such an extent that it is prudent to return to Joe Rosenthal himself for an accurate account. In a letter to the author, he refers to an interview he gave to a well-known magazine in 1955, which he assures me is the genuine account of the event.

Rosenthal, who was attached to the 2nd Battalion of the 25th Regiment, landed on Iwo Jima around noon on D-Day, and began taking pictures immediately. He remained for eleven days in all, and took sixty-five photographs, returning occasionally to the command ship USS *Eldorado* to write captions and to despatch his pictures via the daily seaplane mail service to Guam.

The day of the flag-raising started inauspiciously for him when he fell into the sea while boarding an LCVP from the *Eldorado*. After being fished out, he took a picture of 'Howlin' Mad' Smith and the Secretary of the Navy, James V. Forrestal, gazing towards the beach with Mt Suribachi in the background. Boarding an LCT along with Bill Hipple, a magazine correspondent, he reached the southern end of the beach, and was informed by the boatswain that a patrol was going up Suribachi with a flag. They both made their way to the 28th Regiment command post, and were told that a forty-man detachment had already left with a flag, following two patrols that had reached the top at 9.40 a.m.

At the command post were Bob Campbell, a combat photographer, and Sgt. Bill Genaust, a cine photographer (who was killed nine days later on Hill 362). 'I think we'll be too late for the flag-raising,' Genaust said. 'I would still like to go up, and you two guys are carrying guns and I'm not. How about coming along?' replied Rosenthal.

They started on the tough climb, stopping occasionally while Marines threw grenades and set off demolition charges at cave openings where the enemy were still holed up. Roughly halfway up, they met four Marines coming back down. One of them was Lou Lowery, a photographer for *Leatherneck*, the Marine Corps magazine, who informed them that the patrol had reached the summit and raised a flag, and that he had photographed the event. The flag was from the attack transport USS *Missoula*, and had been carried up in the map case of the Battalion Adjutant. It was raised at 10.20 a.m., tied to a piece of pipe that was part of the wreckage of the Japanese radar station on the summit, and it measured 54 in by 28 in.

At this point, Rosenthal was in two minds whether to continue, but decided to press on and take a picture anyway. With Campbell and Genaust to provide protection, they reached the top a few minutes before noon, and saw the flag flying. As he got closer, he saw a group of Marines dragging a long, iron pipe, and one holding a neatly folded flag. 'What are you doing?' he asked. They replied: 'We're going to put up this bigger flag and keep the other as a souvenir.'

The second, larger flag, had been collected from LST 779, which was beached near the base of Mt Suribachi, by 2nd Lt. Albert T. Tuttle. Ensign Alan Wood, who was aboard LST 779, informed the author:

> I was on the ship when a young Marine came along – he was dirty, dusty and battleworn, and even though he was probably only eighteen or nineteen, he looked like an old man. 'Do you have a flag?' he asked. 'Yes,' I said, 'what for?' He said something like, 'Don't worry, you won't regret it.' The flag was one that I had salvaged from a supply depot at Pearl Harbor. It was found with some old signal flags that I think belonged to a decommissioned destroyer. It seems funny now when I look back on that day, because I hadn't the slightest idea that one day that flag would become the symbol of one of the war's bloodiest battlefields.

Rosenthal toyed with the idea of getting a shot of both flags, one coming down and the other going up, but could not line them up, although Bob Campbell scrambled down to the right and captured the moment. 'I decided to get just the one flag going up, and backed off about thirty-five feet.' As he moved backward, the ground sloped away and masked his view. Putting his Speed Graphic camera to one side, he grabbed a sandbag and some stones to make a platform (he is only 5 ft 5 in tall), climbed on, and set his camera between f8 and f11 at a speed of ¼₀₀ second.

Bill Genaust took up a position about three feet to his right with his cine camera. 'I'm not in your way, am I, Joe?' he called. 'No,' Joe shouted, 'and there it goes!' Out of the corner of his eye he had seen the men starting to raise the flag, and he swung his camera and caught the scene. 'That is how the picture was taken, and when you take a picture like that, you don't come away saying you got a great shot – you don't know – and within the next few minutes, I made another shot of some of the men putting ropes on the pipe, and another of a group that I got together to wave and cheer under the flag' (the posed photograph he was later to admit taking):

On the way down, Campbell and I took 'gag' shots of each other sitting in a chair that was strangely exposed on the mountainside, and I also took a picture of a Marine with an abandoned kitten, and another of a group of Marines holding up a sign they had painted, reading 'Weehawken NJ'.

When they got back to the 28th Regiment command post, he looked at his watch – it was 1.05 p.m., and that was how he knew the picture was taken around noon.

I took eighteen exposures that day, and when I got back to the *Eldorado* later that afternoon, I captioned one film pack of these and a pack from the previous day, and they went off on the mail plane to Guam. The caption for the flag-raising shot read: 'Atop 550 ft Suribachi Yama, the volcano at the southwest tip of Iwo Jima, Marines of the 2nd Battalion, 28th Regiment, 5th Division hoist the Stars and Stripes signalling the capture of this key position.'

When the films reached Guam, they were processed by the Picture Pool Co-ordinator, Murray Befeler, and sent to the US mainland via radiophoto. The flag-raising picture became an immediate sensation.

Ironically, Rosenthal did not get to see the picture until nine days after it was taken, by which time he had returned to Guam. He walked into Press Headquarters, and a correspondent walked up to him:

'Congratulations, Joe,' he said, 'on that flag raising shot on Iwo': 'Thanks,' I said. 'It's a great picture – did you pose it?' 'Sure,' I said – I thought that he meant the group shot I had arranged with Marines waving and cheering, but then someone else came up with the picture and I saw it for the first time. 'Gee,' I said, 'that's good alright, but I didn't pose that one. I wish I could take credit for posing it, but I can't.'

Rosenthal is explicit:

Had I posed that shot, I would have ruined it. I'd have picked fewer men. I would also have had them turn their heads so that they could be identified for AP members throughout the country, and nothing like the existing picture would have resulted.

The first congratulatory messages started at Guam, as did the first misunderstandings. One of the many correspondents had heard the first part of the conversation when Joe was asked about the picture, and wrote that the shot was a phoney, and that Rosenthal had posed it.

The picture had created a sensation in America, and Associated Press ordered Rosenthal back home to deal with his celebrity status:

I, who had never been asked for an autograph in my life, was being asked to sign dozens of them. I was interviewed and photographed, and sent back to AP head office in New York, where I was received by executives, and where, of all things, a 'Rosenthal' desk was set up to deal with the requests for interviews and appearances.

He later went to meet President Harry Truman in Washington, and was awarded the Pulitzer Prize for photography:

I received a raise in salary, and with the Pulitzer Prize came $500, and a further $1000 from *US Camera*. I was presented with three wristwatches as well as numerous scrolls, plaques and medals, and was offered $200,000 for the statuette rights for the picture.

The picture was the property of Associated Press, who very generously turned over the proceeds from its sale to the Navy Relief Society, which benefited over a period of ten years by $12,941,084.

Joe Rosenthal's life would never be the same again. The seemingly endless round of appearances, at one of which he was bizarrely introduced as 'Mr Joe Rosenberg, who raised the flag on Okinawa', became a chore:

> When the *World Almanac* stated in discussing the picture that 'Rosenthal also died later', I realized a truth had inadvertently been written. Joe Rosenthal, who is really just another news photographer, who did no more than any competent news photographer would have done, and a great deal less than some, no longer lives – at least, not as the unknown private citizen he once was.

The picture became the most widely reproduced photograph of all time: it was shown on an issue of 3 cent stamps that had the largest sale in history, a painting was used for the seventh War Loan Drive which raised $220,000,000, it appeared on 3,500,000 posters, 15,000 outdoor panels and 175,000 car cards, it has been done in oils, watercolours, pastels, chalk and matchsticks, a float won first prize in the Rose Bowl Parade, the flag-raising has been re-enacted in films, by gymnasts and children, it has been sculpted in ice, and even hamburgers. The final accolade was the hundred-ton bronze statue by Felix de Weldon which stands near the northern end of Arlington National Cemetery in Washington as a memorial to the United States Marine Corps.

Col. Dave Severence, who was a Captain in 'E' Company of the 2nd Battalion of the 28th Regiment at the time, informs me that the primary reason a second flag was raised was that the Secretary of the Navy, James Forrestal, had indicated that he wanted the small flag, and Lt.-Col. Johnson, CO of the 2nd Battalion, intended to keep it as a battalion memento. It was not intended that anyone would know that a second flag was raised. Col. Severence also clears up a mistake by the Marine Corps Chief Historian, Benis Frank:

> Joe Rosenthal did not accompany Sgt. Strank and his detail as they laid phone wires and carried the large flag to the top of Suribachi. He was some ten minutes or so behind them, and was not aware of a second flag until he reached the top. In an oral history review, Joe told Frank that he 'followed Strank's detail to the top', and Frank has insisted Joe told him he 'accompanied Strank's detail'. I specifically asked Joe about this misunderstanding, and he said Frank was wrong.

Charles Lindberg, who helped raise the first flag, and at this time is the only surviving flag-raiser, tells me: 'You should have heard the noise from down below when we got that first flag up. The troops were cheering, the ships horns were blowing – I got a chill all the way through.'

The six flag-raisers in the Rosenthal photograph are now all deceased. They were, from left to right, Pfc Ira Hayes, Pfc Franklin Sousley, Sgt. Michael Strank, Pharmacist's Mate 2nd Class John H. Bradley, Pfc Rene A. Gagnon, and Cpl. Harlon H. Block. Sousley, Strank and Block were all killed on Iwo Jima. Both flags now hang side by side at the Marine Corps Historical Center in Washington DC.

The final words should go to Joe Rosenthal himself:

I can best sum up what I feel by saying that of all the elements that went into the making of this picture, the part I played was the least important. To get that flag up there, America's fighting men had to die on that island, and on other islands, and off the shore, and in the air. What difference does it make who took the picture? I took it, but the Marines took Iwo Jima.

Appendix 3

US Command and Staff List

EXPEDITIONARY TROOPS (TF 56)

Commanding General	Lt.-Gen. Holland M. Smith
Chief of Staff	Col. Dudley S. Brown
G1	Col. Russell N. Jordahl
G2	Col. Edmond J. Buckley
G3	Col. Kenneth H. Weir
G4	Col. George R. Rowan

V AMPHIBIOUS CORPS (VACLF)

Commanding General	Maj.-Gen. Harry Schmidt
Chief of Staff	Brig.-Gen. William W. Rogers
G1	Col. David A. Stafford
G2	Col. Thomas R. Yancy (US Army)
G3	Col. Edward A. Craig
G4	Col. William F. Brown

3RD MARINE DIVISION

Commanding General	Maj.-Gen. Graves B. Erskine
Asst. Division Commander	Col. John B. Wilson
Chief of Staff	Col. Robert E. Hogaboom
D1	Maj. Irving R. Kriendler
D2	Lt.-Col. Howard J. Turton
D3	Col. Arthur H. Butler
D4	Lt.-Col. James D. Hittle

Headquarters Battalion	Lt.-Col. Jack F. Warner (until 14 March)
	Lt.-Col. Cary A. Randell (after 14 March)

3rd Marine Regiment

Commanding Officer	Col. James A. Stuart
Executive Officer	Lt.-Col. Newton B. Barkley
R3	Capt. Paul H. Groth

NB: This regiment did not land on Iwo Jima, and did not take part in the operation. It returned to Guam on 5 March 1945.

1st Battalion, 3rd Marine Regiment

Battalion Commander	Lt.-Col. Ronald R. Van Stockum
Executive Officer	Maj. Leyton M. Rogers
Btn. 3	Capt. Joseph V. Millerick

2nd Battalion, 3rd Marine Regiment

Battalion Commander	Lt.-Col. Thomas R. Stokes
Executive Officer	Maj. Howard J. Smith
Btn. 3	Capt. French R. Fogle

3rd Battalion, 3rd Marine Regiment

Battalion Commander	Lt.-Col. Ralph L. Houser
Executive Officer	Maj. Royal R. Bastian
Btn. 3	Capt. William R. Bradley

9th Marine Regiment

Commanding Officer	Col. Howard N. Kenyon
Executive Officer	Lt.-Col. Paul W. Russell
R3	Maj. Calvin W. Kunz

1st Battalion, 9th Marine Regiment

Battalion Commander	Lt.-Col. Carey A. Randall (until 6 March)
	Maj. William T. Glass (6–14 March)
	Lt.-Col. Jack F. Warner (after 14 March)
Executive Officer	Capt. Frank K. Finneran
Btn. 3	Capt. James R. Harper (until 27 February)
	Capt. Robert R. Fairburn (after 27 February)

2nd Battalion, 9th Marine Regiment

Battalion Commander	Lt.-Col. Robert E. Cushman Jr
Executive Officer	Maj. William T. Glass (until 6 March and again from 15 March)
Btn. 3	Capt. Laurence W. Cracroft

3rd Battalion, 9th Marine Regiment

Battalion Commander	Lt.-Col. Harold C. Boehm
Executive Officer	Maj. Donald B. Hubbard
Btn. 3	Capt. Joseph T. McFadden

21st Marine Regiment

Commanding Officer	Col. Hartnoll J. Withers
Executive Officer	Lt.-Col. Eustace R. Smoak
R3	Capt. Andrew Hedesh

1st Battalion, 21st Marine Regiment

Battalion Commander	Lt.-Col. Marlowe C. Williams (until 22 February – WIA)
	Maj. Clay M. Murray (22 February – WIA)
	Maj. Robert H. Houser (after 22 February)
Executive Officer	Maj. Clay M. Murray (until 22 February)
	Maj. George D. Flood Jr (after 22 February)
Btn. 3	Maj. George D. Flood Jr

2nd Battalion, 21st Marine Regiment

Battalion Commander	Lt.-Col. Lowell E. English (until 2 March – WIA)
	Maj. George A. Percy (after 2 March)
Executive Officer	Maj. George A. Percy (until 2 March)
	Maj. Michael V. DiVita (after 2 March)
Btn. 3	Capt. Thomas E. Norpell

3rd Battalion, 21st Marine Regiment

Battalion Commander	Lt.-Col. Wendell H. Duplantis
Executive Officer	Maj. M. Jones
Btn. 3	1st Lt. James C. Corman

12th Marine Regiment

Commanding Officer	Lt.-Col. Raymond F. Crist Jr
Executive Officer	Lt.-Col. Bernard H. Kirk
R3	Lt.-Col. Thomas R. Belzer

1st Battalion, 12th Marine Regiment

Battalion Commander	Maj. George B. Thomas
Executive Officer	Maj. William P. Pala
Btn. 3	Maj. Clarance E. Brissenden

2nd Battalion, 12th Marine Regiment

Battalion Commander	Lt.-Col. William T. Fairbourn
Executive Officer	Maj. Oliver E. Robinett
Btn. 3	Capt. Joseph F. Fogg

3rd Battalion, 12th Marine Regiment

Battalion Commander	Lt.-Col. Alpha L. Bowser Jr
Executive Officer	Maj. Claude S. Sanders Jr
Btn. 3	Maj. Wilbur R. Helmer

4th Battalion, 12th Marine Regiment

Battalion Commander	Maj. Joe B. Wallen (until 20 March) Lt.-Col. Thomas R. Belzer (after 20 March)

Executive Officer	Maj. David S. Randall (until 20 March)
Btn. 3	Capt. Lewis E. Poggemeyer

3rd Tank Battalion

Battalion Commander	Maj. Holly H. Evans
Executive Officer	Capt. Gerald P. Foster
Btn. 3	Capt. Bertram A. Yaffe

3rd Engineer Battalion

Battalion Commander	Lt.-Col. Walter S. Campbell
Executive Officer	Maj. Eldon J.C. Rogers
Btn. 3	Capt. Arthur J. Wardrep Jr

3rd Pioneer Battalion

Battalion Commander	Lt.-Col. Edmund M. Williams
Executive Officer	Maj. Howard A. Hurst
Btn. 3	Capt. Jack R. Edwards

Service Troops – 3rd Division

Commanding Officer	Col. James O. Brauer (until 6 March)
	Col. Lewis A. Hohn (after 6 March)
Executive Officer	Maj. Reginald G. Sauls III

3rd Service Battalion

Battalion Commander	Lt.-Col. Paul G. Chandler
Executive Officer	Maj. William E. Cullen
Btn. 3	Capt. Warren E. Smith

3rd Motor Transport Battalion

Battalion Commander	Lt.-Col. Ernest W. Fry Jr
Executive Officer	Maj. Ira E. Harrod Jr
Btn. 3	Maj. Ira E. Harrod Jr

3rd Medical Battalion

Battalion Commander	Cdr. Anthony E. Reymont (USNR)
Executive Officer	Cdr. Owen Deuby (USN)

4TH MARINE DIVISION

Commanding General	Maj.-Gen. Clifton B. Cates
Asst. Divisional Cmdr	Brig.-Gen. Franklin A. Hart
Chief of Staff	Col. Merton J. Batchelder
D1	Col. Orin H. Wheeler
D2	Lt.-Col. Gooderham L. McCormick
D3	Col. Edwin A. Pollock
D4	Col. Matthew C. Horner
Headquarters Battalion	Col. Bertrand T. Fay
Command Support Group	Lt.-Col. L. Krulewitch

23rd Marine Regiment

Commanding Officer	Col. Walter W. Wensinger
Executive Officer	Lt.-Col. Edward J. Dillon
R3	Maj. Henry S. Campbell

1st Battalion, 23rd Marine Regiment

Battalion Commander	Lt.-Col. Ralph Haas (until 20 February – KIA)

	Lt.-Col. Louis B. Blissard (after 20 February)
Executive Officer	Lt.-Col. Lewis B. Blissard (until 20 February)
Btn. 3	Capt. Fred C. Eberhardt (until 20 February – KIA)
	Maj. James W. Sperry (after 20 February)

2nd Battalion, 23rd Marine Regiment

Battalion Commander	Maj. Robert H. Davidson (until 7 March – WIA, and again from 11 March)
	Lt.-Col. Edward J. Dillon (7–11 March)
Executive Officer	Maj. John J. Padley (until 7 March – WIA)
	Capt. Carl O.J. Grussendorf (after 7 March)
Btn. 3	Capt. Edward J. Schofield (until 7 March - WIA)

3rd Battalion, 23rd Marine Regiment

Battalion Commander	Maj. James S. Scales
Executive Officer	Maj. Phillip J. Maloney
Btn. 3	Maj. William H. Cushing

24th Marine Regiment

Commanding Officer	Col. Walter I. Jordan
Executive Officer	Lt.-Col. Austin R. Brunelli (until 8 March)
R3	Maj. Webb D. Sawyer

1st Battalion, 24th Marine Regiment

Battalion Commander	Maj. Paul S. Treitel (until 8 March)
	Lt.-Col. Austin R. Brunelli (after 8 March)
Executive Officer	Maj. Horace C. Parks
Btn. 3	Maj. Irving Schechter (until 8 March)
	Maj. George D. Webster (after 8 March)

2nd Battalion, 24th Marine Regiment

Battalion Commander	Lt.-Col. Richard Rothwell
Executive Officer	Maj. Frank E. Garretson
Btn. 3	Capt. John F. Ross Jr (until 20 February – WIA)
	Maj. Charles C. Berkeley (after 20 February)

3rd Battalion, 24th Marine Regiment

Battalion Commander	Lt.-Col. Alexander A. Vandergrift Jr (until 23 February – WIA)
	Maj. Doyle A. Stout (after 23 February)
Executive Officer	Maj. Doyle A. Stout (until 23 February)
	Maj. Albert Arsenault (after 23 February)
Btn. 3	Maj. Albert Arsenault (until 23 February)
	Maj. William C. Esterline (after 25 February)

25th Marine Regiment

Commanding Officer	Col. John R. Lanigan
Executive Officer	Lt.-Col. Clarence J. O'Donnell
R3	Maj. John H. Jones

1st Battalion, 25th Marine Regiment

Battalion Commander	Lt.-Col. Hollis U. Mustain (until 21 February – KIA)
	Maj. Fenton J. Mee (after 21 February)
Executive Officer	Maj. Henry D. Strunk (until 19 February – WIA)
	Maj. Fenton J. Mee (19–21 February)
	Maj. Edward L. Asbill (after 21 February)
Btn. 3	Maj. Fenton J. Mee (until 21 February)
	Capt. William J. Weinstein (after 21 February)

2nd Battalion, 25th Marine Regiment

Battalion Commander	Lt.-Col. Lewis C. Hudson Jr (until 20 February – WIA)
	Lt.-Col. James Taul (after 20 February)
Executive Officer	Maj. William P. Kaempfer (until 20 February –WIA)
Btn. 3	Maj. Donald K. Ellis (until 20 February – WIA)
	Capt. Edward H. Birkenmeier Jr (after 26 February)

3rd Battalion, 25th Marine Regiment

Battalion Commander	Lt.-Col. Justice M. Chambers (until 22 February – WIA)
	Capt. James C. Headley (after 22 February)
Executive Officer	Lt.-Col. James Taul (until 20 February)
	Capt. James Antink (after 22 February)
Btn. 3	Maj. Lawrence M. Rulison (until 19 February – WIA)
	Capt. Elwyn W. Woods (after 12 March)

14th Marine Regiment

Commanding Officer	Col. Louis G. DeHaven
Executive Officer	Lt.-Col. Randell M. Victory
R3	Capt. Frederick J. Karch

1st Battalion, 14th Marine Regiment

Battalion Commander	Maj. John B. Edgar Jr
Executive Officer	Maj. Charles V. Watson
Btn. 3	Capt. Raymond Jenkins

2nd Battalion, 14th Marine Regiment

Battalion Commander	Maj. Clifford B. Drake
Executive Officer	Maj. Donald E. Noll
Btn. 3	Maj. Ralph W. Boyer

3rd Battalion, 14th Marine Regiment

Battalion Commander	Lt.-Col. Robert E. MacFarlane (until 19 February – WIA)
	Maj. Harvey A. Feehan (19–23 February, and again after 10 March)
	Lt.-Col. Carl A. Youngdale (23 February–10 March)
Executive Officer	Maj. Harvey A. Feehan (until 19 February, and again 23 February–10 March)
Btn. 3	1st Lt. Bernard J. Diggs

4th Battalion, 14th Marine Regiment

Battalion Commander	Lt.-Col. Carl A. Youngdale (until 23 February, and again after 10 March)
	Maj. Roland J. Spritzen (23 February–10 March)
Executive Officer	Maj. Roland J. Spritzen
Btn. 3	Capt. Russell F. Schoenbeck

4th Tank Battalion

Battalion Commander	Lt.-Col. Richard K. Schmidt
Executive Officer	Maj. Francis L. Orgain
Btn. 3	Maj. Leo B. Case

4th Engineer Battalion

Battalion Commander	Lt.-Col. Nelson K. Brown
Executive Officer	Maj. Melvin D. Henderson
Btn. 3	Maj. Melvin D. Henderson

4th Pioneer Battalion

Battalion Commander	Lt.-Col. Richard G. Ruby
Executive Officer	Maj. John H. Partridge
Btn. 3	Capt. George A. Smith

4th Service Battalion

Battalion Commander	Lt.-Col. John E. Fondahl
Executive Officer	Maj. Henry P. Welton
Btn. 3	1st Lt. James T. Willis

4th Motor Transport Battalion

Battalion Commander	Lt.-Col. Ralph L. Schiesswohl
Executive Officer	Maj. Michael J. Danneker
Btn. 3	Unknown

4th Medical Battalion

Battalion Commander	Cdr. Reuben L. Sharp (USNR)
Executive Officer (USNR)	Lt.-Cdr. Eugene G. McCarthy

5th Amphibian Tractor Battalion

Battalion Commander	Maj. George L. Shead
Executive Officer	Capt. William C. Stoll Jr
Btn. 3	Capt. William S. Clark

10th Amphibian Tractor Battalion

Battalion Commander	Maj. Victor J. Croizat

Executive Officer	Maj. Harry T. Marshall Jr
Btn. 3	Capt. George A. Vradenburg Jr

5TH MARINE DIVISION

Commanding General	Maj.-Gen. Keller E. Rockey
Asst. Divisional Commander	Brig.-Gen. Leo D. Hermle
Chief of Staff	Col. Ray A. Robinson
D1	Col. John W. Beckett
D2	Lt.-Col. George A. Roll
D3	Col. James F. Shaw Jr
D4	Col. Earl S. Piper
D5	Lt.-Col. Frederick R. Dowsett
Headquarters Battalion	Maj. John Ayrault Jr

26th Marine Regiment

Commanding Officer	Col. Chester B. Graham
Executive Officer	Col. Lester S. Hamel
R3	Lt.-Col. William K. Davenport Jr

1st Battalion, 26th Marine Regiment

Battalion Commander	Lt.-Col. Daniel C. Pollock (until 19 March – WIA)
	Maj. Albert V.K. Gary (after 19 March)
Executive Officer	Maj. Albert V.K. Gary (until 19 March)
Btn. 3	Capt. Aram S. Rejebian

2nd Battalion, 26th Marine Regiment

Battalion Commander	Lt.-Col. Joseph P. Sayers (until 23 February – WIA)
	Maj. Amedeo Rea (after 23 February)
Executive Officer	Maj. Amedeo Rea (until 23 February)
	Capt. Thomas M. Fields (after 3 February)
Btn. 3	1st Lt. Boyer G. Warren (until 26 February – WIA)
	2nd Lt. William M. Adams Jr (after 26 February)

3rd Battalion, 26th Marine Regiment

Battalion Commander	Lt.-Col. Tom M. Trotti (until 22 February – KIA)
	Capt. Richard M. Cook (22 February only)
	Maj. Richard Fagan (after 22 February)
Executive Officer	Maj. George F. Waters Jr (until 20 February – WIA)
	Maj. Chester E. Bennett (after 6 March)
Btn. 3	Maj. William R. Day (until 22 February – KIA)
	Capt. Conrad A. Pearson (after 22 February)

27th Marine Regiment

Commanding Officer	Col. Thomas A. Wornham
Executive Officer	Col. Louis C. Plain (WIA 19 February)
	Lt.-Col. James P. Berkeley (after 15 March)
R3	Lt.-Col. Justin G. Duryea (until 5 March)
	Capt. Franklin L. Smith (after 5 March)

1st Battalion, 27th Marine Regiment

Battalion Commander	Lt.-Col. John A. Butler (until 5 March – KIA)
	Lt.-Col. Justin G. Duryea (5–9 March – WIA)
	Maj. William H. Tumbelston (9–14 March – WIA)
	Maj. William H. Kennedy Jr (after 14 March)
Executive Officer	Maj. William H. Tumbelston (until 9 March)
	Maj. William H. Kennedy Jr (9–14 March)
	Maj. Ronald F. Adams (after 14 March)
Btn. 3	Capt. Thomas R. Shepard (until 14 March – WIA)

2nd Battalion, 27th Marine Regiment

Battalion Commander	Maj. John W. Antonelli (until 9 March – WIA)
	Maj. Gerald F. Russell (after 9 March)
Executive Officer	Maj. Gerald F. Russell (until 9 March)
Btn. 3	Maj. C.J. Chandler Jr

3rd Battalion, 27th Marine Regiment

Battalion Commander	Lt.-Col. Donn J. Robertson
Executive Officer	Maj. Frederick J. Mix Jr
Btn. 3	Maj. William H. Kennedy Jr (until 9 March)
	Maj. Frederick J. Mix Jr (after 9 March)

28th Marine Regiment

Commanding Officer	Col. Harry B. Liversedge
Executive Officer	Lt.-Col. Robert H. Williams
R3	Maj. Oscar F. Peatross (until 14 March)
	Lt.-Col. Charles E. Shepard Jr (15–25 March)

1st Battalion, 28th Marine Regiment

Battalion Commander	Lt.-Col. Jackson B. Butterfield
Executive Officer	Maj. William A. Wood
Btn. 3	1st Lt. William R. Henderson

2nd Battalion, 28th Marine Regiment

Battalion Commander	Lt.-Col. Chandler W. Johnson (until 2 March – KIA)
	Maj. Thomas B. Pearce Jr (after 2 March)
Executive Officer	Maj. Thomas B. Pearce Jr (until 2 March)
	Maj. James H. Finch (after 2 March)
Btn. 3	Capt. Martin W. Reinemann

3rd Battalion, 28th Marine Regiment

Battalion Commander	Lt.-Col. Charles E. Shepard Jr (until 14 March, and from 25 March)
	Maj. Tolson A. Smoak (14–25 March)
Executive Officer	Maj. Tolson A. Smoak (until 14 March, and from 25 March)
	Maj. Oscar F. Peatross (14–25 March)
Btn. 3	Capt. Robert N. Spangler

13th Marine Regiment

Commanding Officer	Col. James D. Waller
Executive Officer	Lt.-Col. Kenyth A. Damke
R3	Lt.-Col. Jack Tabor

1st Battalion, 13th Marine Regiment

Battalion Commander	Lt.-Col. John S. Oldfield

Executive Officer	Maj. Edward O. Cerf
Btn. 3	Maj. James R. Crockett

2nd Battalion, 13th Marine Regiment

Battalion Commander	Maj. Carl W. Hjerpe
Executive Officer	Maj. Olin W. Jones Jr
Btn. 3	Maj. George E. Moore

3rd Battalion, 13th Marine Regiment

Battalion Commander	Lt.-Col. Henry T. Waller
Executive Officer	Maj. William M. Miller
Btn. 3	Maj. Edwin N. Kittrell Jr

4th Battalion, 13th Marine Regiment

Battalion Commander	Maj. James F. Coady
Executive Officer	Maj. William W. Mitchell
Btn. 3	Capt. Jackson C. Turnacliff

Service Troops

Commanding Officer	Col. Benjamin W. Gally
Executive Officer	Lt.-Col. Robert L. Cooper

5th Tank Battalion

Battalion Commander	Lt.-Col. William Collins
Executive Officer	Maj. Gardelle Lewis (until 26 February)
	Maj. John Frothingham (after 26 February)
Btn. 3	1st Lt. George C. Moore

5th Engineer Battalion

Battalion Commander	Lt.-Col. Clifford H. Shuey
Executive Officer	Maj. Herbert I. McCoy
Btn. 3	Capt. Richard J. MacLaury

5th Pioneer Battalion

Battalion Commander	Maj. Robert S. Riddell
Executive Officer	Maj. Rupert C. Henley
Btn. 3	Capt. Harold A. Hayes Jr

5th Service Battalion

Battalion Commander	Maj. Francis P. Daly (until 22 February – KIA) Maj. Gardelle Lewis (after 26 February)
Battalion Adjutant	1st Lt. William A. Brokaw

5th Motor Transport Battalion

Battalion Commander	Maj. Arthur F. Torgler Jr
Executive Officer	Capt. Herbert E. Pierce
Btn. 3	Capt. William Montagna

5th Medical Battalion

Battalion Commander	Lt.-Cdr. William W. Ayres (USN)
Executive Officer	Lt.-Cdr. John E. Gorman (USN)

3rd Amphibian Tractor Battalion

Battalion Commander	Lt.-Col. Sylvester L. Stephan
Executive Officer	Maj. Erwin F. Wann Jr
Btn. 3	Maj. George M. Foote

11th Amphibian Tractor Battalion

Battalion Commander	Lt.-Col. Albert J. Roose
Executive Officer	Maj. Robert W. Dyer
Btn. 3	Capt. Leopold Fiske

V AMPHIBIOUS CORPS (AND MAJOR ATTACHED UNITS)

CORPS TROOPS

Commanding Officer	Col. Alton A. Gladden

HQ & Service Battalion VAC

Commanding Officer	Capt. Cyril M. Milbrath

1ST PROVISIONAL FIELD ARTILLERY GROUP

Group Commander	Col. John S. Letcher
Executive Officer	Lt.-Col. Marvin H. Floom
Group 3	Maj. William G. Winters Jr

2nd 155mm Howitzer Battalion (1st Provisional FA Group)

Battalion Commander	Maj. Earl J. Rowse
Executive Officer	Maj. Alexander A. Elder
Btn. 3	Capt. Earl N. Lewis

4th 155mm Howitzer Battalion (1st Provisional FA Group)

Battalion Commander	Lt.-Col. Douglas E. Reeve
Executive Officer	Maj. Marvin R. Burditt
Btn. 3	Maj. Joe H. Daniel

138th AA Group (US Army)

Group Commander	Col. Clarence E. Rothgeb

506th AA Gun Battalion (138th AA Group, US Army)

Battalion Commander	Lt.-Col. D.M. White

483rd AAAW Battalion (138th AA Group, US Army)

Battalion Commander	Lt.-Col. A. Roth

8th Field Depot

Commanding Officer	Col. Leland S. Swindler

Landing Force Air Support Control Unit

Commanding Officer	Col. Vernon E. Megee

VAC Signal Battalion

Commanding Officer	Lt.-Col. Alfred F. Robertshaw

VAC Medical Battalion

Commanding Officer	Lt.-Cdr. William B. Clapp (USNR)

Provisional Signal Group

Commanding Officer   Lt.-Col. Harry W.G. Vadnais

HQ Provisional LVT Group

Commanding Officer   Maj. Henry G. Lawrence Jr

2nd Separate Engineer Battalion

Commanding Officer   Lt.-Col. Charles O. Clark

2nd Armoured Amphibian Battalion

Commanding Officer   Lt.-Col. Reed M. Fawell Jr

23rd Naval Construction Battalion (Companies A&B)

Commanding Officer   Cdr. H.W. Heuer (USN)

31st Naval Construction Battalion

Commanding Officer   Lt.-Cdr. D.J. Ermilio (USNR)

62nd Naval Construction Battalion

Commanding Officer   Lt.-Cdr. F.B. Campbell (USNR)

133rd Naval Construction Battalion

Commanding Officer   Lt.-Cdr. R.P. Murphy (USNR)

Corps Evacuation Hospital No. 1

Commanding Officer   Capt. H.G. Young (USN)

38th Field Hospital, Reinforced (US Army)

Commanding Officer   Maj. Samuel S. Kirkland

Appendix 4

US Task Force Organization

In overall command of the Iwo Jima operation was Adm. Raymond A. Spruance, commanding Task Force 50 (5th Fleet).

Subordinate task organizations participating in the assault on the Volcano-Bonins were as follows:

Task Force 51 (Joint Expeditionary Force)

Commanded by Vice-Adm. Richmond K. Turner, Commanding Amphibious Forces US Pacific Fleet. Task Forces functioning under Joint Expeditionary Force command were as follows.

TASK FORCE 52 (AMPHIBIOUS SUPPORT FORCE)

Commanded by Rear-Adm. William H.P. Blandy, included an Air Support Control Unit, Support Carrier Group, Mine Group, Underwater Demolition Group, Gunboat Support Group, Mortar Support Group and Rocket Support Group. The mission of this force was to furnish preliminary (plus D-Day) gunfire and air support, including preparation fires, minesweeping, net-laying, beach reconnaissance and underwater demolition. At 0600 on D-Day, TF 52 passed to the direct command of Vice-Adm. Turner. Rear-Adm. Blandy then assumed command of TG 51-19 (Night Retirement Groups).

TASK FORCE 53 (ATTACK FORCE)

Commanded by Rear-Adm. Harry W. Hill, this force comprised an air support control unit, embarked assault troops, two transport squadrons, tractor groups, LSM groups, control group, beach party group and a pontoon barge, causeway, and LCT group. Its mission was to transport and land the expeditionary troops.

TASK FORCE 54 (GUNFIRE AND COVERING FORCE)

Commanded by Rear-Adm. Bertram J. Rogers, this force was composed of three battleship divisions, one cruiser division and three destroyer divisions, and was reinforced on D-Day by an additional two destroyer divisions from TF 58. On D+1, two cruiser divisions and two more destroyer divisions from TF 58 joined the Gunfire and Covering Force off Iwo Jima. The potent aggregation thus assembled combined their power to furnish shore bombardment and protect the vulnerable invasion shipping from enemy surface attack.

Task Force 56 (Expeditionary Troops)

Commanded by Lt.-Gen. Holland M. Smith, under this command were all assault troops and certain assigned garrison troops. Units under Lt.-Gen. Smith's command were responsible for executing all ground attacks and, in the later stages, certain shore-based air operations during the effort to capture, occupy and defend Iwo Jima.

Subordinate units of TF 56 were as follows:

TASK GROUP 56-1 (LANDING FORCE)

Commanded by Maj.-Gen. Harry Schmidt, Gen. Schmidt's Landing Force Headquarters provided overall command and co-ordination of all troops ashore, including shore-based air units during the attack.

TASK GROUP 56-2 (ASSAULT TROOPS)

4th and 5th Marine Divisions, commanded by Maj.-Gen. Clifton B. Cates and Keller E. Rockey respectively, plus Corps Troops.

TASK GROUP 56-3 (EXPEDITIONARY TROOPS RESERVE)

The 3rd Marine Division (Reinforced), commanded by Maj.-Gen. Graves B. Erskine.

Other Task Forces supporting the Iwo Jima assault included the following:

Task Force 58 (Fast Carrier Force of 5th Fleet)

Commanded by Vice-Adm. Marc A. Mitscher, carrier aircraft of TF 58 supported the Iwo Jima operations through diversionary strikes on the enemy homeland, and supplied close air support at the objective. Fire support vessels of TF 58 also provided valuable firepower at Iwo Jima for several days, commencing on D-Day.

Task Force 93 (Strategic Air Force, Pacific Ocean Areas)

Composed primarily of land-based heavy bombers flying from airfields in the Marianas, these planes, predominantly B24s, of the 7th Air Force, helped soften up the target for assault, and beginning on D-Day, delivered several deep support air strikes on the objective and night harassing and destructive air strikes on the Bonin Islands.

Task Force 94 (Forward Area, Central Pacific)

Commanded by Vice-Adm. John H. Hoover, it provided assault forces with base facilities logistic support and various rear-echelon services.

Source: *Iwo Jima – Amphibious Epic*, Lt.-Col. S. Bartley, USMC 1954. Historical Branch, G3 Division, Headquarters USMC.

CINCPAC-CINCPOA
Adm. C.W. Nimitz

Task Force 93
Lt.-Gen. Harmon

US 5th Fleet
Adm. R.A. Spruance

Task Force 94
Vice-Adm. J. Hoover

Task Force 51
Vice-Adm. R.K. Turner
Air Support Control Unit
Expeditionary Force Reserve
Transport Screen
Salvage & Survey Groups
Port Director Unit
Seaplane Base Group
Defense Group
Garrison Groups Zero & One

Task Force 58
Vice-Adm. M.A. Mitscher

Task Force 52
Rear-Adm. Blandy
Support Carrier

Air Support
Control Unit
Mine Group
UDT Group
Gunboat Support Group
Mortar & Rocket Support Group
Task Force 53
Rear-Adm. Hill
Air Support
Control Unit
Assault Troops
Transport Group
Tractor Flotilla
LSM Flotilla
Beach Party
Control Group
Pontoon Barge Causeway & LCT Groups

Task Force 54
Rear-Adm. Rodgers
Fire Support
Battleships
Cruiser & Destroyer Divisions

Task Force 56
Lt.-Gen. Smith
Landing Forces
Assault Troops
Garrison Units
Expeditionary Troops
Reserve

Task Force 58

The Fast Carrier Force of the 5th Fleet carried out major attacks on the Japanese mainland, were responsible for close support during the D-Day landings, and for several days provided heavy gunfire support for the assault.

Commander: Vice-Adm. Marc A. Mitscher in the carrier USS *Bunker Hill*

Chief of Staff: Cdre. Arleigh A. Burke

GROUP 58-1 (REAR-ADM. JOSEPH J. CLARKE)

Carriers: *Hornet, Wasp, Bennington, Belleau Wood*
Battleships: *Massachusetts, Indiana*
Cruisers: *Vincennes, Miami, San Juan* (plus 15 destroyers)

GROUP 58-2 (REAR-ADM. RALPH E. DAVISON)

Carriers: *Lexington, Hancock, San Jacinto*
Battleships: *Wisconsin, Missouri*
Cruisers: *San Francisco Boston* (plus 19 destroyers)

Group 58-3 (Rear-Adm. Frederick C. Sherman)

Carriers: *Essex, Bunker Hill, Cowpens*
Battleships: *South Dakota, New Jersey*
Cruisers: *Alaska, Indianapolis, Pasadena, Wilkes-Barre, Astoria* (plus 14 destroyers)

Group 58-4 (Rear-Adm. Arthur W. Radford)

Carriers: *Yorktown, Randolph, Langley, Cabot*
Battleships: *Washington, North Carolina*
Cruisers: *Santa Fe, Biloxi, San Diego* (plus 17 destroyers)

Group 58-5

Carriers: *Enterprise, Saratoga*
Cruisers: *Baltimore, Flint* (plus 12 destroyers)

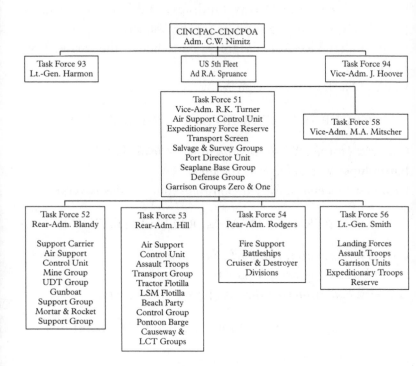

Appendix 5

Japanese Command Structure, Iwo Jima

Order of battle on 19 February 1945

Commander-in-Chief	Lt.-Gen. Tadamichi Kuribayashi
Chief of Staff	Col. Tadashi Takaishi
Fortifications	Col. Monzo Yashida
Operations	Lt.-Col. Takiharu Nakao
Supply	Lt.-Col. Takeo Nishikawa
Intelligence	Maj. Yasutake Yamanouchi
Staff Officers	Maj. Kumeji Komoto
	Maj. Fujio Shirakata
	Maj. Kikuji Nishida
	Capt. Hideichi Toribara

Army Units

109TH DIVISION

Commander-in-Chief	Lt.-Gen. Tadamichi Kuribayashi
Headquarters Group	Not Known (300 men)
Communications	Not Known
109th Division AA Battalion	Maj. Shotaro Azuma (310–40 men)

145TH INFANTRY REGIMENT

Commanding Officer	Col. Masuo Ikeda (2,200-400 men)
1st Battalion	Maj. Mitsuaki Hara

2nd Battalion	Maj. Yasutake
3rd Battalion	Maj. Kenro Anso
Artillery Battalion	Capt. Masuda
Engineer Company	Capt. Kikuzo Musashino
Field Hospital	Not Known

26TH TANK REGIMENT

Commanding Officer	Lt.-Col. (Baron) Takeichi Nishi
Aide	Maj. Akira Matsunaga

2ND MIXED BRIGADE

Commanding Officer	Maj.-Gen. Sadasue Senda (5,100–200 men)
309th Independent Infantry Brigade	Capt. Awatsu
310th Independent Infantry Brigade	Maj. Iwatani
311th Independent Infantry Brigade	Maj. Tatsumi
312th Independent Infantry Brigade	Capt. Osada
314th Independent Infantry Brigade	Capt. Hakuda
Artillery Battalion	Maj. Kazuo Maeda
Engineering Battalion	Maj. Maekawa
Field Hospital	Maj. Masaru Inaoka

BRIGADE ARTILLERY

Commanding Officer	Col. Chosaku Kaido
2nd Mixed Brigade	Maj. Kazuo Maeda
145th Infantry Regiment	Capt. Masuda
2nd Medium Mortar Btn. (Reinforced)	Maj. Jusuke Nakao (700 men)

3rd Medium Mortar Btn. (Reinforced)	Maj. Koichiro Kobayashi (500 men)
20th Independent Artillery Mortar Btn. (Reinforced)	Capt. Mitsuo Mizutari (800 men)
8th Independent Anti-tank Btn.	Capt. Hajime Shimizu
9th Independent Anti-tank Btn.	Maj. Okubo
10th Independent Anti-tank Btn.	Maj. Matsushita (1,200 men)
11th Independent Anti-tank Btn.	Capt. Node
12th Independent Anti-tank Btn.	Capt. Maseo Hayauchi
1st Independent Machine Gun Btn.	Capt. Ko Kawanami (600 men)
2nd Independent Machine Gun Btn.	Maj. Tokio Kawasaki
20th Special Machine Cannon Unit	2nd Lt. Momozaki
21st Special Machine Cannon Unit	2nd Lt. Isamu Kondo
43rd Special Machine Cannon Unit	1st Lt. Tamara (250–300 men)
44th Special Machine Cannon Unit	Not Known

OTHER UNITS

Army Rocket Unit (3 Companies)	Capt. Yoshio Yokoyama (150–220 men)
1st Company, 1st Mixed Brigade Engineer Unit	
5th Fortress Construction Duty Company	
21st Well Drilling Unit	(300 men)
Detachment – Shipping Engineers	

Navy

Commanding Officer	Rear-Adm. Toshinosuke Ichimaru
Commander Naval Guard Force	Capt. Samaji Inouye

125th Anti-aircraft Defence Unit	Lt. (JG) Tamura
132nd Anti-aircraft Defence Unit	Ensign Okumura (2,400 men)
149th Anti-aircraft Defence Unit	Not Known
141st Anti-aircraft Defence Unit	Lt. (JG) Doi
Operations	Cdr. Takeji Mase
Communications	Lt.-Cdr. Shigeru Arioka
Engineering	Lt.-Cdr. Narimasa Okada
Supply	Lt.-Cdr. Okazaki
Suribachi Commander	Col. Kanehiko Atsuchi

Naval Guard Force Coast Defence Batteries (640 men)

Nanpo Air Group Naval Land Forces Capt. Inoue

Southern Air Group (Naval Guard Force Troops, Construction Personnel, Technicians – 2,250 men)

204th Naval Construction Btn.   Lt. Iida (1,410 men)

Technical Air Personnel (320 men)

Total number of Japanese on Iwo Jima on 19 February 1945: 21,060

Appendix 6

US Task Organization

Expeditionary Troops – Lt.-Gen. Holland M. Smith, USMC

CORPS TROOPS

Headquarters and Service Battalion, V Amphibious Corps (less detachments)
Medical Battalion, V Amphibious Corps
Motor Transport Company, V Amphibious Corps
Provisional Signal Group, V Amphibious Corps
  Landing Force Headquarters Signal Section
  Signal Battalion, V Amphibious Corps (less detachments)
  Shore Party Communications Unit
  Detachment – Signal Company, 8th Field Depot
  Detachment – 1st Separate Reconnaissance & Intelligence Platoon
  Detachment – Signal Headquarters Company, VII Fighter Command (USA)
  Detachment – 568th Signal Air Warning Battalion (USA)
  Detachment – 726th Signal Air Warning Company (USA)
  Detachment – 49th Signal Construction Battalion (USA)
  Detachment – 70th Army Airways Communications System (USA)
  Detachment – Communications Unit 434
Landing Force Air Support Control Unit
Headquarters, Provisional LVT Group
2nd Separate Engineer Battalion

62nd Naval Construction Battalion (less detachments)
23rd Naval Construction Battalion (Companies A&B)
8th Field Depot (less detachments, plus VAC Shore Party
Headquarters)
Corps Evacuation Hospital No. 1
2nd Bomb Disposal Company plus 156th Bomb Disposal Squad
Company B, Amphibious Reconnaissance Battalion (FMF Pac.)
38th Field Hospital, Reinforced (US Army)
Medical Section, Civil Affairs
Joint Intelligence Centre Pacific Ocean Area Intelligence Team
Joint Intelligence Centre Pacific Ocean Area Enemy Material and
Salvage Platoon

CORPS ARTILLERY

1st Provisional Field Artillery Group
  Headquarters Battery
  2nd 155mm Howitzer Battalion
  4th 155mm Howitzer Battalion
  473rd Amphibian Truck Company (US Army)

ANTI-AIRCRAFT ARTILLERY

138th AAA Group (less detachments) (US Army)
  Headquarters Battery, 138th AAA Group (US Army)
  506th AA Gun Battalion (US Army)
  483rd AA Automatic Weapons Battalion (US Army)

*4th Marine Division (Reinforced) – Maj.-Gen. Clifton
B. Cates, USMC*

Companies A&B plus detachment, Btn. HQ, 2nd Armoured
Amphibian Battalion
5th Amphibian Tractor Battalion
10th Amphibian Tractor Battalion

1st Joint Assault Signal Company
Marine Observation Squadron No. 4
133rd Naval Construction Battalion
4th Marine Amphibian Truck Company
476th Amphibian Truck Company (US Army)
7th War Dog Platoon
1st Provisional Rocket Detachment
Detachment – 8th Field Depot
Detachment – 726th Signal Air Warning Company (US Army)
Detachment – Signal Battalion, V Amphibious Corps
442nd Port Company (US Army)
Joint Intelligence Centre Pacific Ocean Area Intelligence Team
24th Replacement Draught
30th Replacement Draught

5th Marine Division (Reinforced) – Maj.-Gen. Keller
E. Rockey, USMC

5th Marine Amphibian Truck Company
5th Joint Assault Signal Company
471st Amphibian Truck Company (US Army)
11th Amphibian Tractor Battalion
3rd Amphibian Tractor Battalion
Companies C&D and detachment, HQ Btn., 2nd Armoured
    Amphibian Battalion
Marine Observation Squadron 5
3rd Provisional Rocket Detachment
6th Marine War Dog Platoon
592nd Port Company (US Army)
31st Naval Construction Battalion
27th Replacement Draught
31st Replacement Draught
Detachment – 726th Signal Air Warning Company (US Army)
Joint Intelligence Centre Pacific Ocean Area Intelligence Team

Detachment – Signal Battalion, V Amphibious Corps
Detachment – 8th Field Depot
Liaison Group – V Amphibious Corps
Liaison Group – Fleet Marine Force, Pacific V Amphibious Corps Reserve

3rd Marine Division (Reinforced) – Maj.-Gen. Graves B. Erskine, USMC

3rd Marine Division (less 21st Regiment)
3rd Joint Assault Signal Company
Marine Observation Squadron 1
3rd Marine War Dog Platoon
Joint Intelligence Centre Pacific Ocean Area Intelligence Team
Detachment – Signal Battalion, V Amphibious Corps
28th Replacement Draught
34th Replacement Draught

Garrison Forces (Assault Echelon) – Maj.-Gen. James E. Chaney (US Army)

Detachment – Island Command Headquarters
Detachment – 147th Army Infantry Regiment
Detachment – Headquarters, VII Fighter Command
Detachment – Headquarters, 15th Fighter Group
47th Fighter Squadron
78th Fighter Squadron
548th Night Fighter Service
386th Air Service Group (Special)
1st Platoon, 604th Quartermaster Graves Registration Company
223rd Radar Maintainance Unit (Type C)
Detachment – Administrative Unit, Group Pacific 11
Port Directors' Detachment
Garrison Beach Party

Appendix 7

20th Air Force Command Structure, April 1944–July 1945

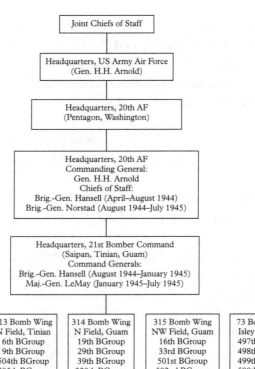

Joint Chiefs of Staff

Headquarters, US Army Air Force
(Gen. H.H. Arnold)

Headquarters, 20th AF
(Pentagon, Washington)

Headquarters, 20th AF
Commanding General:
Gen. H.H. Arnold
Chiefs of Staff:
Brig.-Gen. Hansell (April–August 1944)
Brig.-Gen. Norstad (August 1944–July 1945)

Headquarters, 21st Bomber Command
(Saipan, Tinian, Guam)
Command Generals:
Brig.-Gen. Hansell (August 1944–January 1945)
Maj.-Gen. LeMay (January 1945–July 1945)

58 Bomb Wing	313 Bomb Wing	314 Bomb Wing	315 Bomb Wing	73 Bomb Wing
W Field, Tinian	N Field, Tinian	N Field, Guam	NW Field, Guam	Isley F, Saipan
40th BGroup	6th BGroup	19th BGroup	16th BGroup	497th BGroup
444th BGroup	9th BGroup	29th BGroup	33rd BGroup	498th BGroup
462nd BGroup	504th BGroup	39th BGroup	501st BGroup	499th BGroup
468th BGroup	505th BGroup	330th BGroup	502nd BGroup	500th BGroup

509th
Composite Group
(Atomic)

Appendix 8

Casualties

US Casualties

The official Marine Corps history of the battle lists the dead as 'Killed in Action' (KIA), and 'Died of Wounds' (DOW), and then sub-divides them into 'Officers' and 'Enlisted Men'. The list presented here lists dead and wounded in action, with representative breakdowns of various units.

USMC:	Dead, 5885	Wounded in Action, 17,272
US Navy:	Dead, 881	Wounded in Action, 1916

These figures include 195 Medical Corpsmen, 49 Seabees, and 2 doctors and/or dentists killed; 2,648 Marines suffered from combat fatigue.

The figures give no indication of the appalling losses suffered by individual Companies during the battle. In some cases, as with 'G' Company, 2nd Battalion, 25th Regiment, 4th Marine Division, about 233 men made the initial landing, and the total casualties came to 261. Several drafts of replacements were fed into the battle beginning on 25 February, so the figure of over 100 per cent casualties reflects the additional replacements.

Japanese Casualties

The Japanese force on D-Day, 19 February 1945, has been estimated at 21,060 men. A breakdown of casualty figures is not possible, given the ferocity of the battle and the fact that many Japanese troops died sealed in caves, underground tunnels and bunkers, but 216 Marine and 867 Army personnel were taken prisoner, so a figure of 19,977 Japanese dead can be presumed.

Select Bibliography

Alexander, Bill, *My Private Life*, privately published, 1995

Alexander, Col. Joseph H., *A Fellowship of Valor*, HarperCollins, New York, 1997

——, *Closing In – Marines in the Seizure of Iwo Jima*, USMC Historical Center, Washington DC, 1994

Bartley, Lt.-Col. Whitman S., *Iwo Jima – Amphibious Epic*, Official USMC History, reprinted by Battery Press, Nashville, Tennessee, 1988

Best, Harold C., *My Great Adventure*, privately published

Delano, Jack, *Superfortress over Japan*, Motorbooks International, Osceola, Wisconsin, 1966

Gilomen, Bill, *From This Day Forward*, privately published

Hartman, Mary, *Texas Granite*, Hendrick Long Publishing Co., Dallas, Texas, 1996

Herman, Jan K., *Battle Station Sick Bay*, Naval Institute Press, Annapolis, Maryland, 1997

Kerr, Bartlett, *Flames over Tokyo*, Donald I. Fine, New York, 1991

Lane, John, *This Here is 'G' Company*, Bright Lights Publications, Great Neck, NY, 1997

Morrison, Wilbur H., *Point of No Return*, Times Books, NY, 1979

Nalty, Bernard C. (ed.), *War in the Pacific*, Salamander Books, London, 1991

Newcomb, Richard F., *Iwo Jima*, Holt, Rinehart & Winston, New York, 1965

Ross, Bill D., *Iwo Jima – Legacy of Valor*, Random House, New York, 1985

Tatum, Charles W., *Iwo Jima: Red Blood – Black Sand*, Tatum Publishing, Stockton, California, 1995

Thomas, Otis M., *Come Walk With Me*, privately published, 1994

Vat, Dan van der, *The Pacific Campaign*, Simon & Schuster, New York, 1991

Waterhouse, Col. Charles, *Marines and Others*, Sea Bag Productions, Edison, New Jersey, 1994

Wells, John Keith, *Give Me 50 Marines Not Afraid to Die*, Quality Publications, 1995

Wheeler, Keith, *Bombers over Japan*, Time/Life, Chicago, 1982

Wheeler, Richard, *Iwo*, Lippincott & Crowell, New York, 1980

Index

Note: The names of units which do not appear in the body of the text are shown in Appendix 3, US Command & Staff List, Appendix 4, Task Force Organization, Appendix 5, Japanese Command Structure, and Appendix 7, 20th Air Force Command Structure. A full list of Medal of Honor winners is shown in Appendix 1.

The island of Iwo Jima is not included in the Index, all events pertaining to the island are described from the Preface onward.